THE SILENCER'S WIFE

AF112921

THE SILENCER'S WIFE

Copyright © 2025 by Katelyn Beck.

All rights reserved. Printed in the United States of America. No part of this book may be used or reproduced in any manner whatsoever without written permission except in the case of brief quotations em- bodied in critical articles or reviews.

This book is a work of fiction. Names, characters, businesses, organizations, places, events, and incidents either are the product of the author's imagination or are used fictitiously. Any resemblance to actual persons, living or dead, events, or locales is entirely coincidental.

For information contact:

Katelyn Beck

www.writtenbykatelynbeck.com

Email: writtenbykatelynbeck@gmail.com

Book Designer:

Katelyn Beck with Written By Katelyn Beck LLC

ISBN: 979-8-9878280-7-6

First Edition: May 2025

Dedicated to my Daughter, L.K.P, and my Son, E.R.T. In addition, dedicated to my Dad, G. Beck (Wife R. Beck).

Note from Author:

This book is a work of fiction. Names, characters, businesses, organizations, places, events and incidents either are the product of the author's imagination or are used fictitiously. Any resemblance to actual persons, living or dead, events, or locales is entirely coincidental.

This book does contain abortion request, murder, and rape. I want my readers to be fully aware that if they ever experienced this in real-life that this novel is a complete work of fiction that did not resemble my life or any others. I will not know the pain you suffer as each suffer pain differently. I hope you enjoy the novel as much as I've enjoyed working on this project.

Special "Thank you" to my Beta Readers. I appreciate you all for dedicating your time to read it in its early stages, provide feedback, and overall help.

Another Special "Thank you" to Anton Anderson. Your strong feedback helped me realize things that needed enhancement that weren't clear at first. In much appreciation of your honesty throughout the story, time and effort.

Anton Anderson, author of "The Seekers" fantasy series. The two published books are The Seekers: Soul Ties and The Seekers: Kirin (Kirin made it to the shortlist of the Ozma Awards for Fantasy Fiction 2024) The third book, The Seekers: Perrin Peters.

https://anton-anderson.com/

THE SILENCER'S WIFE

Pre-face

"LIZ," I SNAPPED AS THE ANTICIPATION of my presence in her office rose! "I'm not here for a social visit." Liz, twenty-six years old now, dirty blonde hair pulled back in a ponytail, became silent, forming her lips into a line. "I need your help with something," nervously fumbling my fingers in my lap, not able to look at her.

"Stacy," she said with anger in her tone. "It's been four and a half years since any of us have heard from you."

Tears formed in my eyes. "I know that you're upset with me, but I need your help."

"What possibly could I do to help you?" She sounded frustrated as she interlocked her fingers and sat them on her desk.

"You're an OBGYN," I said glancing up at her. "I need a pregnancy terminated."

Her mouth fell slightly, and then she sat back in her chair and folded her arms across her chest. She looked away from me as if she were in pain to hear the words from my mouth. "How far along are you?"

My mouth felt dry as I looked back down at my hands. The pain inside of me rose as this was something I wanted for the longest time. I licked my lips, and then I looked back at her. "I should be seven weeks," I dabbed my eyes as I sniffled.

She got up from her chair and walked around to me, placing her hand on my shoulder. "You don't look like you want to terminate this pregnancy," she said kneeling down beside me. "Are you sure this is the route you want to go?"

I nodded as I glanced over at her, another stream of tears rolled down my cheeks. "If it wasn't for *how* this baby was conceived then I would keep it," I paused. "But it's not my husband's child."

"Oh Stacy," she said as she wrapped her arms tightly around my neck. I grabbed her arm as the tears flowed out of me. We sat there for a few minutes, and then she grabbed a few tissues and handed them to me. "Let me get a room set up to ensure how far along is accurate," she said. "And then, we will set a date for when you want this done."

"Thank you," I whispered as I dabbed my face with the tissues.

"Of course," she said patting my shoulder. "It's what family does, look out for each other." She gave me a light squeeze, and then she left her office.

I sat there crutched over, my elbows on my knees, and my face buried in my hands. It had been seven weeks since the incident. Seven weeks that turned our lives around for the worse. I moved my right arm around my stomach, as if this tiny thing could feel my hand. *I'm sorry that I have to do this to you. It's not fair for you to be brought into this world from a tragedy that occurred to me.*

Knock. Knock. I looked up to see Liz had returned. "I've got a room for you," she said holding onto the doorknob. Her face looked in as much pain as I felt for what I was about to do. We both were raised better than this, but if it wasn't for that wrongful act I would be making a different choice. I nodded as I slowly got up from the chair, looking in front of me at her desk. A picture of her and her husband Eric on their wedding day sat there. I slightly smiled as it reminded me of my own wedding.

Chapter One

Five Years Earlier…

I was twenty-four years old; Liz had just turned twenty-one. We were at a bar an hour away from the ranch we lived on. I had worn my blue jeans, white tank top, and blue plaided button-up partially done. My blonde straight hair hanged down past my shoulders. Liz wore a similar outfit, but a red plaid shirt and a sash that stated, "Twenty-One Today." Her hair was partially pulled back, her bangs flushed against her cheeks.

We sat at the bar where the bartender put our first shots in front of us. "A toast to the birthday girl," I said with a smile as I picked up the shot. "May you kick ass in Medical School! And don't have any regrets after this night!"

"Is that what you call a speech?" She laughed as we dinged our shots, and then we flung them back.

I slammed mine down, waving at the bartender for another. "It was the best I had," I laughed.

"I'm going to miss you," she said as we took a moment and stared at each other.

I looked away as I didn't want my departure brought up on her night. "Let's not talk about me," I said as I looked back at her. She embraced me with tears streaming. "Hey, hey," I said patting her back. "This night's about you, not me."

"Why do you want travel across the states to one of the biggest cities in the world," she cried. We let go of each other's embrace as the bartender pushed our shots at us. I took mine, and then I sat it back down. "Brian," I said to the bartender. "Get me a cold one, enough of this sissy stuff." Brian nodded as he walked towards the cooler behind the bar. Looking over my shoulder at Liz, feeling the pain that emerged from my own heart. Liz and I were nearly like twins, close in age and done everything together. "You know ever since I was younger, I wanted to do something better with my life."

"Going to New York is better?" Liz wiped her face, and then she turned her shot glass up as she faced the bartender.

I sighed as this wasn't how I expected the night to go. "Liz, it's your birthday. Don't spoil it this way," I said feeling the shattering pain of doubt slip into my soul. A couple of guys were walking up to us. "Besides," I smiled as I nodded at the two men, wearing button up shirts and blue jeans, came closer to us. "These two guys want to help celebrate your birthday."

They introduced themselves, but I don't recall their names. Liz and I drank so much the bartender took my keys away. The guys offered to take us home, but I refused as we sat there with Brian who poured us coffee. Around four in the morning when I had sobered up and Liz was two whistles in the wind, I put my arm around her and took her to the car. I got in and drove us home where mom sat on the front porch waiting for our arrival.

After bringing Liz to her room, tucked her in bed, and then went back downstairs to the front porch. I sat down on the porch swing with mom. "Fun night?" She asked.

I nodded. "Yea, I think she'll have a perfect first hangover," I laughed.

Mom snickered as she patted my leg. "Stacy, you know you can find work here," she said looking over at me. Mom had aged so much over the past year that she had fine wrinkles and gray hair. I leaned my head over and placed it on her shoulder as we stared out at the ranch. It was a hot simmering July night, the bugs were singing, the stars were bright, and the air was thick.

"Ma," I said. "We've talked about this; I'm going to New York. I've been out of school for years and hadn't found a tech job yet."

"Why not look at the cities an hour or so away," she begged as she wrapped her arms around me. I grabbed her arm as it was a moment I enjoyed, snuggled in her arms of comfort like a fuzzy blanket. My mother's embrace was better than any best tasting food around, better than a first kiss, and the most enjoyable moment a girl strived to have her around.

"I'm leaving at nine," I said. "Catching the first bus out, and then I'm heading North."

She sighed, and then she kissed the top of my head. "Remember to take care of yourself," she said squeezing me tightly. "Check in with me every day. Don't get into any trouble." She loosened her embrace as she kissed the top of my head again. "And if you do get into any trouble, come home immediately!"

I giggled as I knew she meant it truthfully. It was the first time in my life where I made a plan outside of our hometown. Through High School, I became fascinated with computer coding and used it as a project to code different data sequences for small businesses. After successfully learning the basics, I received my bachelor's degree in computer science and also majored in physical education as a back up to teach at a school. My first month as a Substitute Teacher at the high school, I found out quickly that teaching wasn't in my future. Life at the farm became my world when I wasn't in school, helping dad tend the animals, fields, and enjoying the natural peace that was brought forward from it.

The work allowed me to think of what I wanted to do with my life, reach further than the small town where everyone knew everything about you. A small town knew more about you than you knew of yourself. Secrets were no longer secrets, but the way of gossiping. It urged me to look beyond this state to go. I wanted to be in the middle of everything unnoticed. New York felt like the place to be where no one would speak of you because of its chaos. The greatest escape from being as if under a microscope in the small town. A place to find new adventure within a fast paced world.

Unlike me, Liz knew what she was going to do with her life. She had always been fascinated with the medical field, even volunteering at blood drives or anything in the medical related. Her work drive in the medical industry profound her as others in the community wrote letters of recommendations, and with her outstanding grades, she was accepted in the local community college medical school at the young age of sixteen. The day she was accepted, she knew her heart was set to become a Gynecologist as the local care in our small town wasn't always the best.

Mom and I went to bed shortly after our talk, and then it wasn't long before the alarm went off. Liz was throwing up in the toilet. I laughed at her light weight and assisted in getting her some medicine. Then, I got ready for the final time at the ranch as I knew tomorrow I would be getting ready in New York. Grabbing my suitcase and taking a final look around my bedroom. The memory filled photos around my walls, the posters of coding, and then took a breath as I closed the door behind me. We all loaded up in dad's bright red pickup truck. Silence filled the ride to the bus stop as I embraced the beautiful country sight, knowing it would be my goodbye for a while. I knew I would miss this part of country living, neighbors a couple of miles apart, and the sights with fresh air that nature provided. However, I also knew that a new calling in my life to go for something greater somewhere else.

My bus ticket tightly gripped in my hand as we made our way towards the bus I would depart on. I gave my suitcase to the driver, and then turned around, hugging dad first who didn't want to let go. Since his stroke a year ago, he hadn't talked. Mom already had a few straggling tears escaped her eyes as she hugged me. "None of those," I scolded with a smile as I kissed the side of her cheek. "This is a good thing for all of us."

She smiled as she kissed my cheek. "Be strong, brave, and courageous. And remember where your roots are grounded at," she whispered in my ear. "I love you."

The goodbye felt as if I weren't returning, but I knew that the adventure would probably result in me returning sooner than they expected. My years of planning moves always failed, and that was why I continued to live with my parents. To be hopeful, I wanted to move away from them to not rely on them to keep me afloat. I kissed mom's cheek, and then I pulled away from her. Liz had been crying all the way here. I wiped her face, putting my hands on her cheeks. "This isn't a goodbye forever," I said as we locked eyes.

Her lips trembled as she tried to hold back tears. "This isn't fair," she cried clutching my wrists. "You and I were supposed to do everything together."

"Maybe when I become a millionaire," I laughed. "We can travel the world together."

She giggled as she wrapped her arms around my back. I hugged her back, holding her for a few seconds. We were three years apart in age and nearly inseparable until now. We pulled back from each other's embrace. She reached into her back pocket. "I got you something," she cried as she wiped her face. She handed me a small black box with a gold bow on top.

I smiled in shock as I felt bad that I only had given her a hangover from the night before. "Shouldn't I be giving you something? I mean it was your birthday," I said as I took the box from her hand.

"Just open it," she said tapping my arm.

I opened the box to discover a golden chain with a gold cross that was about an inch in length. I pulled the necklace out, admiring its beauty, and dropped the box. "Here," I said turning around. "Put it on my neck now." I smiled as I loved it. Liz helped put the necklace around my neck.

"Don't forget your roots," she laughed and kissed my cheek.

We gave a last embrace, and then I walked back from them. I waved as I got on the bus and then made my way to a seat. Taking a spot in the middle next to a window, and I waved until the bus drove off. The bus ride took several hours, and then I switched buses several times. I finally made it to New York and was overwhelmed by its multitude. The first thing on my to-do list was to find an apartment. Dad had helped me cash in all my savings before departure, so I had enough for three months' rent.

I found the smallest one-bedroom apartment, a small kitchenette, living area, and a single bathroom. After settling with the owner and paying the three months in advance, I immediately went to look for work. My clear-concise resume ready for potential employers to view. Adjusting to the city, people slamming into each other, no personal space, and the loudest noise on earth, was chaotic at first as I grew up where we hustled but kept space between us.

Each day coming back to the apartment, I was exhausted, dropping back on my bed like the defeat of the day. A pain growing inside of me that I had made a mistake. A smalltown country girl like me had no business being part of a huge chaotic city. Even with doubt rumbling it's way through me, I urged to continue and be hopeful.

I called mom as promised, daily, sounding positive as I didn't want her to get worried. She would insist I come back home and not ever attempt to do something like this again. So, to ease her mind and avoid confrontation that I wouldn't make it, I made up a job and pretended to sound like I made friends and was adjusting to this new lift well. I had to reevaluate my action plan in this city, and it was driving me crazy internally. The pain that emerged deeply continued to grow, however, I decided that I would give it till my advance on rent was out before I went back home.

Three weeks passed; the struggle was almost unbearable. Each day I woke up, determined that I could find a good paying job and not have to face my parents with defeat. I took the subway daily to discover potential places of businesses that would hire a new IT Tech. The process was long as I interviewed at a few places and was turned down due to lack of experience. To bring back a small part of my life from home, I found a bar near my apartment, ready to drink away some of this new aching pain that continued to grow inside of me.

"You look terrible," the bartender said. He was in his mid-thirties, with a black T-shirt, jeans, shaved face, long hair that was combed.

I smiled as I sat some money down, and laid my jacket to the chair to my left. "That was the goal," I said. "Double shot."

"You have ID?"

I pulled out my ID and slid it across the bar. He looked over it and then tossed it back towards me. I left it laying on the bar as I glanced over at my shoulder, a few people scattered throughout the bar, drinking and socializing. He pulled out two shot glasses, poured the shots, and then slid them towards me. "So, what brought you here?" He asked as he picked up a towel and started to clean glasses.

"Looking for work," I said as I wrapped my fingers around the one shot glass, looking down at it. "But, may have to pack up and move back home."

I took the first shot, letting the burn sting my throat. I coughed a little and then placed the glass back down. I picked up the other, shot my head back, and then sat it down. "I know a few guys needing some help," he said. "But it may not be up your alley."

"If it's not computers, I'm not interested," I said pushing the glasses towards him.

He laughed and then poured two more shots. "These are on the house," he said.

I nodded as I picked one up, flung it back and sat it back down. I felt the wind beside me as a man sat down next to me. I looked over at him, dark brown hair that had enough hair to be glaze over his forehead, green eyes as we slightly glanced at each other, sparking an interest with his appearance. He wore a black leather jacket, jeans, and moved his hands to the bar interlocking them. "Wade, the usual," he spoke a slightly deep tone that intrigued my interest furthermore. I looked back at my second shot, hesitating whether to take it now that I had someone beside me who was fine looking, and then realizing that I wasn't in a place to be falling for someone or even having a night affair. I glanced over at the man as the anticipation built up if he were looking at me as well, he glanced at me.

Our eyes met and it felt like a spark burst between us. I quickly looked away as a flood of embarrassment over this stranger rose inside of me. His charming appearance and voice caused the hair on my arms to rise. I got up from the chair, grabbing my coat from beside me. "You going to take the other shot?" Wade asked.

I glanced at the man beside me, who now looked at me with a twinkle in his eyes, and then back at Wade. "No," I said and turned away quickly. I rushed out of the bar, not really understanding my emotions over this man that only sat beside me. We didn't even talk to each other, and I was interested. That was the first time I've ever laid eyes on someone and was immediately covered in goosebumps.

I got back to my apartment, locked up, and then took a shower. Confusion settling as I've met several people at a bar, but no one had ever interested me with their voice and complexion as he did. Shoving the thoughts away, I contemplated the idea of Wade's suggestion on him knowing people that had work lined up and curiosity rose. If they were willing to hire me, would it be bad to investigate the work he knew further? Night had fallen, I called mom, made up more lies to get past her interrogation and confrontation, and then got off the phone.

A month had passed since leaving the ranch, no progress on job hunting, and my motivation felt as if it were slipping from my hands. The next day, I got onto the subway as usual and then exited. An unusual settling feeling was with me as I felt different with this exit of the subway. I clutched my bag closely as I walked towards the platform stairs. A screeching sound of the subway swarmed passed the platform. I turned as it startled me, suddenly knocked down by a tall bulky man in black attire. He had black hair, mustache, and beard as I mentally notated his facial features. As I was getting up from the ground, he snatched my bag from my shoulder and then started running for the stairs.

"Hey," I yelled as I scrambled to my feet. I ran up the stairs, beginning the chase for my bag back.

The man got into the street, shoving people out of his way. Groans and yelling erupted from those people, I quickly gained speed, running after him for my bag. He crossed the car trafficked street with me on his heels. We crossed into the sidewalk with more people, shoving his way through as he tried to desperately gain space between us. "Hey, stop!" I shouted as I got close to him, a lady running, knocked into me, both of us stumbled. "Sorry," I grunted as I quickly retaliated, getting to my feet and dashing after the man.

Glancing back at me, a man with a cart came around the corner and he fell into it. The pause in his running allowed me to catch up to him as he rushed to his feet, keeping my bag clutched in his hand. I grabbed his shirt and shifted my weight to slam him into a building wall. "Geez, lady," he said turning around to face me, dropping my bag.

The anger rose inside of me as I pulled him towards me and then shoved him hard into the wall. "You don't take what's not yours," I said through gritted teeth. I let go of his shirt and picked up my bag from the ground. He took off running, not looking back, as I watched him disappear into the crowd.

"Ma'am, are you okay?" A man asked as he was picking up his cart.

I nodded. "Yes, I'm fine," I said, and then assisted him with the hats, scarfs, and wallets scattered around the sidewalk.

After ensuring the man with his car was in order, I left the scene, walking back towards the subway as I looked around to see where I was at. Moving to the side, towards a building entrance, I stopped and investigated my bag, the shoulder strap was broken, and my ID was gone. *Great!* I sighed in disappointment as now my photo ID card was stolen. *Damn!* The anger that already was there grew deeper as I made my way back to the subway. Defeated by the way the day had started, and decided it was best to go back to the apartment and enjoy a bottle of liquor.

I walked back down the stairs and waited for the next subway. A hand grabbed my arm and pulled me around to the other side of the wall. "Hey, stop," I said as he pushed me to the wall. Caught off guard, I looked as it was the man in the black leather coat from the other night.

A hardened lump formed in my throat as our eyes met again. Suddenly, I looked away as I wasn't sure whether to be grateful or to be terrified that it was him. "Wade said," he stuttered.

I looked back into his eyes as we locked gazes. "Wade said?" I asked arching an eyebrow with curiosity.

His eyes blinked a few times as his cheeks became rosy flushed, and then he reached in his pocket. I threw my hands up as I wasn't sure what he had in his pocket, a threatening fear rose inside of me as my breathing hardened. He stepped back as my emotions rattled him, "Woah," he said. "I'm not going to hurt you. I have your," he stuttered, as I looked down at his hand that slowly moved from his pocket.

I put my hands down to see he had a white plastic card. "My ID," I gasped as he reached his hand out to me with it. A flush of excitement rushed over me as I felt a sense of relief. "I thought the guy-"

"The guy you chased stole it?" He asked without stuttering.

I looked up from my ID to him, unsettling how his stuttering disappeared. Our eyes met as I stepped back into the wall, a chill moving up my spine. I looked away as my cheeks flushed in embarrassment. The hair on my arms rose as I didn't understand why my body was reacting so oddly with this man that I hadn't even had a conversation with since we met. "You saw?" I asked keeping my eyes on the ground.

He came closer to me, putting his hand on my cheek. I quickly looked up as our personal space was now a combined space. Our eyes met as another hardened lump formed as anticipation rose if our lips were to meet. "Stacy Edwards, bachelor's in computer science and physical education," he said moving my hair behind my ears. His breath fluttered against my skin, sending another wave of chills down my spine. The air thickened as my breathing hardened, *was he going to kiss me*? "Why come to New York?" He asked as we stared intensely into each other's souls.

"I," I stuttered with my mouth suddenly drier than a hot humid day in North Carolina. "I wanted to work in the city."

He moved closer to my face as I felt the anticipation grow intensely, allowing a small gasp escaped my lips. *Do I want him to kiss me?* I didn't fight him as we kept our eyes locked on each other. "How is New York treating you?" He asked as his breath flushed over my face. I felt the hairs on my body stand as I couldn't unload this overwhelming sensation. My mind and body a mess from how awkwardly but unalarming this felt.

I licked my lip and glanced to see if anyone was nearby. No one in sight, *of course!* "I say it's New York," I said nervously as I moved my fingertips to the wall behind me. Allowing the cool sensation to calm my now heated body.

"You still need a job?" He asked breathing into my face.

I swallowed the hard lump that formed in my throat. Beads of sweat forming as I wasn't sure whether to be afraid of him, or if he wanted to kiss me, or the idea of him now bringing up work. Mesmerized by him, my mind juggled the entire scene as I wasn't even drunk to kiss a stranger, yet alone unsure how I felt about his way of a job proposal. He touched my cheek, my body flinched in reaction to his touch, looking more intensely into my eyes. "I'm not a prostitute," I blurted out as it felt like he had me pinned to a wall.

A slight chuckle escaped his mouth. "That's not the kind of business I'm in," he said moving his hand from my cheek to the wall beside my face.

My heart beating out of my chest. I licked my lip, glancing around again, no one in sight. I dropped my ID and bag on the ground as I kept my fingers touching the wall behind me. Every hair on my body stood straight up in anticipation whether I was about to be attacked or kissed. I took a deep breath, trying to calm myself as I was ready to kick him in his groins and get out of the stance I was in. A sense of reassurance that he wasn't going to hurt me raveled through me. I locked my eyes with him again.

"What kind of business are you in?" I asked as a smile swept across his face. As if he were happy to hear the question, he pulled back away from me as he kept the hand on the wall beside me. The space grew apart between us as my body became less tense.

"Here's my card," he said with a smile as he pulled out a card from his jacket with his other hand. "Call me if interested."

I took the card as he backed away from me, and then he turned away. Another screech from the subway roared through the pass. A sigh of relief swept through me as I put my head back on the wall behind me, looking up at the ceiling, and taking a few breaths as my rapid heartbeat calmed down. After gathering my composure, I bent down and grabbed my bag and ID from the ground. I looked over the card he gave me, nothing but a number on it in bold black font. I got on the subway and made my way back to my apartment.

I tossed my bag on the counter with the card that the estranged man gave to me, who I didn't even get a name. I went to the kitchen sink, splashing cold water on my face. The coolness washed away the anxiety from the day off of me. Grabbing the dry cotton towel next to the sink, I patted my face and then grabbed a cup from my cabinet and poured a glass of cold water. I leaned against the counter, staring at the card that sat face up on the countertop island.

I have to be out of my mind. I sighed as I sat the cup down on the counter by the sink, reaching to the card and reading over the number. The memories of our interaction rushing through me as I remembered the way this man compensated my feelings, making me feel nervous but calm in his presence. His voice tender but stern, sending chills up my spine, pricking every goosebump across my body. His stuttering at first as if I caught him off guard. I smiled as the thought was intriguing that I made a man stutter at the sight of me.

I sat the card back down and then grabbed my cellphone. I called mom to have my daily chat with her. The lies that I fed her of my fictional job had burdened me as I knew it wasn't the right thing to do. Today, I told her about a specific co-worker that I had bumped into on the elevator. Mom fed by my web of lies was also interested in this mysterious man and advised me to find out more about him. She was excited to hear that I may have bumped into my soulmate.

After getting off the phone with her, I went back over to the card, propping myself on the counter and fiddling with the card in hand. I contemplated the worst idea of this mysterious number being a door to my deepest darkest devastation. And then I entertained the thoughts of the number being the best thing that was to ever happen for me. I put the card down on the countertop, and then went to bed.

That night I dreamt of the estranged man who had caused me to have overwhelming mixed emotions. I dreamt of our conversation on the platform where he had me cornered, desperate, stuttering, but also insanely courageous. The hair rose on the back of my neck, the chills rolling down my spine, and the anticipation of whether he was going to kiss me or not. I woke up when he had his lips nearly touching mine.

I looked over at the clock that read 11:57. I rubbed my hand over my face as I was now knee deep in the mud with emotions over this man who've yet has given me his name. I rolled over towards the clock, looking at the minutes slowly pass as the thoughts of him dwelled on my mind. I slid my hand around the necklace Liz gave me and closed my eyes.

A week had passed since the mysterious man's encounter. My search for a job continued, ending up at home staring at the card each night, lying to mom on the phone. I fumbled the card in my hand for hours at end, thinking of the mixed emotions I felt and desperately wanted to feed into them. The feelings growing deeper as each day went by, continuously remembering the interaction between us, allowing the urge to want more grow. The idea of what could come of the job he had to offer, and the possibility of him becoming the true soulmate of my life intensified every second my mind thought of him.

Liz called me that evening after mom and I talked. "Stacy," Liz said with sadness in her tone. "I wish you were here with us. It's just not the same without you here."

"Liz," I scolded. "I told you all that I'm doing this my way. Plus, I got a job and will hopefully earn enough time to come see you all a week or so."

"I'm going to hold you to it," she said as I felt a smile slide across her face. I slightly smiled as I knew with the way things were going that I may be going back home for good if I didn't make a change soon.

"I got to hit the hay sis," I said rushing myself off. I didn't want to lie to her too. Lying was weighing deeply on me, and I knew better than to continue to feed the weight.

She sighed. "Miss you, big sis," she said. "Remember your roots."

I laughed as we disconnected. Placing my phone down on the counter, and I started pacing back and forth in the apartment. The card that seems to be the only light in this apartment, I picked it up and fumbled with it and then sat it down. Butterflies swarmed as the anticipation grew stronger with each second at the thought of calling him and inquiring about the work he had. Every part of me wanted more information about this estranged man. A different rhythm fluctuated in my heart at the thought of him. I sighed as I looked over the card one more time and then slid it in my new small shoulder black bag. The idea of having a drink first drew to my mind.

I locked my apartment and went to the bar around the corner. It was a busy Thursday night, crowds all around the bar. As I caught Wade's attention, I stood near the bar, keeping my attention in his direction. "I will take a double shot," I shouted over the loud noise of music and conversations.

Wade nodded as he pulled the glasses out. "You're not afraid of taking double shots," a familiar voice spoke in my ear as chills raced down my spine. A hardened lump formed, a shallow breath escaped my lips, my body shuttered as I shifted away from him. He lightly grazed my arm, goosebumps immediately popping up as he pulled himself next to me. "But you're afraid of me."

I gave a slight nod to Wade as a gesture to thank him as he pushed the two shots towards me. I went to put money down and was beat to it as the man behind me slid his money onto the bar. "Those are on me," he said as I turned to face him, an inch space between us. A smile rushing across my face as I put my money back in my purse, he grabbed the double shots.

We made our way over to a tall skinny black table that had no chairs. He placed the shots in front of me. "Thank you," I said pushing my hair behind my ears. I took the first shot in my hand. He wrapped his hand around mine with the shot, sliding both the glass and my hand down on the table.

"You haven't called," he said keeping his hand on mine, eyes locked with mine.

My mouth suddenly dry as he inched his way closer to me. He leaned down to my ear. "I thought you needed a job," he whispered. A roaring sensation fluttered my entire body, from ear to toe as his hot breath tickled my ear.

I made myself slightly cough to escape the feeling. "You intimidate me," I said shifting my sight to the shot glass. "And I don't even know your name."

"You haven't asked for it either," he said moving his hand off mine.

I glanced up to meet his eyes staring at me. I swallowed the lump that formed in my throat, and then licked my lips. "What is your name?" I asked curiously.

"Mason," he said as a smile slid across his face.

"Stacy," I said looking back at the two shot glasses. "May I?" I asked, side glancing at him.

He picked up the shot glass and handed it to me. I flung it back in my throat, letting the burn tickle my throat as I placed the glass back on the table. He handed me the second one locking eyes with mine, his eyes shown tender side of him. He put his hand around mine and the shot glass. "Do you still need a job?"

Beads of sweat formed, chills falling down my spine, goosebumps rose as my breathing hardened. "What do you do for work?" I asked.

He smiled as he moved in closer to my side, putting his arm around my back, and then shifting his mouth to my ear. I looked down at the table as every sensation he unraveled built up more steam. "I train people to work on my team. I need them to be soberminded, physically fit, and determined. The job itself is difficult, but the payout is worth every cent," he whispered in my ear. "I also need them to not fear as that will only cause a disturbance."

I gasped as I turned my face to where our faces nearly met. We stared at each other, breathing on each other. My body jumping at the thought of wanting him to kiss me, unsure why, but I wanted our lips to meet. "I'm not scared of you," I said as we intensely stared at each other.

He smiled as he moved his face to the side of mine, barely grazing my cheek as he whispered, "then put down that shot and follow me."

He pulled back from my ear, as our eyes locked on each other. Before realizing, my hand with both the shot and his wrapped around it slowly moved to the table, sitting down the shot. He let go of my hand, turned away from me, and started towards the exit. A sense of shock washed over me as none of this made sense, and then without hesitation I followed him out of the bar.

Chapter Two

We walked down the street, keeping at his heels, feeling a sense of overwhelming emotions. I wanted to stop, but I knew if I did then he would leave me where I stopped. Shoving any fear of the unknown behind me as we hurriedly down the streets. We walked for what felt like an hour to an abandoned warehouse, slowing my pace, the fear that I shoved away crept back in. "Wait," I said as I stopped at the door. He turned around to face me, locking his eyes with mine. "I just need to know one more thing." I put my fingers through my hair as he took a step towards me. "I need to know you're not going to kill me."

He put both hands on my chin, pushing the hair back, keeping our eyes locked as he got an inch from my face. I grabbed his hands that felt amazingly great on my face. My body reacting as if it knew that we were about to kiss. "You have to trust me," he insisted. "Every step of the way, from here forward."

My breathing hardened as the darkest deepest devastation choice that I contemplated every time I fumbled that card in my hand rushed through me. I saw through his eyes the sternness that rose every cold chill in my body, forming the goosebumps. A sense of fear fled through me as I knew I couldn't overpower his strength, and then it was the moment I became scared. "Can you trust me?" He asked.

Another lump formed in my throat, my mouth as dry as the desert, and my heart beating out of my chest. His lips were a centimeter from mine, and then I closed my eyes. I had to take the second of letting myself breathe again as I knew I was scared, but now I was even more scared of losing him. My eyes opened and looked into his stunning green eyes. "As long as you will be there with me," I said.

He smiled as he pulled away from my face, letting go of my chin. Shocked as I didn't get a kiss from him. Disappointment flooded me as he turned away. I followed him as he put his hand on the doorknob. "Once you enter this warehouse, your training will begin," he said sternly not looking at me. "I will be there, but you have to put in the work. This isn't for the weak."

I nodded as the anticipation of what was behind that door rose inside of my veins. A part of me battled whether I should turn around and run, but the other part of me that wanted Mason knew to fight the first of many battles. It's an old saying that when you find your soulmate, it's hard to let them slip away. The intense feelings I felt towards Mason assured me that he was mine. I could tell he felt the same about me, or else he wouldn't have waited for me at the bar.

He opened the door and entered first as I followed behind him. The pathway was dark as we approached a lit section ahead. Glancing back at me as the sound of the door slammed shut behind me. A shutter rattled through me as we kept walking towards the light. It felt like a sign that I was about to leave behind everything that I once loved and cared about before entering this warehouse. I heard footsteps around as we continued to approach the lit section.

"Mason," an elder man said. I looked around Mason as we got underneath the light. The man wore a light blue suit, white button up, black tie, and black shoes. His hands were in his pockets as we stopped. "Is this her? Your choice for the job?"

"Yes," Mason said not looking back at me. He walked over to the man. "We now have five prospects to train."

"Then let the training begin," the elderly man stated. "I hope none are a disappointment."

"Yes sir," Mason said. "I'm only training for one week. Anyone who doesn't make the cut will be-."

The elderly man interrupted Mason with clearing his throat. "We'll handle business as needed."

Mason nodded and then turned around to me. "Best of luck, Stacy," he said as we locked eyes. The sound of footsteps grew louder behind me, I turned quickly but wasn't quick enough. An arm with a black cloth bag covered my head, quickly, I grabbed the arm to fight back. Ropes were tied around arms and legs, and then I was picked up. A world of panic flooded me as I couldn't find my voice to yell or scream as shock settled in, and then I recalled Mason stated it wasn't going to be easy.

I was placed in a chair; my hands were tied to the chair behind me as my ankles tied to the legs under me. Someone snatched the black bag off my head, my hair a mess across my face as I shook it to the sides. In the middle of a line of chairs, two to my right and two to my left, sat other men bound to their chairs like me. The other men were looking to their left and right as well. Looking around the now fully lit warehouse, seeing multiple doors out of this room, but only one door with an exit sign lit up above it. All of the doors were blackish gray with small lights above them that illuminated the color yellow. I began to work my hands with the rope to get myself free as I knew that I was ready to get out of there.

A big hanging light with buzzing noise rocked slightly in the air above us. Mason walked to the center of us, parallel to me. "Welcome," he said with one hand in his pocket and the other out towards us. "Tonight, you begin your training." He put his hand in his other pocket and started pacing in front of us. I kept moving my hands, building the sweat and friction to remove them from the knots. "What we do is top dollar, and we need nothing less than perfection. I plan to build a team for my work that excels in every fear-stricken situation." He pulled out a gun from his left side holster.

I stopped moving for a moment, as another wave of emotions rolled through me. "I need skilled, trained professionals, nothing less to take on challenges that are far worse than you will ever face. I need men," he paused, "and women," glancing at me for a second, and then looked away. Instinctively working my hands to free them. "To only be afraid of getting caught." He turned back towards me for a brief moment. "Because if you do get caught, then you must know that you will have to do everything in your power to be let go with no charges. If by chance you get caught and found guilty, know that we have people on the inside of every slammer there is to mankind that will kill you."

A cold sweat formed on my forehead as I could feel my breathing hardening again. *What kind of mess did I get myself into?* I steadied my breathing as the others were chanting, as if praising this kind of behavior, beside me. Another lump formed inside of me as I felt every inch of fear striking through my body. The prickling of the hairs on my body stood as the energy around me felt unnerving. My only thought was that I have now entered the arena of fight till death, and if I didn't fight I would become death's next victim. "Your first assignment," Mason said. "Getting out of these chairs and finding your way to the bunkroom before time is up."

"What do you mean?" The guy to my left asked. He had glasses on, curly brown locks, looked to be in early twenties, wore a white tank, red bandana around his neck, blue jeans, and red sneakers.

"You have two minutes to get yourselves free once I leave the room," Mason said. "Once time is up, the dogs will be in. They go after anything that runs or isn't known to them, and they will chew until I call them off. You must figure out which door is the one with the bunks and safely secure yourself into the room. All who make it out alive move to the next phase of training."

"You have to be kidding," another man to my right said. "Attack dogs, really?"

Mason shrugged his shoulders. "In a real-life situation, you may be attacked by professional police K9s," Mason said interlocking his fingers. "I need to know you can get yourself out." The men beside me were swearing and jerking in their chairs. Mason turned away and walked into the darkness. "Oh yes," Mason said. "One more thing, the lights will be off."

Sounds of aggressive dogs barking and growling grew as his footsteps drifted away. I quickly got back to working on my hands. A door closed; the lights flashed off and then panic settled in for all of us who were bounded to the chairs. The men on either side of me started screaming and grunting as it sounded like they were trying to get free. I worked diligently as I got my left hand out, and then quickly rushed to get my right hand. Barking and growling grew louder as my breathing hardened with every anxious second that passed. Freeing my right hand, bending down to untie my ankles. My hands sweating as I freed my ankles, not able to see anything but the doors with the low-lit yellow lights above them. The red exit sign was the only one boldly standing out.

I started to run towards it but slammed into someone else, falling to the ground, both of us groaned in pain. Rolling over to my knees, I got back up and started for the exit sign. *The exit sign is a trap!* The idea that it was placed as a decoy to throw us off raged through my mind. I shifted my direction as the sounds of the dogs got closer. A shriek slipped through my teeth as the door I went to was locked. I slapped the door hard in frustration and then ran to the next one.

The dogs entered the area as a man screamed in agony. Looking around for another door, the aggressiveness of the dogs roared the warehouse with panic shrieks from others. I stopped in my tracks as one leaped in front of me towards a man next to me. Slight scream slipped my lips as I ran hard, hearing the barking and growling all around me. Fear of being bit pounded my chest as it felt like back at home when we had to coyote hunt.

I ran into a chair as it fell in front of me, bringing me down on one knee. Looking around as the sounds screamed in my ears from others and the dogs. I grabbed a rope that dangled on one of the chairs and dashed for another door across the room. A growl pierced beside me as a dog leaped towards me. Avoiding the leap, I ducked falling to my knees as it flew over my head. Rushing to my feet, I ran towards the door I had my sight set on. I was a few steps away, and then another person collided with me, knocking me into a wall. A pain shattered through my side and a groan left my throat as I fell down. I gripped the rope tightly in my hand as a large black and brown dog charged towards me.

Its teeth showing, snapping barks, and then it jumped after me. Throwing my hands up, to pull the rope tightly, the dog's mouth gripped the rope as I quickly lunged forward, wrapping it around the neck. Pain emerged from the dog's paws clawing at my skin. As a country girl, having to defend myself from a dog was unnatural, allowing my heart to sink as I strangled the meat-eating dog. I couldn't allow my sensitivity to overpower at a time as this where I needed to survive.

THE SILENCER'S WIFE

The dog went from barking to a gasp. I let it go as it died, letting it go as I took a breath, holding back tears.

The sounds of footsteps running flew past me as I looked at their path, seeing the door I originally was headed towards open. One of the men had a dog on its ankle, as it tried to kick it off. Scrambling to my feet, dashing towards the open door where another made it inside, revealing the bunks. *Yes!* A sensation of a hand grabbing the back of my neck as I ran towards the door. Not enough time to react, I was shoved towards the ground. I threw my hands to protect my head as I rolled, retaliating with a jump up. The door was slowly shutting as I shoved into the man in front of me as he had his hand on the doorknob. Rolling onto our backs as we both fell into the room, looking up as another dog was dashing towards us. Panic rushed through me as I tried to crawl backwards. Another man slammed the door shut as the dog leaped towards us.

Panting from the adrenaline, I got up from the ground next to the man who had attempted to ensure I was left for the dogs to kill. I looked around when someone had turned the two light bulbs on. "Thomas, you made it," the man said as he got off the ground from beside me. He wore a red toboggan, plaided button up and jeans with white sneakers.

"Jackson," Thomas said, who was a white man wore a regular t-shirt and jeans with black sneakers. They both had dark brown hair with little length that could use haircuts.

Glancing over at the man by the door who wore a green jacket with glasses, jeans, and had blonde hair. "Do you think they will let us know when we can exit?" He asked. I walked over to him and then placed my ear on the door. The noise of barking and growling dogs was gone.

"I don't hear anything," I said pulling my ear back from the door.

He put his hand out. "Preston," he said with a smile.

I turned around, ignoring his greeting, at the small closet room we were in. There was a total of four bunks with no sheets just mattresses and a pillow on each. The room had one vent next to the upper left bunk, no markings on the walls, or anything else in the room but us. Jackson, who shoved me down, came over to me. I felt myself back into the bunk bed corner near the door.

"Sorry about earlier," he said invading my personal space.

I shoved him back. "Stay away from me," I snapped.

"Jackson, leave her," Thomas said.

I crossed my arms over my chest as I put my head against the wall next to the door. Preston put his ears to the door. "Should we try to go out?" He asked.

I shrugged my shoulders as this became more awkward than any situation I've ever been in. I'm in a room full of men, and an exit with flesh eating dogs. Preston's hands shook, sweat dripping as he put his hand on the doorknob. Uncrossing my arms and placed them by side as I stood up straight while anticipation of what to come rose. We all became silent as he went to turn the knob. He jiggled the knob.

"Open the door," Thomas yelled.

Preston with a panicked look turned around to us. "It won't open," he hesitated.

Jackson shoved him out of the way, glancing at me with a smirk across his face, and then grabbed the doorknob. He attempted to twist the knob. "Well," Preston said as he went and sat down on the cot to the door's left. "Can you get it open?"

"It's locked from the outside," Jackson said as he slapped the door.

I turned away as I felt the tension rise in all of us. It was unsettling as they all started showing emotions of rage, fear, and panic. "He said the next phase would begin after the first," Thomas said. "Maybe that means we need to rest."

Jackson brushed my arm. "Hey," he said lowly. "If you get scared, you can sleep next to me."

"In your dreams," I snapped as I jerked my arm away from him.

Jackson took the bunk I stood next to and shifted himself over. "Well, it's here if you need a shoulder to cry on," he said as he interlocked his fingers behind his head.

I walked over to the door, trying the doorknob for myself as it felt extremely nauseating and uncomfortable in this room with these pigs. In hope that if I jiggled the knob, it would unlock, nothing. I finally gave up as I watched the others lay down on the cots. Thomas took the cot above Jackson with Preston across from him. I waited till they all had their eyes closed as I made my way to the cot above Preston. He didn't alarm me as much as Jackson.

The two single lightbulbs that barely lit the room remained on. I kept my eyes open, listening to the others snore, focusing on the ceiling above my head, afraid of the unknown with these three men. This wasn't just a test of endurance and survival, but it felt like a test of how we would act with each other. Every emotion that I felt of Mason disappeared as I wasn't afraid of him. Now, I'm completely terrified.

The dreadful hours passed as I clutched the cross around my neck, eyes wide open, listening to strangers' snoring around me. I rubbed my eyes, trying to keep them awake. "Psst…" I heard the sound. I rolled over and looked down at Preston.

"Have you slept any?" He whispered.

I shook my head. "If you want to get some shut eye, I will stay awake for you," he said.

I rolled back over onto my back and contemplated trusting this person. The first person I trusted threw me to the wolves figuratively speaking. I rubbed my temples as I thought of mom's words on the porch back in July. *If you find yourself in trouble, come home.* The fact that I was in trouble, and I couldn't go back to the ranch rumbled in my thoughts. Mixed emotions about a man that persistently made his way in my life from the bar to the subway platform, then allowing him to completely manipulate me into following him. Mentally and physically, I was drained and unsettled with where I lied.

The door lock unlatched, I jumped up to a seating position, shifting off the bunk, and falling onto the floor. The others got up from their bunks and followed behind me. "Well," Jackson said. "Ladies first."

I rolled my eyes, walking towards the door, and then slowly twisting the knob. It opened, shocked by the motion. We all held our breaths as I slowly opened the door. The lights shone brightly into the warehouse with the chairs and ropes. A table was present to the right with food on it, another table to the left with a cloth over it. I took a step out of the room, glancing around to see or hear any dogs. The dog I killed lay with its rope over to the right. Saddened more by the sight of it, I looked away.

"Good morning," the elderly man said as he clapped his hands. We all came out of the room, spreading out into a line. "Congratulations to you all making it to phase two."

"Who are you?" Thomas asked as he crossed his arms.

"Henderson," he said as he moved towards us. I took a step back as the others stood firmly in their positions. "Breakfast anyone?" He asked as he put his hand out towards the table. Preston and I glanced at each other and then looked at Thomas and Jackson. They slowly made their way over to the table. Preston nodded and then went on to the table. I hesitated as Henderson stared at me. He didn't stare at me as if he were a creep, but as if he were surprised. "What a treasure you are," he said as an uneasy feeling rolled over me. "Do eat, I know with last night's events you must be starved."

"Sorry about your dog," I said glancing at him who had stepped to my side.

"It's all part of business," he said. "Some live, some die."

The words scorned me as if fire were flooding my veins. The hair on the back of my neck stood as my cheeks flushed. Henderson and I stared a few seconds into each other's eyes. A strange feeling crossed me as the uneasiness settled in. It was nauseating as everything about this place felt abnormal to me. I glanced over at the others who had taken seats at the table with the food and started to fill their plates.

"Shall we eat?" Henderson asked.

I folded my arms as I looked back at Henderson. "There were five of us," I said. "What happened to the fifth?"

"I wouldn't want to spoil your breakfast," he said as he placed a hand on my back. I jumped forward, uncrossing my arms, and then walked towards the table with the others. I took a seat beside Preston, regardless of Jackson motioning for me to desperately sit beside him.

"Jackson, Thomas, Preston, and Stacy," Henderson said as he took a seat at the head of the table. "Your next phase will begin shortly. You each will need to deliver something to Mason somewhere in the city without being detected by my men." Four men appeared at the other side of the table, wearing black sunglasses, black shirts, jeans, and all were bald. "Each will be given a package," Henderson said. "You will have a handler assigned to you, your job is to escape and stay undetected by the others."

"Where will Mason be?" Jackson asked as he tossed his fork on his plate.

Henderson smiled. "You will have to find him."

"What kind of game is this that you all are playing with us?" Thomas asked.

Henderson folded his napkin on his lap. "No games, just training. We need the best of the best," he said looking at each of us. "Either you complete the trainings, or we can let you go."

"How much does these jobs pay out?" Preston asked.

"Each pay is different depending on our client's wealth," Henderson stated. "Now, Scott, Kyle, James, and Ryan-."

"Wait a damn minute," Jackson interrupted.

Henderson formed a line with his lip. "You have more questions?" Henderson asked glaring at Jackson.

"What if we don't want to go any further," Jackson stated. "You all tried to kill us last night. What makes you think we want to keep going?"

"Scott," Henderson said. The man closest to Jackson came forward, locking his arm around Jackson's neck. We all jumped back, shocked at the commotion. Jackson fighting to get free of the grip around his neck. "Loosen your grip slightly," Henderson said. Scott listened by loosening his grip around Jackson's neck, and Jackson gasped. "You're free to let me know when you've had enough at any time, but do know this," Henderson said glancing at each of us, and then locking eyes with Jackson. "You have one exit when you entered at your freewill."

I heard Preston gulp beside me. I glanced at him as he looked pale as a ghost. "Do you want in, or do you want to leave, Jackson?" Henderson asked.

"In," Jackson gasped as he let go of Scott's arm.

Henderson nodded and Scott released his grip and then stepped back into formation with the others. "Now, Scott you're well acquainted with Jackson," Henderson said. "He will be your handler for this assignment. Kyle with Thomas, James with Preston, and lastly, Ryan with Stacy. You each have until lunch," Henderson stated as he stood up. We all stood up in accordance with him. Henderson turned around and walked away, exiting at a door across the room.

My stomach was in knots, all the food on the table appeared unappetizing. The others quickly ate, and then we got up from the table and went to our handlers. Scott and Jackson walked out first, followed by Kyle and Thomas, and then James and Preston. Ryan didn't speak as he kept his shades on and turned away, walking out of the room. Keeping up with his long pace, we left the warehouse. Each pair went separate routes as we walked several streets over. We went to the Subway, Ryan handed me an envelope as we entered the cart.

"Where are we headed?" I asked as I clutched the envelope close to my stomach.

Silence, Ryan didn't speak or make a sound as his facial expression remained serious. He looked to his left up the subway cart of people. Glancing down at his phone that was face out in his clip holster, had a map open on the screen. Shifting my eyes away as Ryan looked back towards me, and then stood up as if he were going to exit. I followed, getting up from the seat, clutching the package in hand. The cart came to a stop, everyone started to line up. Snatching his phone off his clip as the people shifted within the cart, bumping into each other as their impatience showed. Hydraulics sounded as the doors opened, the crowd flooded out like a herd of cattle. I ducked to blend in with them as I got close to others, grabbing a lady's brown coat from her black rolling suitcase she had beside her. Keeping low as I slid the jacket on, letting my hair be tucked inside the coat. I saw a hat on the ground by another lady who was reading a newspaper on the subway cart bench. Snatching the gray hat and quickly putting it on as I slid out of the cart with the crowd.

Walking in the opposite direction of most people that got off the cart, walking beside a man I pretended to grab his coat, but staying close enough to appear as being with him. Hastily, I got to the top of the steps, and made a hard right, hiding in the crowd of people, glancing at the phone with the map on. A blue 'M' icon was on the screen. *Mason!* Keeping myself on the path in his direction and blending my way through the crowd, seeing Preston rush past me. Moving in on him as I turned around, quickly grabbing his arm and pulling him into a nearby clothing store.

"What are you doing?" I asked frustrated as if this idiot had any idea of how to blend and track someone.

"Stacy," he said amazed once we got in a dressing room at the store. "How did you see me?"

"You idiot, you haven't even attempted to disguise yourself," I whispered as I glanced out the door, not seeing any of the handlers.

"Have you seen the other two yet?" Preston asked.

I shook my head and pulled out the phone. I swiped this off Ryan's clip. We looked at it together, seeing the initials of the handlers in different colors. They were all swarming towards one location. I zoomed in on the map of Mason's location. It was one of the finest hotels in New York. "He's at this hotel," I said pointing to it.

"How do we know where to find him once there?" Preston asked.

"Hotel bar," I smiled.

"Alright, you want to stick together?" He asked as we glanced at each other.

I shook my head. "We don't want to risk getting caught," I whispered.

I glanced out at the dressing room door, still no sign of any of the handlers. "I'm going to go this route, you take this one," he said pointing at different directions. I nodded in agreement. Leaving the dressing room first, seeing a red cocktail dress on my way out. I slid it off the hanger and went towards the cashier. Eyeing their tool to take the clip off the dress that sounded their security alarm if exited with their device. The cashier was busy ringing up a customer and in deep conversation when I slipped the clip and tossed it in the trash. Swiftly grabbed a bag and stuffed it in it, walking out of the store.

I knew being a criminal wasn't necessary part of the job, but I remembered what they said about being caught. A disguise and change of an outfit were the best way to keep blending. Whistling once outside, stopping a cab as I entered it and gave them an apartment building two blocks from the hotel. Once there, I got out, dashing through the crowd, not paying as I ran to the side street. I glanced at the phone, seeing the initial 'S' around the corner of my location. Pressing the buzzard on a building as someone exited and slid into the door before it locked. Made my way down the hall to the rear exit. I found a storage closet and entered it. Hurriedly, I stripped off my clothes, shoving them into the retail bag as I slid on the red cocktail dress. Looking down at my sneakers that were on the floor by the retail bag and scolding myself for what a mess that outfit appeared.

Fixing my hair back as I smoothed it into a partial ponytail and then put on the large brown coat that I took earlier from the subway cart. Grabbing the phone and envelope, glancing to see the letter 'S' had moved away from my location. Ensuring the hallway was clear, I made my way out the back exit, sliding on my sneakers, terrible combination with the cocktail dress. Scurried through the chaotic streets towards Hotel. Slowing down as I entered the Hotel's main entrance. I glanced at the phone to see that I was near Mason's location and looked around to find the bar entrance. Keeping the envelope clutched to my stomach, hiding it under my coat as I made my way over to the Hotel's bar entrance.

"May I help you?" A male hostess in black tuxedo asked, holding out his hand to prevent me from entering the bar area. His brown eyes and facial expression showed concern as he glanced over me from head to toe.

"I would like a seat at your bar," I said.

"Do you have ID?" He asked.

Realizing that my bag was taken from me, not recalling when they snatched it. A lump hardened as the challenge of this phase hardened by the moment. Slightly chuckling, I looked back up at the hostess with a smile. "I'm not here to drink," I said trying to think of anything to get past him and to Mason. "Meeting a friend."

"I see," the hostess smiled. "Security," he called out.

Jumping at his swift words, I shook my head as I turned seeing security coming towards us. "I'm leaving," I said turning away from him. He called off the guards as I went towards the entrance, running my hand over my forehead as a small deception came forth that I may be at a position where I couldn't get inside of that bar. It seemed that defeat followed me everywhere I went these days.

A blonde hair lady near my age with a man to her side in a tuxedo walked past me to the front desk. A slight hold of my breath as I made my way over to her, grabbing a magazine, acting as if I were interested in its content. The couple were laughing with the receptionist, unnoticing me sliding closer to her. She had her black purse over her shoulder closest to me with her wallet bulged out of it. A smile slipped across my face as my defeat was turning into victory. I glanced around, not seeing anyone noticing my appearance and snatched her wallet. Moving away from the couple as I glanced at the photo and age inside of the wallet, similar to mine.

I walked over to the hostess, smiling. "I went back to my room and retrieved it," I said.

Forming a line with his lips, he took the ID and glanced over it, and then at me. Hesitant for a moment and then handing the ID back to me with a genuine smile. "Where is your friend?" He asked as we both looked around.

Across the room in a rounded booth, Mason sat with his back towards us. "He's there," I said with a sigh of relief that the phase was almost completed. The hostess led me toward the booth as I walked hastily over to the table, sliding in across from Mason. Mason nodded at the hostess who then took a small bow in response, turning away and leaving us alone.

Mason and I locked our eyes, a rattling sensation flooding down me as my body temperature suddenly became hot. My emotions unfolding once again in his presence, never have I ever did this with any other man. He smiled as he chuckled, looking down at my dress, and then back at my eyes. "Should we go to the bar?" I asked breaking the silence as I sat up.

"You really should think about cutting out the drinks," he chuckled a little more. "They seem to be wearing off on your attire."

I smiled as I pushed my hair behind my right ear, breaking eye contact from him. He got up, forcing me to look back up at him as he moved over to my side, sliding an arm behind my shoulders. "However," he whispered in my ear. His hot breath forming goosebumps on my skin. "We better keep it professional."

A slight breath slipped from my lips as the sensation overwhelmingly compensated my entire body, craving more than just a tease. Clearing my throat to regain composure, I pulled the envelope from my coat and pressed it against his chest, pushing him away from me as I looked into his green emerald eyes. "You keep leaning towards me like you do, and professionalism will be out-."

"Shh…" He interrupted. Silencing myself as he grabbed my hand that was still on the package against his chest. "I heard you snatched another possession that isn't yours," he whispered. "I'm going to need that back as well."

I smiled as I placed the phone on his left leg. He looked down at my placement and then back up into my eyes. His eyes changed as a look of surprise rushed over him, and then he took his other hand and moved my hair behind my ear for me as we leaned closer towards each other. Appearing as if he were finally going to give me the kiss I've been desperately craving. The hair on the back of my neck rising as the anticipation of wanting our lips to touch lingered.

A clearing of someone's throat broke our trance of a stare as I shifted away from him. We looked up to see Preston, in a suit with his same sneakers on entering the circular seating. Preston held his hand out to shake Mason's. I moved my hands away from the items pressed against Mason. Mason shifted his body and stood up. I slid an inch more away from him as they shook hands. My cheeks were feeling warm as I watched the two interact. Preston secretly handed a package to Mason as he sat back down beside me.

As Preston sat down, Thomas entered, following close behind, Jackson. All shook hands and provided their envelopes. Mason didn't have anyone else's phones to collect. I was the first to him, and the only one who took a phone. A slight boast of confidence silently flooded my spirit as we all sat there. A server came by as Mason ordered a glass of wine for all to taste. Keeping a causal conversation as we sipped on the wine, and then we left separately. Mason led me out of the hotel, catching a cab for us to share.

Chapter Three

THE CAB DRIVER DROVE OFF from the hotel as Mason and I sat with space between us in the backseat. "Do you trust me now?" He asked.

"Not with an inch of my life," I whispered as we looked at each other. A look of seriousness as he slightly smiled at me with those eyes that pierced through my soul. "But I know that I'm now of your possession."

He chuckled as he looked out the window. "I don't possess you," he said lowly. Keeping my eyes on him, he looked back over at me and slid over next to me. Placing his arm over my shoulder and pressing his other hand on my chin. Our combined space sent my mind in rushing thoughts as the way he continuously closed in on me. I stared into his eyes, melting inside out. My eyes closed as I took the initiative to lean in. He shifted his lips to my ear, slightly grazing my cheek with his, and pushing back my hair. "I don't kiss women," he whispered. "That are not mine."

"How am I not yours?" I asked opening my eyes to look at him. "I can't leave this job you've thrown me in." Confusion rushing over me as none of this made sense to me.

He shifted his head to look at the cab driver who didn't look at us, and then back at me. "I don't claim you as mine," he paused as his breath tickled every hair on my neck, forming goosebumps all over my skin. "Unless I'm married to you."

I gasped as I turned away from him. He slid his hand on my chin, and I glanced back at him. "You have nothing to fear with me," he said. "I just met you, and I won't marry you." He slid away from me and part of me slid with him as my confused thoughts flooded. I looked back out the window as I thought of the past twenty-four hours. My entire self was a mess with all the encountering events, and then I've become a criminal from stealing.

This wasn't the woman my parents raised me to be. I thought of my mother as she was the one person who knew how to get me out of this situation that I'm in. Her words of *if you find yourself in trouble, come home immediately* broke me more as the world I was falsely forced into didn't appear as if that were an option. This mess was much greater than anything we've ever experienced at the ranch.

I shifted myself uncomfortably away from Mason as the trip back to the neighborhood of the warehouse was long with traffic. We made it back by lunchtime, everyone at the table where we all sat. My stomach still in knots kept me again from eating as I wasn't sure how to process my new life. Henderson didn't join us for lunch, and Mason had left as well. I had changed back into my jeans, white tanktop, and blue plaided shirt.

Over the next several hours we were provided weapons and target practicing as the handlers taught us techniques. It was our turn to shoot the targets, Preston on my left, Jackson on my right with Thomas on his right. "Getting cozy with the boss," Jackson stated. "Smart technique."

"You don't know what you're talking about," I snapped as I focused on the gun in hand at the target. Ryan was behind me, pointing with his hand where to shoot.

"We all saw how the two of you interacted," Jackson edged on. "Rode in the same cab as you. Bet that was spicy."

I turned to face Jackson, shoving Ryan's arm out of my sight. "Is there a problem?" Ryan asked stepping between Jackson and me.

Shaking off the anger boiling, and then my head as I stepped back. "Sorry, it won't happen again," I said repositioning myself to be lined up with the target. Jackson chuckled as he took a few shots, shooting the target in the head, and then putting his gun down on the table between Thomas and him.

Ryan stepped back as I took a deep breath to shoot. I hadn't shot anything besides a shotgun at home. Coyotes and snakes were the most I've ever shot at, and now I was faced with a target before me. Jackson crossed his arms as he stared at me, building up unwanted tension between us. "Stacy," Jackson chuckled. "Tell us. Do you plan on making your way here by sleeping with him?"

"That's it," I shouted as I moved over to Jackson, placing the gun under his chin.

Ryan had stepped forward. "Ryan," Mason shouted as he approached us. "Back off. Let it be."

"Look there, Stacy," Jackson said staring me in the eyes. I curled my lip as I felt anger rage inside of me. "Your boyfriend is here to save you."

I felt a hand touch my shoulder. A cold chill rushing down my spine as my anger continued to boil. "Stacy," Mason whispered. "It's not the time or place to do this."

"Look, you wedged between two men," Jackson chuckled. I shoved the barrel further into his throat. "Must be your favorite position."

The hand slid off my shoulder behind me. "You kill him," Mason said sternly as he took a step back. I glanced over my shoulder to see him cross his arms. "Then you will ultimately have to face consequences. Training isn't a dog-eat-dog world. It's to bring out the toughness inside of you."

Shifting my eyes back to Jackson who smiled wickedly. "Come on, Stacy," Jackson edged on. "Get some balls and shoot!"

The word *consequences* suddenly felt pressurizing as I pulled back from Jackson, taking a step back with the pistol clutched in my right hand. A burst of laughter slipped from Jackson, almost falling over as he stumbled backwards. "You couldn't do it if your life depended on it," he continued.

I turned, facing the target, and pulled the trigger until the gun quit firing. A raging roar left my throat as I turned back to Jackson who stood up straight, no longer laughing, staring with the rest of them at the target. Placing the gun down on the table beside Preston and walked away in frustration. Everyone was silent while I walked over to the chairs with the ropes that sat in the middle of the room.

"Let this be a lesson to all of you," Mason said loudly while I took a seat placing my elbows on my knees and my hands on my forehead. "We're not here to choose one of you. You're here because you made the cut. You edge one or the other to do the unexpected," Mason paused as I glanced over at him. He locked eyes with me for a moment and then turned back to the others. "Then you're betraying your team."

"Scott, Ryan," Mason said. I watched as they grabbed Jackson, startled by their reaction, I sat up to watch their motives. Jackson tried to fight them off as they walked him over to a trough filled with water.

Surprised at how far they were taking this training, I got up from the chair and took a few steps over as Preston and Thomas sat their guns down. We all watched as they forced Jackson's head into the trough of water. Jackson gasping as he struggled with them submerging his head. Like statutes, the rest of us were afraid to move as they jerked his head up and then submerged it again. He constantly gasping and coughing, desperate for them to stop. The punishment went on for several minutes, and then they pulled him up and threw him backwards on the ground. Jackson coughed, rolled over onto his stomach with his hands out in front of him. His face was bloodshot from spitting the water that filled his lungs.

Mason walked over and squatted down to Jackson. "You ever antagonize another individual on this team again, then you will meet the body bag." Jackson nodded as Mason stood up and walked over to me, stopping when his shoulders aligned with mine.

"Be glad you listened and didn't kill him," he said keeping his face forward. "Or else it would be you over there coughing your guts out."

I turned to look at Mason as I realized I had confined in his warning and made the right call. "Thank you," I whispered. A small bond of trust formed within my soul.

"Keep your head up," he whispered. "Don't listen to their remarks."

I looked back over at Jackson who pounded the ground and then rolled over to sit up. Mason walked away from me, leaving me there alone. I glanced at Preston who dropped his head and then turned back to the shooting range. Thomas went over to Jackson and helped him to his feet. Anger and frustration left Jackson as he got to his feet, swinging his arms, and then he glared at me. He walked over to the shooting range, jerking his head away from looking at me. I glanced over at the target and looked at mine that I didn't notice beforehand. It was squared in the head each round.

Ryan walked over to me. "You need any more target practicing?" He asked as he folded his shades into his pocket, his eyes were brown.

I shook my head. "Do you know when I will get my bag back?" I asked.

Ryan glanced over at the others, and then back at me. "You need your phone?" He asked lowly.

I nodded. "I check in with my mom daily. If she doesn't hear from me, she will more than likely file a missing person's report," I said crossing my arms as a small tear pierced my heart.

"I would be more worried if they find you on your phone," he said taking a towel from his back pocket. "I will give you a few minutes, but you may want to make up something."

I nodded. He motioned for me to follow him, and then we went through a room that looked like an interrogation room. It had a table with two chairs in the center, and a black locker cabinet at the back of the room with twelve lockers. "It went off earlier as we were in phase two. I silenced it," he said as he put it on the table. I reached for it as he put his hand up. "Put it on speaker."

I nodded. The low battery flashed as I dialed the ranch house number. She answered in the first ring. "Hey Stacy, you will never believe what I'm making," she started rambling.

The phone beeped in my ear. "Hey mom, my battery is about dead. I have to take a work trip and won't have access to my phone for a while."

"Wait," she said as her mother instincts took over. "What is going on?"

"I have a work trip," I said as I wiped my face that tears dripped. "I will call you as soon as I can. Love you."

Another beep noise came across, and then the line disconnected as the phone went black. A small breath slipped through my teeth as I put the phone down. A new pain emerged through me as I realized that I should've never put down that shot glass and followed Mason. He's taken more than my feelings as now trapped in a job that I had no business being placed in. "I will get a charger," Ryan said interrupting my thoughts.

"No," I said. "Just let it stay dead. As long as it's off, it won't cause any problems."

"You sure?" Ryan asked as he picked up the phone.

I nodded. "Can I just have a minute?" I asked as I sat down at the table.

He took the phone back over to the lockers, placed it back into the second one from the left, and locked it back, moving the combination numbers a few rounds. I took a moment as he stood by the lockers and wiped my eyes. Allowing my hardened breaths release, I knew I was in big trouble with this job. None of it felt right and it definitely wasn't something I would have signed up to do. Regaining composure, I knew having contact with family would make it difficult. Wiping my eyes for the last time and then got up from the table. "Thanks," I said. "Let's go."

I went over to the door and placed my hand on the knob. Ryan walked up behind me, and then I turned it and rushed out of the room quickly. Mason had gathered all around the center of the room. "You all will eat and then rest. Tomorrow will be more training tactics," Mason said glancing at Ryan and me walking up. "Grab a sandwich, chips, and a drink and head to the bunk room."

"Will we be locked in this time?" Thomas asked.

Mason chuckled. "You think we trust you all to roam free?"

Thomas and Jackson crossed their arms as they looked at each other, and then back at Mason. "Get some rest," Mason said as Kyle had a white bag for each of us. We grabbed the bag and headed to the bunk room. Mason and Ryan had turned to have a private conversation.

We entered the bunk room, not speaking to each other. The door closed and a latch sounded, it was locked. Jackson sat on the bunk he had last night, Thomas climbed above him. I tossed my bag up on the top bunk. Preston glanced over at me, and then back at the other two. "You can take the lower one if you want," he said.

"I will take the top bunk," I said, and then climbed up to the top bunk. I crossed my legs as I opened my bag. Jackson got up from his bunk and snatched my sandwich from in front of me. He went back and sat down on his bunk, opening the sandwich and eating it while staring at me. "Too soggy for me anyways," I said as I moved the chips and drink to beside my pillow. My stomach pain grew as I lay back, putting my hands over my stomach and staring up at the ceiling.

They threw their trash on the ground. Thomas sat up on his bunk, feet dangled off the side. Jackson had lied back down, and I wasn't sure what Preston did. They started to engage in conversation as I kept quiet, listening to them. Thomas and Jackson grew up in the same neighborhood and had been friends since childhood. Recruited through Kyle who scoped them out at a drug heist that went bad. The two were not using drugs and got out before the cops arrested or known of their presence there. Kyle found them through a mutual friend that happened to be there that night of the bust.

Preston's cousin got him recruited through Ryan. They gave him a trial run when he went to a casino and stole rich millionaires' money. Preston was able to think quickly and keep a conversation alive to distract others. His sleek motives landed him in the arena with the rest of us. Thomas had asked for my story, but I didn't talk as they all knew Mason had a part to play in it.

"I don't get why he puts you in here with us?" Jackson snapped. "You're nothing but a snitch."

"Leave it alone, Jackson," Thomas said as he shifted himself to lay down on his bed. "She isn't our concern."

"Not yours," Jackson said. "You didn't get submerged in water for an hour."

"If you learned to shut up," Thomas said throwing his hands up. "You wouldn't have been submerged."

"Yeah," Preston chuckled. "Bet your glad she unloaded on the target rather than you."

"Shut up," Jackson shouted.

Breathing steadily, I kept still as I wasn't about to engage with them that could go south quickly and there was no escape route in this bunkroom. After a few moments, snores erupted in the room as they had fallen asleep, allowing some peace to enter my soul. The ceiling became my new window of opportunity to view and ponder my thoughts. My mind drawn to how Mason acted around me, the mixed signals with his closeness to his awkward statement in the cab. "I don't kiss women that aren't mine. Mine is the one I marry." The words wouldn't shake as he's entrapped me into this dangerous game.

Hours passed as I sat in silence, not allowing the darkness or exhaustion to overwhelm me. The room was unsettling with my bunkmates as I knew I had already grown tension with Jackson. Suddenly, exhaustion fled me as I lay there in silence. Shifting myself upright, trying to fight the exhaustion, and then hearing a cough. Shifting my sight to Jackson who moved and turned over, facing our bunk. His eyes opened and locked with mine immediately. I rubbed the back of my neck and looked away from him as an uncomforting sensation rushed through me. My body tense as I wasn't sure if I was entirely safe in a room with a stranger who wanted multiple things with me. As my thoughts rambled, he acted like he wanted me as his side piece, another time as a friend, and then suddenly the thought of him wanting me dead crossed my mind.

The sound of movement as I glanced back over at him. He shifted to sit up and then stood up. Taking a step towards our bunk, he put his arms on my bed as he interlocked his fingers. I shifted away from him uncomfortably as my body was alarmed. "How'd you end up in this mess anyways?" He asked soft tone. "You look educated," he paused. "Definitely fit enough to outsmart my shove to the ground in phase one."

A dead lock stare between us as he continued to talk. "You don't talk but to the higher ups," he chuckled as he glanced behind him, seeing Thomas still asleep. "Sucks to be you. The only girl locked in a room full of men. Even out there, you're just the only girl they have here. What makes you think they don't have you here for a particular reason?"

Silent and frozen as I was unclear of his motives towards me. He looked at me with a smile of terror crossing his face. Reacting to the unwarming smile, I jumped to get off the bed. Grabbing my arm, Jackson pulled me off the bunk. My body pounded the ground as pain shot through my back. He kicked me in the side, a shriek slipped my mouth as more pain emerged. Sounds erupted the room as the others woken up. "Dude," Thomas yelled. "What are you doing?"

Jackson grabbed me up by my neck, strangling as it became harder to breathe. My feet struggled to get under me as he swung me into the back wall, another pain spiking through my back. Preston jumped off his bed as he side-tackled Jackson who released his grip on me. I fell to my knees, gasping for air. Jackson rolled Preston to the ground, punching him hard. Preston had blood running from his nose as his eyes rolled back, collapsing from the blow. I rushed to my feet as Jackson turned around. Rushing towards him to fight him the best I was skilled to do. He shoved me back on top of Preston's bed.

A scream slipped through my lips as he pressed his knee down on my stomach. I reached for his shirt as he palmed my nose, warm liquid running down my face as sweat drew over my body. A pain shot through me as my head fell backwards. I spat blood out to my left. Jackson grabbed my throat, putting his face to mine. "I think they brought you here for entertainment," he said as he swung my head back, releasing my neck in the process.

Throbbing pain flooded my face, my sight spinning as I felt lightheaded. Preston had come to and had stood up behind Jackson. He went to attack Jackson when Thomas jumped off his bunk and elbowed him in the back of the head. The lock unlatched and Jackson quickly jumped off of me, stepping back to the back wall. Thomas grabbed Preston and swung him over on top of me.

Preston's body pressing on me, letting out a slight scream as the room swayed while the door opened. Suddenly, Preston was pulled off of me and the pressure was released. "I don't know what he was thinking," Jackson stated. A hand grabbed my arm, pulling me up from the bunk. I looked to see Scott as he drew me to him as my knees buckled and walked us out to the main room.

"What happened?" Mason asked rushing past us to Jackson. They sat me down on the ground outside of the bunk room. The room swayed so much as I couldn't sit up, pain radiating throughout my body as my head thudded to my heartbeat. Looking beside me, Preston lying on the floor. I moved Scott's hand off my shoulder as I didn't want to be touched by anyone. Kyle was aiding Preston with Ryan. The swaying shifted to the room spinning with the thuds loudly pounding my ears. Closing my eyes, my body fell over to the left.

Sounds of chatter around me, unclear of their conversation as I felt myself come to. My head pounded as I grabbed my forehead, opening my eyes while I sat up. My back and sides radiated pulsating pains. "Stacy," a voice said. A ringing sound flooded my ears as I closed my eyes to attempt to get it to stop. Another whistling ring emerged, and then it vanished, and I could hear clearly again. "Stacy," Mason said soft spoken as someone touched my shoulder. Opening my eyes, Mason kneeled beside me with his hand on my shoulder. "Stacy, can you hear me?" He asked.

I nodded and turned to look around the room. Preston had several band aids on his face and stood several feet away from Thomas and Jackson. They stood near the bunkroom door, staring at me, as Jackson had his arms crossed with a look of disgust across his face. Scott, Ryan, Kyle, and James stood behind Mason in formation.

"Don't look at everyone," Mason said sternly. I jerked my head to look at him. "What happened in the bunkroom?"

I focused on his face as I could tell he wasn't happy with these circumstances. The disconcerting feeling that I was in the spotlight grew as I glanced over at the handlers who were in stance ready to grab someone up. Shifting my sight to Preston who stared at me with a look of concern. Mason grabbed my chin and carefully moved it to where I was focused on him. Our eyes locked, worrisome rushing through me as I couldn't even embrace the stare as the pain shot through my back. "What happened?" Mason asked more sternly than beforehand.

Disorientated as I wasn't sure how I wanted to talk about it, and recalling Mason's words earlier to Jackson, *you antagonize another person of the team, and you meet the body bag.* Grabbing his hand, I pushed it off my chin as I cleared my throat that was dry. "A misunderstanding," I coughed as I broke our eye contact. The air shifted around me as everyone stances shifted, leaning in to hear of this *misunderstanding,* as they stared at me intensely. "I accidentally brought it on."

"Brought what on?" Mason asked.

Clearing my throat, "I fell getting off my bunk, hitting Preston." I glanced over at Preston, who looked confused. Shifting my eyes back to the ground to avoid eye contact with Mason. "Which startled him awake, where he swung unintentionally."

Mason grabbed my chin again, forcing me to look up at him less carefully than beforehand. "Are you lying?" He asked as his tone shifted with irritation.

I shook my head and glanced over at Jackson and Thomas who kept their stance the same as when I first looked at them. Ryan bent down to whisper in Mason's ear. "It may be too soon to question her," Ryan said. "Shock can-."

"I'm telling the truth," I interrupted as I shoved Mason's hand off my chin. "It was a complete misunderstanding."

I glanced up at Mason who looked over his shoulder, and then at Preston, and then back at me. Mason stood up and walked over to Jackson and Thomas. "Is she telling the truth? Because now would be the best time for you all to come clean," Mason shouted.

"She's telling the truth," Preston said. "I guess from everything we've been through, I dreamt another dog was attacking me."

Mason looked back at Preston, and then at me. His irritation grew as he turned and walked away from them and headed over to the handlers. "Make them move their mattresses out here," Mason demanded while pointing his finger. "For now on, we all sleep out here."

The room started to spin again as I placed my hand on my forehead. "Something doesn't look right with her," Scott said as he dropped his bag beside me. Jerking from the sound, but unable to focus as the room continued spinning intensely. I fell over to my side, my vision blurring, and I heard the ringing again. "Her blood sugar is super low."

"Did she eat anything?" Mason yelled.

Jackson cleared his throat. "No, she gave her sandwich to me," he yelled.

I heard the ringing again as sweat formed all over my body, chills rushing through me as my body shook. "Stacy, drink this," Scott said putting something cold to my lips. I sipped it slowly, tasting orange juice, hearing the rings fade away. I sipped it again as the blurriness faded into clearness.

"Mason," Henderson said.

Scott helped me sit up as I took the cup and sipped on the juice. "We may need to look at disposal," Henderson said.

"No," Mason said grabbing Henderson's arm. Mason pulled him away from us but still within earshot.

Henderson glanced over at me as I back to him, and then at Mason. "She appears compromised enough to not be able to move further," Henderson said.

Fear settling in as I glanced over at Jackson who formed a slight smile at the corner of his lips. Uneasiness formed as my body quivered while I finished the cup of juice. Placing it beside me as I wrapped my arms around my stomach as I looked over at Henderson and Mason. "She isn't compromised," Mason snapped. "Trust me on this one."

Henderson nodded. Scott pricked my finger again, letting the machine read my blood sugar, and then nodded at Mason. "Each of you," Mason said turning as he spoke. "Go grab your mattresses. You're sleeping out here."

Shaking as fear rose, I slowly got to my feet, feeling lightheaded, and then allowing myself to regain my stance. I moved towards the bunkroom as Preston walked beside me. "Why did you go with that story?" He asked lowly.

I shook my head as all the eyes were on us. "It was the truth," I snapped, looking down at the ground to avoid others eye contact. Jackson grabbed his mattress and pillow first, sliding by me with smirk across his face. Thomas grabbed his next, and then Preston. As they left, I grabbed mine which was heavy weighted down. Trying to fight the resistance of its weight, a noise behind me as if someone were watching me. I glanced over my shoulder as Mason stood at the doorway, looking in at me struggle to pull the mattress.

"You can sleep in here," he said then grabbed the doorknob and closed the door.

"No, wait," I shouted as the door slammed shut. Rushing to it and slapping it with the palm of my hands as I heard the latch sound. Tears rolled down my face as I hit the door again in frustration. "No," I screamed. "Let me out of here!" Turning my back against the door and sliding down it. The familiar pain of defeat, allowing weakness to flow through my mind. *You're not weak! He's protecting you from the others.* The thoughts of Mason placing me in isolation to prevent another mishappen lifted my broken spirit. Mason trapped me to secure me from the dangers of them. *From this point forward, you must always trust me,*

Mason's words before entering the warehouse surrounded me as I looked around the empty bunkroom and knew I was safe for the moment. I wiped my face as I got up from the ground and climbed up on the bunk, clutching the pillow underneath my head. Feeling my bag of chips and soda by my pillow, I sat up and ate. Relief that I could eat, drink, and sleep without a sense of feeling threatened. Tossing my trash on the ground as I lay down. Exhaustion weighed in my body as I drifted off to sleep.

Chapter Four

I WOKE UP FEELING REFRESHED, it was the best sleep I've had since following Mason to the warehouse door. Climbing down from the top bunk, I made my way over to the door and twisted the knob, still locked. Pounding the door with the palm of my hand. "Hey," I shouted. "I'm awake. Let me out!" Pressing my ear against the door, hearing nothing, frustration rushed through me as I hit the door again. Pacing to the opposite side and propped myself against the wall, crossing my arms.

Time passed as I stood propped on the wall, waiting for the door to unlatch. My body feeling tensed as now I was trapped in a room, unknowingly what was being planned outside of the room. Anxiously, I paced back and forth in the room, exhaustion rushed through me again. I climbed to the top bunk and lay down, falling asleep effortlessly.

A peaceful sensation flooding me as I woke up, feeling refreshed again. I climbed down, twisted the doorknob with no luck of it turning, frustration lingered as I turned away from the door. Pacing back and forth in the room and then starting to do a few exercises I knew to stay limber. No longer feeling pain from my back as the result of Jackson's force on the ground and wall, I felt much better. Several hours passed, propped against the wall opposite from the door, and crossed my arms.

Boredom settled as I nodded off, jerking in reaction as I stood there waiting to be let out of the bunkroom. The sound of the door unlatched. I shot straight up, uncrossing my arms and dashed towards the door. A bag was tossed in quickly, and then the door closed again. "No, no, no," I said pounding on the door. I tried to twist the knob but the latch sealed. "You can't keep me in here forever," I yelled. Water surfaced my eyelids as tears streamlined down my face as my fist pounded the metal surface. Turning around in defeat, pressing my back against the door and slid down, putting my face in the palms of my hands.

Sobs fled the room as I were cut off from everything, my family, Mason, and my life. Wiping my face, I saw the white paper bag beside me and peeked inside, finding a clear wrapped chicken sandwich, chips, and a soda. I ate all of it allowing it to comfort me. Leaving the trash to the side, I explored the room, climbing above Thomas's bunk. Discovering a vent where I attempted to open it, unable to get the door to pop open. Investigating the room further, I located a door with a lock under Preston's bed. Shaking the lock, in hopes that it would open, didn't budge as I wanted to free myself. After several failed attempts, I paced around the room allowing the memories of Jackson rush through me as if the entire night reappeared before me.

Anxious from the memories, I propped myself against the wall opposite of the door. Anger rose inside of me as it was unfair that I felt conflicted to lie and be placed as a prisoner for this much time. Distracting myself, I did a few more exercises, and then after several hours climbed on the top bunk and lay down.

Pain erupted in my lower abdomen as I woke up. Cramps, feeling nauseated as the first day of my menstrual caused it. Climbing down from the bunk, walking over to the door and attempting to twist the knob, locked. I hit the door in frustration as I knew this wasn't good for me, no way of cleaning up and no medicine. "Hey," I yelled. "I want out of here!" The cramps intensified as I slowly turned around and moved down the wall between the door and the bunk beds. Holding my stomach as the cramps continued, aching my muscles, my head ached. Slowly made my way to the opposite side of the room, keeping my knees bent, and arms wrapped around my stomach.

The door unlatched, I got up from the ground slowly, keeping an arm around the stomach. Slowly opening, the door widened than beforehand as I kept on the opposite wall. My free hand was balled up, ready to hit if the opportunity presented itself. Suddenly, it swung open wide, Mason stood propped on the doorframe. His eyes looked at me, and I felt embarrassed as I knew my jeans were ruined and I were a mess.

"You ready to tell me what really happened that night?" He asked with his arms crossed. I folded my other arm across my stomach as I sat back down on the ground. He watched me as I slid to the ground, tightly squeezing my stomach.

"I need to be let out of this room," I said lowly. "I need to change clothes, and."

He positioned himself straight up. "You're on your cycle," he said glancing behind him.

I nodded feeling embarrassed as I wasn't sure what to do now. I've never felt so disgusted and soiled. "I need to know the truth of that night," he said staring back at me. He stepped into the room, closing the door behind him.

"I told you what happened," I said keeping my eyes lowered.

He sighed as he walked over to me. "How bad is your menstrual cycles?" He asked squatting down in front of me.

"Pretty rough," I said. "How long have I been in here by myself?"

"Two days," he said as I looked up at him. "But I can't let you out of here until I know the truth."

My mouth dry as I looked down, a hard lump forming in my throat as I cleared it. "I fell off the bunk and hit Preston. He attacked as he thought I was attacking him. A complete misunderstanding," I said as I glanced away from him.

"I almost believed you that time," he said propping his elbows on his knees. "Why are you defending Jackson?"

"I'm not," I said looking up at him.

He stared at me, our gazes meeting, mesmerizing my soul. I wished I were in much better-looking attire and stances to fully be swept off my feet.

He got up, grabbed my arms, and pulled me to my feet. "I don't care for liars," he said as we stood there.

"Why can't you believe it?" I asked looking into his eyes.

He moved me back into the wall, pressing my shoulders into the wall as he moved towards me. "Because I saw the truth that none of you care to say," he whispered into my ear. I forgot about the cramps as I felt the shivering chill run down my spine. Slightly shifting my face to where mine was near his, and he looked at me with a twinkle in his eyes.

"Then why are you insisting that I confess," I said.

He slapped the wall with his right hand. Jerking from the reaction to it as I felt my body quiver. "All you have to do is confess and he's gone," he said. "Don't you see, I'm trying to give you the benefit of doubt. I'm trying to ensure he's gone for good and won't hurt you again."

A deep breath slipped as I felt the sincerity in his voice. "You're in love with me," I gasped.

He shook his head, glancing away from me. "You're not worth anymore to me than them," he whispered.

"Is that what you keep telling yourself?" I asked nearly laughing at him.

He looked back at me with all seriousness. "I determine who stays or goes," he snarled. "And if you lie to me once, then how do I know I can trust you."

"Why do you think I am lying for him?" I asked as our eyes met.

He put his hand on the back of my neck, and then he moved his lips towards mine. Maybe this time he was actually going to kiss me. The anticipation rose as I closed my eyes, hoping to feel the magic this man has released on me. I could feel his breath near mine, and then he moved to my neck. "I told you," he whispered below my ear. His hot breath against my neck that now felt my racing heartbeat. "I don't kiss women-."

"Unless they're yours, meaning if I were married to you," I said looking up at the ceiling as suddenly the air in this room had vanished. Breathless as the anticipation fell from the devastation of disappointment he caused again. "You give me mixed feelings," I confessed.

"Yea," he said moving his mouth away from my neck. "You give me the same."

My heartbeat calming back down as he pushed away from me. He turned around to walk towards the door. I pushed my hair back off my face that came across me. "Wait," I said pushing off the wall. "I really need to get cleaned up. I feel disgusting."

"They're going on another training exercise soon," he said putting his hand on the door. "I will come back for you then."

"Don't I need to train with them?" I asked.

"You've already proved to me your loyalty to the team," he said pressing his hand on the wall beside the door. "You're training is over."

"Wait," I said as he opened the door and exited, closing the door behind him. Hurriedly, I twisted the knob, but it was too late, already latched. "No," I shouted hitting the door with the palm of my hand. Turning away from the door, feeling so many emotions rushing in me as I wasn't sure if that meant I were to be killed off. Fear sending every alarm in my body as I was scared that I had met my expiration time with them.

No, he's in love with you. He wouldn't admit to it if he were in love with me. I felt like an idiot for trusting him that night at the bar. A feeling no other has ever given me. His staring sent me in some sort of trance, making me risk my life. The mixed emotions petrified me of my life being locked up in this room, in this warehouse.

Time passed, and finally the door unlatched. I quickly got to my feet, twisting the knob and opening the door. Scott had stayed behind this time, sitting at the table with food. I ran over to him as he looked up at me. "You have clean clothes here, some other stuff, and showers in that room there," he said and pointed to the door behind his left side.

"Where are the others?" I asked grabbing the bag from the table.

"Training," he said and looked back down at a magazine.

"Can we catch up to them?" I asked clutching the bag in my hands.

He looked up from the magazine. "I was told you needed this and that your training is finished. Take it for the win and go get cleaned up," he said then looked back down at the magazine. I walked past the table to the room with the showers. I turned the water on, ready for this desperately needed shower, but I had to work fast.

I stripped quickly, tossing my clothes in the trash as I jumped into the shower, washing my hair and my body. Rushing as I dried off, dressing and finding pain relief medicine for cramps. I went over to the faucet, cupping my mouth with water and taking the medicine. Looking around the room for anything to be used as a hair tie, seeing a clipboard with papers and a rubber band hanging around the top of the board. Pulling it off the clipboard and then shoving my hair back as I made a messy ponytail.

Refreshed with new clothes and a clean body, I looked around, seeing Scott's medical brown bag on the bench in the center of the room. Siffling through it, finding a bottle of chloroform. I opened it, holding my breath as I drenched a rag in it. I washed my hands, hiding the rag in my back pocket. Regaining composure as I knew what I needed to do to get to them. My training wasn't complete, and I was going to make sure they knew it. Walking out of the shower room, Scott had his head buried into the magazine, not paying any attention to me behind him.

"Are you able to bring me to them?" I asked walking towards his backside.

He sighed. "Take it as a win, you're done," he said shaking his head.

I slowly pulled the rag from my back pocket. "Then I hope you forgive me later for this," I said as I wrapped my arm around his neck, pressing the rag over his nose and mouth. Shocked by my surprise attack, he grabbed my neck, trying to grip it as I held tightly, grunting as I fought him. His energy quickly suppressed as his head and arms fell down on the table. I tossed the rag to the side of him, mentally apologizing as I didn't need any more tension between these men and myself. Quickly, I found his phone on the side of his belt and pulled up their tracking devices. Running out of the warehouse to the door I knew led to the exit. Following the tracker's direction, I ran up the street, catching a cab, and then headed to their location. Informing the cab driver to let me out a block from their location.

Making my way to what appeared to be an apartment building. I approached the rugged looking building, going behind it to the fire stairwell. Jumping up and grabbing the ladder, pulling it to the ground. I quickly climbed up and then made my way up the stairs to the fifth floor, finding a cracked window. Peeking inside, seeing no one around, and then pushed the window up. Quietly climbing inside the apartment, not making a sound as I made my way to the front door.

Closing the door lightly behind me, I walked hastily down the hall, grabbing the phone out of my pocket. All of their locations appeared in this building. Locating the stairwell door, I made my way up the stairs as I glanced between the phone's tracker and each hallway. Arriving at the eighth floor, I peeked out the door, seeing Ryan down the hallway. He had his phone to his ear. The others weren't in sight. I took a deep breath, unsure what I was walking into, but determined to not allow them to dispose of me.

Slowly opening the stairwell door as I watched Ryan enter an apartment, I made my way down the hallway towards the room. Picking up my pace, anxiously getting to the open door, and then sliding next to it. Noises of shifting weight and walking inside the apartment room as I stayed put. Unsure what I was going to do when I got inside. Looking down the hallway as a door opened up at the other end of the hallway, I turned myself as if I were going to enter the apartment and then took a step inside.

Closing the door lightly as I heard more footsteps behind me. I peeked around the corner, seeing Mason and Ryan by the window. A hand reached around my face, entering my peripheral vision, and pulled me back. Breathing hardened as I turned around, seeing Preston push me against the apartment entrance door as he kept his hand over my mouth. His face was all busted up from where Jackson smashed and punched him.

Preston didn't speak as a look of desperation and fear flooded his face. A look as if to say what on earth are you doing here of all places. I grabbed his hand to pull it off and started to open my mouth; he quickly pressed his hand over again as if he were protecting me. He shook his head in a panic manner. As if lightning were hitting a tree, fear sparked throughout my body, pounding my heart out of my chest. Obviously, he knows more of what has been said and why we were here than me.

"Mason," Ryan stated. "I just got a call from James. He went back to the warehouse and found Scott passed out."

"Where's Stacy?" Mason asked.

Ryan shifted more towards the door. "Said she made a run for it."

I heard what sounded like a slap on the wall. "She's not a talker," Mason said. "Tell James to get Scott awake and go to her apartment."

I moved Preston's hand from my lips as I wanted to speak up. Preston shook his head again at me. A whistling noise sounded from behind Preston as

Jackson was walking towards us. "No need to search her apartment, boss," Jackson smiled as he grabbed my arm. He pulled me into the room where Mason and Ryan stood. Jackson shoved me to the ground. I fell on my hands and knees, and then quickly looked up at Mason who took a step forward. "Look what the cat brought in," Jackson said walking around my right side. I glanced over at him. "Preston had his hand over her mouth at the front door."

Mason glanced over at Preston who moved over to my left side. "I wasn't sure if she was to be here," Preston admitted.

"Hiding her like a-."

"Enough," Mason interrupted Jackson, throwing his hand up towards him. "Jackson, you're on thin ice. I would stop while the thin sheet is still frozen from beneath you. Stacy, what are you doing here?" Mason's eyes shot from Jackson to me. Everyone else jumped from Mason's to me as well. I sat back on my knees, slowly getting to my feet.

"I'm still in training," I said glancing at Jackson. "Just as much as the rest of them."

Mason shifted his weight as he glanced over at Ryan. "Take her back to the warehouse," Mason snarled as he threw his hand up.

"No," I said taking a step towards him. "You said my training was up. Does that mean I end up in a body bag next?"

Mason quickly turned around to face me. Jackson took a step towards me. I glared at him as my fist balled up by my sides. The sound of the apartment door opened behind us; I glanced over at Mason's face as a look of shock filled his face. He rushed past me, shoving me to the ground as he quickly went to the person behind me. I fell into Jackson, as we both tumbled to the ground. I quickly got up, seeing Mason and Ryan grab the man that entered the apartment. Preston had his hands on his head, in full fledge panic as we watched.

Mason pinned the man to the wall, forcing his nose and mouth closed. Ryan assisting in pinning him down. Kyle coming up from the hallway with Thomas, assisting Mason and Ryan as the man lost consciousness quickly. Jackson stumbled to his feet, falling into the wall behind him as I took a step back with shock flooding me. We just witnessed a murder! My breathing hardened as I really am screwed in this situation. Preston and I both took another step back as Jackson and Thomas pulled their composures together. A hardening lump formed in my throat as my breathing shallowed.

"You just-." I felt the air being sucked from my lungs. Mason, Kyle, and Ryan brought the body into the living area with the chairs and television that we all stood in. I stepped back into the window, feeling a small gap under my fingertips. I pressed my hands behind me as I watched them. The three men quickly staged the incident, spilling wine, planting papers, and pills near the man. They made it look like he overdosed. The air thickened around me as I pressed my fingers deeper under the window to the fire stairwell.

Preston combing his hands through his hair, pacing in a circle. Jackson fully composed, watching closely as the men reacted and orchestrated quick work. I watched them in terror as I now understood why I was supposed to stay behind. Glancing over my shoulder, seeing the fire escape, contemplating how to get myself out of this staged scene. I looked back as they continued to stage the scene. Preston glancing at them, Jackson and Thomas, and then looked over at me.

I took a deep breath, and then turned around, jerked the window open, and climbed out. "Stacy, no," Preston yelled. I glanced back as I saw hands flailing out the window as I started running down the stairwell. My heart raced as I glanced back every few seconds, falling down a few steps, quickly retaliating and jumping up. I heard the sounds of another running down the stairs, and looked back, seeing Jackson two flights above me. Quickly looking over the railing, seeing a dumpster that lied down below. Lunging myself over and jumped. I felt the wind of hands missing my body as I fell into the dumpster. I rolled it over, quickly getting out and running down the street.

I glanced back seeing Jackson get off the fire stairwell. Running hard as I could, dashing to the street with chaos, people walking in every direction, cars honking, bikers making their way through the sidewalks. I ducked down and swept through the crowd, snatching someone's newspaper as I kept running. Sharply jumping into the entrance of a bakery shop, going inside, running past their register to the back. I missed a person pulling cookies out of the oven, shoving them back. People were shouting as I ran to the back door, pushing the release handle. I ran out the back and down the strip, finding a fire staircase. Hustling as I ran up it, finding a cracked window three floors up. Shoving open the window, slamming it shut behind me.

A man yelled from behind me. I turned quickly, running past him to the front entrance. I went out the front door of their apartment, heading towards the elevator. I jumped inside pressing the top floor, looking down as my hands shook. Panic continued to shiver its way as I couldn't control my shakingly body. I knew I was in trouble and feared for my life. The sound of a notification from a phone went off. *Shit!* I grabbed Scott's phone from my pocket, pulling up the tracking system. They were closing in on this building. Running off the elevator, heading to the roof access, I got out the door, slamming it shut behind me. Out of breath as I tossed the phone down on the ground by the door.

I ran behind the door, seeing a jump to the next building. Without hesitation, I ran as hard as I could, jumping, and falling into the next building. A pain shrieked as I held tightly, kicking my feet up the side of the building, trying to pull myself up. Climbing up and rolling over the wall, a slight breath of relief, and then got up. Running to this building's roof access door, I quickly opened it and dashed down the stairs to the eighth floor. Gasping for air as I peeked out, looking to see if this building was busy. I saw a server closet across the hallway. A short inhale to gain composure as I opened the door, quickly getting to the access room of the computer panel. I locked myself inside and looked around for the IT laptop. Locating it in the back of the access room. Breathing hard as the anticipation of being caught in here grew.

I jumped on the laptop, pulling up the building's surveillance cameras. Shifting myself in the corner of the room, my eyes were on the locked door as I glanced between the cameras and it. Finally able to calm my breathing as I felt my heart was going to pound out of my chest. Viewing the footage, Ryan entered the building and began speaking with the receptionist. He pulled out a badge. *He's a police officer!* He showed a picture on his phone of me as if asking them if they saw me. Everyone he asked shook their heads, and then he pulled out a card and placed it on the counter before them. Shortly afterwards, he exited the building. A breath of relief escaped my trembling lips.

Sitting in the confined sever room for hours, watching surveillance cameras and the door. No one else checked this building for me, and I was relieved. Clearing the past settings and erased my image from the footage of me on the roof access. Rebooting the system and shutting off the cameras to allow for a clear exit, and then I closed the laptop. Gaining composure, I unlocked the door, peeking out and not seeing anyone in sight and walked out of the room. Locating the window with the fire stairwell case and shifting out the window. I made my way down the stairwell and walked along the alleyway, keeping my eyes moving around me as I were afraid of them locating me.

I've become part of a nightmare where I desperately needed to escape, except there was none. The idea of going back to my apartment ran through my mind, then recalling Mason's action at that man's apartment stating for them to look for me at mine first quickly changed my mind. Going to Wade's Bar seemed pointless since Mason waited for me there and definitely would be their top places to locate me. A sigh of insecurity released from my mouth as every motive to hide was bound to be found. Leaving by Subway crossed my mind, realizing they more than likely already had spectators waiting on my appearance, and then it would result in being caught. Shaking while walking towards the hotel where our second phase of training led us since I was in the neighborhood. Recalling that many who were there appeared to be rich millionaires. Maybe I could snatch another purse and find me a cab to take me back to the ranch.

My parents never acted in the manner that I had to do so, but in that area of my life, I felt I had to in order to survive. The idea of stealing from another motivated me to want to go home, causing anxious thoughts that they would go after my family. Jackson was likely to find me before the others. My breathing felt heavy as my throat felt like it was closing in as the thoughts of what he planned to do with me once he located me. My legs weighted as I walked, feeling faint. The painful cramps overpowered, and I stopped, hugging the wall as I bent over to let it pass. It passed, regaining composure, I slowly got back up and headed towards the chaotic streets of New York.

Slipping onto the main strip, blending in with the crowd, scanning for any familiar faces, none. Locating a pharmacy, quickly rushing in and grabbing a few necessities. I headed to the bathroom, cleaned up, and then headed back out. People crowded around the door, joining the chaos, snatching a coat off the rack on my way out. A lady had a small black cap on as she looked on the top shelf of the pharmacy entrance. The hat slipped off her head and without hesitation, I slipped by, snatching it before it fell to the ground, continuing my way towards the exit. People walked without space in between, shifting into the crowd along with them, looking for other possible prospects to gain for my new disguised look. Swiping a pink scarf from another lady's bag that she kept at her side as she posed for a picture.

Snatching a wallet from the back pocket of a man on his phone, quickly turning in a different direction to blend in another form of the crowd's direction, not looking back to see if he had recognized. I headed towards a payphone, ready to make the one call that gave me greater motivation to get home. Insecurity settled as I took a breath, knowing that the call would not be easy, inserting the change and called home.

"Stacy," mom's panicked voice came across the receiver.

"Mom, I'm fine," I said calmly. "I wanted to call to let you know I'm still on my work trip. I will call you the next time I get a break and check in with you."

"Stacy, please don't hang up," mom begged.

"I'm fine," I snapped trying to end the call quickly. "I will check in with you when I get another break."

"Stacy," mom squealed.

"Mom," I said calmly. "Listen to my voice."

"I want you home immediately," she squealed in panic. "I will come up there myself."

I breathed into the phone as I looked around to ensure I didn't recognize anyone. "I love you," I said softly. "I will check in with you in a few days."

"I love you," mom said calmer.

Swiftly hanging the phone on its receiver, letting out a breath as the sting prickled my eyes from tears that drawn. Sliding the door open, walking into the crowd, heading North. As I blended myself through the crowd, fear rushing through me, but having to keep a straight face to not draw attention to myself. My mess of a life unfolding at every step since I was young, my decisions to full forcibly do something ended with me in either a confrontation room with some head of security or an unreasonable amount of debt. The thoughts weighed on my shoulders as I never seemed to be the person to stay out of some sort of trouble.

Sizzling sounds with the aroma of pizza filled the air near an Italian restaurant. I went inside and ordered a quick meal. Eating as much as I could in as little time. Tossing some cash down as I left, bringing the wallet with me. Counting the remaining cash, a few dollars left, shaking my head as I headed East. The bus station was a few miles away according to the map that I snatched from a park bench.

I made my way on foot to the bus station. The crowded lanes were busy but at a standstill. An uneasy feeling swarmed my stomach from being at the station, clutching the jacket around me, readjusting my scarf. Recounting the money, walking towards the teller to purchase a bus ticket. I waited, reminding myself to stay patient while keeping my head down, not to be detected by cameras. "Next please," the female black teller said. I walked up to the window. "I need a ticket to North Carolina."

"It will be two hundred and ten dollars," she said looking me in the eyes.

I looked down in the wallet with only eighty dollars. My eyes started to burn as the salty liquid formed at the bottom of my eyelids. Glancing up at her as the pain of wanting to cry, holding back the tears. "How far will eighty dollars get me?" I asked with my lip slowly trembling.

She sideways glanced at me as she tilted her head, looking back down at her screen, she pressed keys, and then looked up at me. "South border of New York State," she said glancing at me with her eyes wide as she knew I looked as if I were about to cry.

I nodded and grabbed the eighty dollars out. Pushing it under the window in the tin that was between us. She looked down at the money, picked it up, and counted it. Moving my head down as she printed my ticket. She pointed to the bus area where I would get loaded at. "Thank you," I said taking my ticket, turning away from the teller, and made my way to the bus waiting area. Scoping out the waiting area while leaning against a pillar and watching people. The sight of a mid-age blonde lady in a black business jacket and skirt that went past her knees, sat her coffee down that was recently purchased as she adjusted her luggage wheel. The cup sat on top of the bench near me. Watching as she fumbled with her bag, making my way towards her, snatching the coffee, and then turning sharp right away from her.

I sipped the latte, absorbing the caramel latte that made my taste buds lit up with excitement for the first time in a hot minute. Keeping my pace like others as I spotted another seating area, taking a seat while enjoying the delightful taste. Taking the last sip while standing up and then making my way to the trash can and throwing the empty cup away. The minute of allowing myself to enjoy a latte warmed my spirit as I walked back towards my waiting area, seeing the woman with a fresh brewed cup, sipping on it. Taking a seat on the bench next to hers. "Is that a caramel latte?" I asked as with a grin.

"Yes," she snapped. "My second cup in less than thirty minutes."

I sat back as I crossed my legs. "You must really like your lattes."

"The first cup I had was taken while I was fixing the wheel on my luggage," she said pruning her lips. "It makes me madder than the dickens."

"A thief?" I asked.

"Yes," she exclaimed. "There is no reason to steal when so many good jobs are available."

I nodded as I readjusted my scarf. "Where are you headed?" I asked.

She sipped more on the latte. "Georgia," she said as she glanced over at me. Her blonde short hair lay flat as it reached her chin, green eyes, and pale skin. "I always take the bus as it's easier for me than driving myself."

"Are you on bus two sixteen?" I asked.

"Yes," she said. "Then we have a layover at the state boarder where I get on a different bus to head to Georgia."

"Do you mind if we sit together?" I asked. "I'm headed to North Carolina. I rather sit with someone properly dressed and maintained."

Her lips formed a line as she glanced me over, and then nodded with a grin. "Agreed," she said breaking the silence. "I rather sit by a woman any day of the week."

An announcement came over the intercom as they called our bus number to load up. "Do you have luggage?" She asked.

"Yes," I said as we walked to board the bus. I snatched a lady's silver luggage as she turned to her child's stroller. I handed my bag to the attendant, seeing this lady's tag number and last name, Franklin. We boarded together, finding seats in the middle of the bus, she sat down by the window as I sat next to her. "My name is Sarah Franklin," she said putting her hand out.

"Stacy Edwards," I said shaking her hand.

She started talking about her family in Georgia, and then discussed their family known recipe for peach pie. The trip was never going to end as she continued to talk about her family's wealth. We exited the bus at the South border of New York State. She and I walked over to the next bus's waiting area. "Stacy," she said. "Do you mind watching my items while I run to the bathroom?"

"Not at all," I smiled as she left her purse and luggage beside me. I watched as she entered the restroom door and snatched up her wallet, counting out her cash as she had over three hundred dollars inside it. *I guess her wealth outweighed her common sense.* I stuffed it into my pocket. Sliding her wallet back into the purse as I waited for her return. She came out immediately as I turned to look an opposite direction. "Ah, thank you so much," she giggled. "All the coffee that I drank finally caught up to me."

"No problem at all," I stated. "I'm going to go over to the café area. I will meet you on the bus."

She nodded as she sat down. I got up and grabbed my luggage. "I'll take my things so you're not waiting on me." She smiled, and then pulled out her phone.

I walked away, leaving her with her cashless wallet as I made my way to the teller's station and purchased a ticket to home at the ranch. The bus was already loading as I hastily left with my ticket. I gave my belongings to the driver, and then boarded the bus, not seeing Sarah Franklin again.

For a moment, fascinated with how far I've come to get back home. Relieved as I was going to be home soon and embraced in mom's arms. Excited to jump back to the reality of hearing about how Liz was doing with school. Ready to feel the breeze from sitting on the porch swing, enjoying the peace that the ranch provided. The peace of not being wrapped up in Mason's world of death. I was ready to be back in the comfort of my own home, putting away what I've done this past week and what I witnessed. Trickling down my spine, the memory of how Mason shoved me out of his way to execute his target haunted my sight. Every emotion that attracted me to him shoving its way back as it petrified me to witness the terror. Keeping my head against the window as I wrapped my arms around my abdomen, thinking of him.

The bus stopped in Virginia where we had a short layover to eat and use the restroom. I took advantage of the cash taken from Sarah and purchased a meal and another latte. Taking a seat at the back of the small restaurant area and eating in silence. I reflected on my actions, not happy with the person I've become, but was happier to be a mile closer to home. Finishing my meal and tipping the waiter, I headed for the restroom, cleaning up, washing my face, and adjusting the hat and scarf.

Exiting the restroom, seeing a small shop across from the bus parking. I walked over to it, picking up a few shot bottles of alcohol, and then a few more necessities with a magazine and some light snacks. Purchasing with cash, the clerk didn't ask for my ID as he didn't look like he was enjoying his job anyways. I walked out and headed back towards the bus, smelling the Virgina air, embracing the thickness of its humidity. The bus driver wasn't back yet to allow us to load, so I walked over to the wall next to the doors and propped against it. Grabbing one of the small bottles of alcohol from my bag, unscrewing the cap, and then took the shot allowing the burn to sting my throat. I lifted my head up, looking up at the ceiling of the overpass, and then closed my eyes as I enjoyed this familiar taste that washed away my nerves of being caught by Mason's people.

Chapter Five

"Hey," a man's voice said. I looked down from the ceiling of the overpass to the man walking up from my right. He wore a thick heavy coat, black pants, and looked very homeless. "You got a smoke?" He asked.

"Get lost," I said as I glanced over at the buses.

The man got up next to me. "Hey, I just want one smoke, please," he said putting his hand on my arm.

I shoved it off. "Back off," I said stepping back away from the wall.

He threw his hands up. "Sure thing," he said taking a step back.

Staring him down as the whistle blew behind me, alerting us that it was time to get on the bus, glancing over my shoulder to see the driver motioning other passengers on. "Only one more thing," he paused.

"Look buddy," I said turning back to the man.

A gun barely out from under his coat was pointed at me. My mouth went dry as my body began to feel the heat of fear rise from my feet up. The stinging of the alcohol had nothing on the sting of being held at gunpoint. "Stacy," he said slowly. "You run and I will shoot." His eyebrow arching as he spoke as if he were anticipating me running.

My heart aggressively pounded faster as I kept still, not moving an inch, afraid of what to come if I did. "Look," I said as a lump formed in my throat.

"You follow me," he demanded motioning me with a few fingers.

Stay calm. I took a step towards him to follow his command. He turned sideways to block people from seeing his gun as I took another step towards him. He glanced at the crowd, and then at me. A pattern as he didn't want to draw attention to us, every few seconds he exchanged looks between me and the crowd. Allowing my mind to focus, the next second he looked at them, I grabbed his hand with the gun and shoved him backwards, flinging my bag of items into his head. Shocked by my attack, he stumbled backwards as I twisted his wrist, releasing the gun. Pulling him towards me, lifting my knee into his groins, he fell to the ground. I kicked him one more time, snatching the gun, and then shoving it in my bag as I ran to the people loading the bus.

Taking a breath, I followed in, blending and entering a random bus. They didn't check tickets as they closed the doors of the bus. I watched as the man who I snatched the gun from got on his phone. He stared at me as the bus backed up and drove off. I sighed in relief, looking in my bag and shakingly grabbed another shot bottle. Twisting the cap off, flinging it back, as I wanted to use it as a way to calm my aroused nerves. The alcohol burned my throat as I sat the bag with a gun in it beside me.

The moment overwhelmed, feeling the continuous heat from the man who had me in full panic. Slipping off my jacket, scarf, and hat, I looked around as the darkness of night surrounded the bus. Pain emerged as I wasn't sure that going home was in my best interest now. The salty water pricked my eyes as burning sensation arose, blinking my eyes and wiping them, I sat back in my seat, placing my head on the window. *I need to get away.* Looking around the bus, for my opportunity of a new disguise, as most had either closed their eyes, reading, or occupied in conversation, I snatched and replaced color coat with a white checkered coat and slipped it on. I grabbed sunglasses from another person, and then pulled my hair down, fluffing it out. The next stop was in North Carolina, rushing to the front as we pulled into the bus station with my bag in hand, exiting first. I slid the shades on and snatched a purse laying on the sidewalk by a woman, stuffing my bag with the gun inside.

Inside the station, I headed towards the bathroom to figure out my next move. I cleaned up, and splashed water on my face. A nausea feeling erupted as I went back into a stall, recalling the man who held me at gunpoint, and threw up as I processed the scene by myself. The thought of being back in my hometown knowing they were already here sent fear-stricken signals throughout my body as I pushed my hair back. If I went to the ranch, my family's safety would be jeopardized. I exited the stall and contemplated my thoughts while rinsing my mouth, fluffing my hair, and then pressing the shades back on my face.

Exiting the restroom felt uneasy as the uncomfortable feeling that eyes were watching me rumbled through my body. Remaining calm as I knew better than to draw attention to myself, I walked with confidence to the front of the bus station. Exiting their terminal, I watched as cars and people entered and exited the drive. Walking up the sidewalk to ponder on where I should go next to avoid the ones after me.

Surfacing with sting, tears prickled my eyes as I wanted to go in the direction of home badly. Understanding that if I did go their death would follow at my feet, I stopped and stared at the road. Glancing back at the cars going through the drive, taking a moment to allow the defeat of another disappointment settle on my shoulders, I headed back inside the terminal. Made my way to the teller line where I waited, taking the shades off of my face, and folding them up. I slipped them down in my new possessed pocketbook. A security guard went past me towards the **Security** door to the left of the tellers. Realizing that the right thing to do was seek help with them as I was in no predicament to escape this alone.

A hard breath slipped through my teeth, squeezing my hands and releasing them as I slowly made my way towards their door. Immediately, a person walked up and slipped their arm around me, leading me past the security guard door and to the left of it, a hallway. Unable to stop them, I looked up, seeing Mason, my breaths were short as he pulled me towards the small hallway. Unable to speak or scream, unsure how I should get away as led us towards a rear exit.

He didn't look at me at all. My body formulated sweat as my breath shortened, eyes forming tears as I looked at him, the exit door, and then my bag. Bringing myself to a halt, I reached for the gun inside of my purse, Mason looking over at me. He grabbed my arm and pulled me away from the exit door, pushing me lightly into the wall. "Drop it," he demanded as he had my wrist of the hand that held the gun discreetly of others view.

I shook my head in fear of what may happen next to me. He moved his eyes from my hand with the gun inside the purse to my eyes. Tears slid as a welp slipped through my teeth. Mason's facial expression shifting as he placed his other hand on the back of my neck. "Drop it, Stacy," he said calmer as we stared into each other's soul. The sound of his voice wasn't scary as it never sounded to me, but instead as if he feared my life. Confusion from his tone and facial expression, I gripped the gun tightly. My lips trembled because my life was over if I went with him knowing that I ran was a sign of weakness. He already told us multiple times that they don't need weak beings.

"Stacy," he said glancing down at my hand, and then back into my eyes. "I can't help you if you make a scene."

Continuing to shake my head, lip quivering, the sound of footsteps neared from around the corner. He glanced over with sweat forming above his eyebrows, and then back at me as he feared we would be caught in this unpredictable circumstance. The footsteps sounded louder as I wanted to scream in panic that I was at the end of my life. Sensing my fear, Mason leaned in and pulled me closer to him, drawing his lips to mine. Closing my eyes as it was the kiss I'd anticipated but better. I felt my hand lose the grip of the gun and purse as the sound of it hitting the floor erupted. He moved his other hand from my wrist to my chin, our lips kissing, and then the tongues exploring each other's world. I grabbed onto his wrists as the air around me suddenly felt lighter. The terror that consumed me dissipated with every second our lips were together.

He pulled back away from me, looking me in the eyes. "Not a word," he snapped sternly.

Taking a deep breath, I nodded as he wiped my face. Mason snatched up the purse from beside us and we looked at the security officer who turned around, heading back in the opposite direction. Mason grabbed my arm and pulled me towards the exit, tires squealed as a dark blue Nissan stopped in front of us. Mason opened the door swiftly, pushing me into it. I slid over in the seat as he got in and shut the door behind him. The car drove off and sped down the road. Scott drove us onto the main road, and in the direction of North. We were headed towards New York.

The butterflies that swarmed inside me from our kiss no longer felt as butterflies as fear slowly crept back inside of me. Glancing between Scott and Mason, I looked at Mason who kept his eyes and face towards the window. The high of our shared kiss lingered as I sat up and tried to comb my hand through my hair to distract myself from wanting another. I glanced out the window to my right, and then at Scott who was in full focus, and then over at Mason. Mason had moved his left hand over his mouth as he swiped it in a motion.

I looked back out the rear window, and then back at Scott. "I-."

Mason jerked his head around to look at me. "Not a word," he interrupted.

I slumped back in my seat and folded my arms across my stomach, staring out the window. The ride was silent to a gas station. Mason and Scott got out, bringing the purse that I had taken with them. I tugged on the handle; the child lock was engaged. Attempting roll down the windows, it was child locked as well. My breathing hardened as the air inside of the car disappeared. Anxiously, I looked around as Scott went to pump gas and Mason walked towards the dumpsters with the purse.

Allowing the heat of panic to rise inside of me, rocking in the seat, I combed my hand through my hair as fear settled in. The door opened and I jumped as I looked up. Mason leaned into the car, getting near me. "You need to use the restroom?" He asked.

I nodded. He stepped back and then let me get out of the car. Keeping my composure as made our way to the gas station, Mason followed closely behind me. Heading towards the sign as I wrapped my arms around my stomach, entering the hallway that led to the restrooms. Mason propped himself across from the lady's door. "I will be right here when you get out," he said putting his hands in his coat pockets.

Nodding, I walked in and went to the sink where I cleaned up, splashing water on my face and wiping it with a dry paper towel. Allowing the cool wet feeling to calm my fear, giving me a moment to clear my head and process my next move of escape. I looked around the restroom, seeing a small window behind the stall. I climbed onto the toilet and pushed the window open. Using my strength to pull myself up and through the window. The sound of the door squeaked behind me as if it were opening, I dropped out the other side, stumbling back where I fell on my butt.

I rolled over, scrambling to my feet as I ran back South. Slowing my run after several moments, I crossed my arms over my stomach and slowed down to a walk beside the road as the thoughts of our kiss left tread marks on my heart. Mason's reaction to me, making the one rule he placed on himself, confirmed that he had fallen for me as I for him. That rule where he only kissed ones that were his rushed in my thoughts as confusion knocked its way inside my thoughts. Disappointed with myself for allowing him to take advantage of me in that manner felt demoralizing to my womanhood. Devastated by the idea that it may have been our first-last kiss as the entire situation wasn't right. He feared that the security guard would have caused a scene and kissed me in desperation of his own selfish needs of the circumstances.

Tires squealed as the Dark Blue Nissan slammed on their brakes and turned sideways in front of me, blocking my path. Mason jumped out of the backseat driver's side, holding my breath as he came up to me. "I need to talk with you," he said grabbing my arm.

"Stop," I said shoving him back. He glanced back at Scott as if he didn't want us to talk in front of him, and then looked over at the woods. Shifting himself towards them. I shook my head as tears emerged to my eyes, shaking at the thought of being killed right here.

Mason looked back at me loosening his tightened jaw as he walked over to me. "I need to talk to you, right now," he calmly said lightly touching my arm. Our eyes met, calming my shaking body as they didn't look like they were going to harm me.

Breaking our gaze, I glanced over at the road of cars driving passed us, and then back at him. "I'm scared of you," I admitted as my mouth came dry. "I don't want to talk in the woods."

Mason glanced at the woods, and then over at Scott. He walked over to the passenger side of the car, opened the door, and talked with Scott. Scott got out of the driver's seat. I took a step back, keeping my hands balled up by my sides, getting prepared if I needed to run. Scott walked over to the woods as Mason opened the rear passenger door, looking over at me. "Can we talk, please," he said.

I glanced over at Scott who was moving towards the woods, his back facing us, and then back at Mason who held his hand out to me. Hesitant as my thoughts went in every direction, *he's not going to kill you,* and took his hand. I slipped inside the back seat looking down at the floorboard, feeling every hair on my body rise.. He walked around the tail of the car and got inside the car. He placed his hands on his knees as I glanced over at him. "You kissed me," I said putting my hand over my mouth and crossing my other arm over my stomach. Unsettling twists formed in my stomach.

"It doesn't change how I feel," he said shaking his head. His hands stroking his pants legs as if they were sweating. *Why was he so anxious.* "I need to ask you some serious questions." His tone changed which seemed worrisome. "Did you talk with anyone?"

I shook my head.

"Your family?"

I nodded. "I didn't say anything about what I'd done or witnessed," I said staring into his emerald, green eyes.

"Do they think you're coming home?" He asked turning his body towards me.

I shook my head.

"You understand that what you saw was part of what we do," he said lowly.

I broke eye contact with him, moving both arms around my stomach. I nodded.

He sighed as he moved his hand to the back of my head and lightly pulled me to him. Confusion with his mixed emotions towards me, hesitant at first, and then confided in his motion, moving into his arms as he embraced me. The hug felt comforting and definitely needed at that moment. Unable to hold back anymore, I sobbed as the thought of what I witnessed swarmed my mind. He stroked my back and kissed the top of my head, taking a deep breath that showered my hair, and then he nuzzled his head to my cheek as he moved my hair away from my ear.. "Stacy," he whispered in my ear. "I'm sorry that I brought you into this world of mine."

My arms tightened around him, tears continued to flow, as I gripped onto him. "You have to understand that now with you doing this," he paused.

"I'm terminated," I sobbed. "You have to kill me."

He pulled me away from him, grabbing my face, stroking my hair back. He shook his head. "There's always a consequence, but not termination," he said staring me the eyes. I moved my hands to his wrists as I felt his words of security rush through me. "I won't allow them to terminate you."

I nodded as I moved back to his chest, hearing his heartbeat through his chest. He stroked my hair for a few moments, and then I pulled away from him. I wiped my face as I glanced back at the woods where Scott was still facing them, off the road a few feet. "We have to start heading back," he sighed. "Just know that your reaction of the apartment is exactly why I wanted you to stay back. I was going to bring you later on."

"Why are you killing people?" I asked as we moved to opposite sides of the car.

Mason rubbed his face pulling his fingers in on his forehead as he didn't want to speak about it, and he sat up straight in the seat moving his hands down to his knees. "We have clients who bring us money to dispose of a mole within their company," he admitted. "We get paid top dollar to ensure it looks like a suicide."

"Do you enjoy killing people?" I asked biting my lower lip.

He shook his head. "It's not about killing people," he said sliding closer to me. "We simply help ensure the mole is properly disposed."

"You silence them permanently," I said looking away from him.

"Yes, we are considered the silencer," he said lowly. "You understand by me telling you this, I'm giving you access that your bunk buddies don't know yet."

I nodded. "I'm not much of a friend to them anyways," I said folding my arms. "Let's just get going. I don't know how I feel right now."

"I can't just let you walk away now," he said lightly grazing my arm. I looked over at him and nodded. He stroked the hair on my cheek to behind my ear. I looked down at the floorboard as he exited the car. He whistled, and then moments later got back into the car. Scott into the driver's seat. We got back on the main road, turned around and headed North.

The idea of him being a murderer feared me as I was always raised to stay away from danger. It was safer to find gentlemen than to find boys. I glanced over at Mason as he stared out the window with his hand on his chin. Unlike other times, his facial expression was tightened as he looked angry with himself. Not drawing attention to his expression, I looked back out my window as the idea of him being a *boy* didn't fit right with me. Mason from the moment we met to the interaction at the subway cart has always shown me a gentleman's side. I know that this went against all of my raising, but I also knew that he was breaking as many rules as possible by keeping me alive. When you become a rule breaker for the one you've fallen in love with, was it worth destroying that love?

My body feared him, as I knew now that if ever crossed, he could kill me and set it up as if I got depressed and killed myself. The thought was unsettling. His title of a silencer didn't settle well as a woman from the South enjoyed finding love, raising kids, and living the simple life. And when life didn't feel simple anymore, the women of the South keep trucking along the twisted highway of hell. The thought of marrying this man who has captured my soul and wanting to have babies with him broke into a million pieces. Like shattered glass on the floor, I couldn't imagine how I would be able to explain his lifestyle to the kids or raise them to be proper if we were breaking every rule meant to mankind.

My heart felt torn in two as I knew he was mine and I was his, because no person puts their life at stake to save a stranger. And no person who was willing to put one's life at risk ever apologizes. I also knew that the life I ever dreamt of on the ranch of marrying and having kids was washed away. He didn't strike me as a person to settle, but then again, he was settling now for me. I glanced over at him and stared as he kept his eyes on the view outside. The long ride back was the beginning of my lengthy journey with him.

*****

We arrived back at the warehouse, Scott pulling the car around back into a garage area. Scott exited first, and then Mason looked over at me. "Once we get in there," he said. "Everything that you done these past few days will come to light. You will have consequences, and then you will be forever on thin ice. I won't show you any mercy," he said staring me in the eyes.

I nodded as I knew this moment forward was no longer going to be easy. "Mason," I said grabbing his wrist.

"You have to keep it as it was," he said touching the side of my face. Sweat formed as the humidity of the car rose. "Best of luck, Stacy." He grabbed the door latch, and then exited quickly before

I could say another word to him. I turned to look as they gathered behind the car. Mason, Scott, Ryan, and James. Ryan walked around to my door and opened it. He grabbed my wrist and pulled me out. I couldn't loosen or fight against his grip as he walked hastily inside the arena, dragging me. I looked back at Mason and Scott. James followed behind Ryan as I turned back around to see the bright lights.

Jackson, Thomas, and Preston were in the center of the room. "Look who's back," Jackson said as he walked with Ryan and James. They led me over to the trough. I knew what was about to happen as James grabbed my other arm. A hand went on the back of my neck, and then my face was submerged into the cold water. I screamed as the coldness shocked me at first, tingling my face. My mouth quickly filled with water. I was jerked up taking a moment to breathe and submerged again.

It lasted for a couple of minutes, and then I was pulled out of the water and swung backwards. I coughed, rolling over to my side as Jackson done when he was submerged. "Feels rough, right?" Jackson edged on as he walked over to me. I spat the water out as I rolled over to my knees.

"Again," Mason shouted.

I looked up as I saw Ryan and James making their way back to me. I threw my hand up to block them. They pulled me to my feet, turning me around to the trough. A hand went on the back of my neck, and I was submerged again. I tried to hold my breath, making the impact less painful, but still managed to swallow water. I came up coughing. I took a breath, and then I was submerged again. This round was shorter as they pulled me back out, tossing me onto my back. I coughed and rolled over to my side. A kick to my side, rolling me back over to my back.

I lost my breath for a moment, and gasped as I looked up. Jackson was clapping his hands as he admired the torture I was getting. "Again," Mason shouted.

"Mason," Henderson said. I looked up as Ryan and James grabbed my arms pulling me to my feet. "You don't want to kill the girl."

"She will survive," Mason said.

Ryan and James dragged me over to the water trough, turning me around. My face inches in front of the water. "Bet you wished you stayed put," Jackson edged on. A hand was placed on the back of my neck. I looked up at Jackson who smiled as my head was submerged. I held my breath as long as I could. They jerked my head out of the water, swinging me back onto my back. The breath knocked out of my lungs as I looked up at the ceiling.

"Bring her to the bunkroom," Mason shouted. Ryan and James grabbed my arms, pulling me to my feet as we walked to the bunkroom. I was tossed inside, rolling onto my back as they closed the door. The sound of the latch locked the door. I coughed as I rolled over to my side. I spat up water again. I rolled over onto my elbows and knees, coughing.

It felt like forever till I regained strength to stand. I got up and crawled onto the top bunk, shivering as the cold water froze my body. Quivering and trembling as I curled up into a ball, laying on the cot. I finally fell asleep and dreamt of Mason. We were lying in bed together, holding each other, and then he started to kiss me. I woke up as I had moved over top of him.

I got up from the bunk bed and walked over to the door, locked. I turned away from the door and walked to the opposite wall, propping myself against it. I thought of the idea of being locked in here with no escape. I worked on doing sit ups, pushups, twisting my torso. I ran in place to build endurance. After a few hours, the door unlatched, a bag was tossed inside. It was a chicken sandwich with chips and a bottle of water. I ate all of the contents, finding a napkin in the bag folded into a triangle. I unfolded the napkin reading a note.

Keep up the good work, -Mason. I folded the napkin back and got up and continued to exercise. I rested, exercised, ate the food that was tossed once a day. I received another napkin with a different note. **Your punishment will be over soon, -Mason.** I folded the napkin back up and continued to exercise. The third day I woke up and got down from the bunk. I heard a commotion outside of the door but couldn't make out the sounds. A few moments later, the door unlatched. I stood back as the door opened up, revealing Scott as he stepped to the side. I took it as for me to exit and walked out of the bunk room.

Mason was over by a different door near the exit sign. "You each will be given an assignment," Mason said as I walked up and stood behind the others. "You locate your target and decimate it." Mason had his hands crossed over his chest. "Each will be assigned a handler, get the job done and approved."

"When is this training over with?" Thomas asked.

I walked over towards Preston who stood shakingly. "Consider this your graduation," Mason said. He and I locked eyes for a moment, and then broke contact. "Any questions?"

"Do we get paid for this?" Jackson asked as he had his fingers interlocked in front of him.

Mason nodded. "We don't waste your time, and we don't collect off of earned work," Mason said. "Scott with Thomas, Ryan with Jackson, Kyle with Preston."

I looked up as the others looked back and forth. "Who's Stacy's handler?" Jackson asked.

Mason glanced over at him. "Me," he said pointing at himself.

Jackson shook his head. Mason caught a glimpse and took a step towards him. "You have a problem?" Mason asked.

Preston shifted uncomfortably as he balled up his fists. I touched his arm, and he looked down at me. I nodded to let him know that Mason has this one. "I think she should have a different handler," Jackson said. "Since you two are romantically involved and all."

"Who said anything about romance?" Mason asked.

My eyes shot over towards them as Jackson looked back at me, and then at Mason. "I want you as my handler," Jackson said. "You're their leader." Jackson took a step back and spun around pointing at everyone. "So, since you're the best. I want you as mine."

Mason glanced around at each individual, locking eyes with me for a few seconds. "Scott with

THE SILENCER'S WIFE

Stacy, Ryan with Thomas, and Kyle with Preston. I'm with Jackson," Mason said looking at each one of us. "James you stay post, listen for scanners," Mason said. "We each have separate missions, but ultimately, we're one team. Do the work as if your life depends on it. Because it may very well do so."

Aa large lump formed in my throat as most of everyone parted. I looked over at Preston, who turned and walked away, going towards the wooden chairs. Realizing something was off with him, I followed behind him and sat down beside him. He propped his elbows on his knees, and then started to rub his hands through his hair. "You okay?" I asked as I leaned over towards him.

"No," he said looking up at me. "I'm not okay with any of this. If I'd known what my cousin was involved in, I would have stayed away."

"You can do this," I said licking my lips. "Pull yourself together."

"Easy for you to say," he said as he rolled his eyes.

Anger rose as they all assumed things about Mason and me, but we've only shared one kiss. "I'm just as nervous," I said. "I could screw this up just like any of us."

"Yeah, you will," Jackson snorted. "But unlike us, you have the most powerful person in this arena keeping you safe."

I rolled my eyes as I touched Preston's shoulder. "Just stay alive," I said, and then turned away from them. Jackson started to laugh. I couldn't hear their remarks but moved on towards the gun range. I grabbed up a pistol and loaded the gun. The air shifted behind me as I moved over to in front of a target. I glanced over my shoulder.

"You feel confident enough?" Mason asked as he shifted to my peripheral vision, crossing his arms.

I nodded. Focusing on the target, I pulled the trigger, unloading the clip on the target. I sat the gun down looking away from the target. Mason nodded as an approval of my shooting. "Who taught you to shoot?" He asked as he glanced over his shoulder, and then back at me.

"My father," I said looking over at the target with multiple bullets in the same location, left eye.

"Your mother gave you your looks," he complimented.

I smiled as I turned away from him. "Professionalism," I commented as I walked away from the target. The day gearing up for our assignments was long as we ate, washed up, and then got with our handlers.

Scott who looked over the folder. "I wish I could say we had an easy case," Scott said as he handed me the folder. "Unfortunately, we got the worst case of the four. But these were specifically given to us by Henderson himself."

I glanced over at the center of the room where Henderson sat, staring back at me. He put his hand in the air as to wave good luck to me. I looked back down at the folder. The image of the man was a three hundred pound IT Tech at a major corporation. "You realize this guy is nearly four times my weight," I exclaimed as I folded the file close.

"Let's go get staked out," Scott said as we walked towards the exit. Mason and Jackson had left the arena first, saddening my heart as I wanted to say goodbye.

Chapter Six

THE IT TECH LIVED IN CALIFORNIA. We got on a flight and headed West. We were given a hotel near the major corporation, staying in a suite, acting as tourists in the area. I was provided with a laptop, and lattes. I took the laptop to the Hotel's bar and sat near the back closest to the Corporation's building. As I revived my computer skills, I hacked into their network, and then downloaded our targets computer files. Scott brought over double shot glasses.

I looked a little impressed with the knowledge of my favorite drinks. "Mason advised that you could have a double shot."

I smiled as I leaned forward, collecting a glass. "Send him my thanks," I smiled.

Scott slid towards me to pretend that we were a couple. I downed the first shot, letting the alcohol burn my throat. I handed it to Scott as I worked on the files. Scott leaned his head back as if he were going to take an afternoon nap. I looked over the files in hopes of finding out why we were even assigned this case. "This doesn't make any sense," I said as Scott popped his head up to view the data with me.

"Stacy," he warned. "We're not here to prove innocence."

I nodded. "I know, but if I could-."

Scott closed my laptop and pulled it away from me. He grabbed the second shot glass and handed it off to me, leaning over to whisper in my ear. "We complete the task and leave."

I downed the second shot, letting the alcohol burn my throat. I glanced around the room as to distract my now curious mind. "Let's go back to the room," he said as he stood up. He held out his hand to me. I accepted the offer and held onto his arm as he carried the laptop in his other arm. We got back to the room where he went to the bathroom. I opened the laptop back up and reviewed the files. I moved to his email data and pulled his calendar data off. I reviewed the information as it appeared he would be getting a pedicure later this evening. It was the perfect time to attack.

I went back to the files to review the information about the company. It was certain product testing software that had bugs which led to missing files and inaccurate data. This man was to die because he had saved all the information about the company. He was planning to release it as he had already begun leaking snips to the public under a coded name.

I closed the laptop as I moved over to the suite's balcony. I leaned against the railing, viewing the out over the coast. Seagulls squawking as beach waves crashed onto shore. Scott appeared beside me as I stared out over the horizon. "Do you have an action plan?" He asked.

I nodded. "I know the perfect time to complete the assignment," I said hesitantly.

"You're not here to do anything other than the job," Scott scolded.

I nodded as I looked down at my flip flops. Scott turned to face me. "How did you get wrapped up in all this?" I asked as I crossed my arms.

"Wrong city, wrong time," Scott said turning back to the overlook.

"How old were you?" I asked.

"Same age as you," he said glancing over at me. "I was just a kid who went to the wrong street looking for work."

"Who recruited you?" I asked.

He shook his head. "You're getting yourself too involved."

"I know this will be my life now," I said. "How do you face not seeing your family?"

He gripped onto the balcony as if it were a sore subject and then glanced over at me. "When you don't have one to face, you don't worry about those things."

I nodded. "Want to talk about it?" I asked.

He shook his head. "You need to interest yourself into some beach therapy," he said. "Go relax on the beach."

I looked down at the crowd, and then turned away from it all. "I promised my sister I would travel the world with her," I said leaning against the rail. "I can't enjoy the beach right now."

He sighed as he leaned forward on the balcony. "Getting involved with Mason is far more dangerous than any other on this team," he said keeping his eyes towards the overlook.

"You warn me now?" I asked as I giggled.

He smiled as he chuckled slightly. "I guess I should have picked up on the clues when he first brought you in."

"What's his story anyways?" I asked as I glanced over at him.

He shook his head. "Not mine to tell," he said. "When the time is right, he will let you know."

We ate lunch in our suite. Scott lounged on the balcony as I sat inside the suite, constantly going back over the files in my mind on the IT Tech. The hours passed, and then it was time to complete the mission. We went to the spa that was listed on the calendar. I followed the lady that prepared stations, scoping out a spot to stay hidden until I needed to be present.

I watched as the man entered the Pedicure room. He sat down, lounging back, turning on the chair massage, sipping on a mixed drink. The girl started working on his pedicure. I watched as it came time for him to get a foot massage. I went around and found an organized tray with wheels. I started to wheel the tray and supplies down the middle pass. I had a syringe in my apron that would be used to induce a heart attack.

The man was fitting for this type of death. As the lady who was completing the pedicure started the leg massage, I tripped the cart, spilling it over the main floor. She stopped the massage, apologizing to the IT

Tech, and then coming over to the pathway to help clean up. I grabbed a pair of gloves and made my way back to him. "While she's away, would you like me to complete your massage?" I asked.

He nodded as he went back to sipping on his drink. I sat down on the stool, pouring the lotion onto his skin, and then mimicking massage techniques. I pulled the syringe out of my apron and pricked his big toe. I quickly hid the needle as he glanced down at me. Continuing with the massage until the lady walked back towards us. "I hope you enjoy the remainder of your pedicure," I said pulling the gloves off and walking away.

The girl gave me a soured look as I turned the corner. I made my way back to Scott as we pretended to be touring the spa. As soon as we rounded the pedicure room, a lady blocked the hostess that was showing us around and turned us around immediately. A few moments later, paramedics were on the scene. Scott and I refused any services as we felt the medical personnel made it a bit uncomfortable. We finished our night out as we strolled along the beach back to the hotel, keeping beside each other as to play our part of being a couple appearing to be romantically involved.

We stayed the remainder of the weekend and then caught a flight back to New York. The plane ride back was long and exhausting. The entire incident felt wrong as I remembered the files. Scott had fallen asleep on the plane as I grabbed the laptop out of his bag. I went to the bathroom, snatching a flash drive from another person with a laptop. Their flash drive contained gaming data which I erased and downloaded the files of this corporation.

I hid the flash drive in my coat pocket and then placed the laptop back in its place. Scott woke up with turbulence from us arriving back at the airport. We exited the plane and caught a cab back to the usual a few blocks from the warehouse. Walking in silence as I kept the flash drive hidden in my pocket. We made it back to the warehouse, meeting up with Preston and Thomas.

"Any news on Jackson?" Thomas asked as I side-hugged Preston.

I stepped back and shook my head as if I had any news of Mason. "Well, maybe he will be back soon," Thomas said, and then departed.

The three of us sat off near the water trough, facing the gun range. Preston discussed his case, giving details of the profile, and then how he accomplished the mission. Thomas kept it simple, "the job is done."

The hours continued to pass as we paced, shot rounds at the range, and then paced more. The uneasy and nervous that Mason wasn't coming back rushed through my mind as time elapsed. Every moment that passed I felt myself falling apart inside out. "You know he will be back," Preston whispered. "Mason's the best here."

"What if Jackson did something to him?" I asked as we propped ourselves against the wall. Thomas threw a ball at the wall near the bunkroom.

"Mason would outsmart him," Preston said nudging my shoulder.

"Their back," Ryan shouted.

Preston and I jumped up and made our way over to the table, quickening my pace before the others. Thomas quit throwing the ball and walked over to us.

Jackson came through, pumping his fists in the air, and then shook hands with Thomas. Mason shook hands with the handlers, and then with Henderson. A breath of relief left my lips when I saw him in the same confident condition as when he left.

Mason and the handlers gathered a distance away from us. I turned to face Jackson who was gloating about himself and his fine work. Preston kept his arms crossed as I stayed back, letting him gloat, but not engaging. I glanced over at the handlers as they continued to talk. Preston nudged my shoulder. "Told you he'd be back," Preston smirked.

I smiled as I stroked the hair behind my ears. "Don't worry Princess," Jackson said as he moved to in front of me. "I made sure your king returned." I rolled my eyes at his remarks.

"Knock it off, Jackson," Preston said shoving him back.

I put my hand up to stop Preston. Jackson got into Preston's space, shoving his face forward. "Why don't you listen to your little girlfriend," Jackson said poking Preston's chest.

"Knock it off," I said wedging myself between the two of them.

"You screwing him too," Jackson said getting into my face.

Preston swung over my head and punched Jackson in the face. "Preston, stop!" I shouted as I went to grab Preston's arm. He shoved me off as he punched Jackson again. Jackson rolled him on the floor. I went forward grabbing Jackson by the arm. Thomas tackled me from the side as we both rolled on to the floor. Thomas pinned me down.

I lunged my face forward, hitting Thomas's nose. He fell backwards as I got my arms free. Rushing to my feet, seeing the handlers were now her with us. Ryan and James grabbed Jackson as Kyle and Mason had Preston. Scott pulled Thomas to his feet, keeping him back. No one was blocking me. "Even after all we've been through, you're still starting-."

"Enough," Henderson shouted interrupting Mason.

I looked over at Henderson who walked to the center of this chaos. "Mason, Jackson, let's go for a walk."

I took a step forward as I wanted to follow him. Ryan and James let go of Jackson who shook off their arms in anger. Scott moved between Thomas and me as we watched the three walk out. Mason glanced at me for a few seconds and then looked back ahead of him. *No!* I wanted to chase after him as I felt it was going to end badly over me. Preston was let go by Kyle, stumbling over to the water trough. I walked over to him.

"What were you thinking?" I asked as I hit the back of his head.

Preston splashed water on his face, cleaning up the blood that was drawn, and then rubbed the water over him. "I'm tired of Jackson's mouth about you," Preston confessed. "Since day one, he's done nothing but make you out to look like a whore."

"That's a little stretched," I said crossing my arms.

"You're so blinded," Preston said as he turned around and sat on the ground.

I glanced over at the door, waiting for them to come back inside. "I'm not blind," I said. "I just chose to ignore Jackson." I sat down beside Preston. "You know you're going to have to suffer the consequences now."

"He edged it on," Preston said slapping his knee. "If anyone deserves to be cut, its him."

I shook my head. "You know that cut means-."

"I know," he interrupted waving his hand to wave off my statement.

The door sounded as Henderson returned, but no signs of Mason or Jackson. I got up from the ground and ran over to the handlers. "We will see them both soon enough," Henderson said as he walked past us.

"What does that mean?" I asked looking back at Henderson who kept walking, and then back at Scott. Scott looked away from me. The handlers separated and went on about their business. I stood at the table, pacing back and forth as time lapsed. The door finally sounded, and I looked over to see Mason with Jackson behind him. My heart leaped as I was glad to see Mason come through the door.

Mason motioned for Preston and Thomas to join us. "Tonight, we celebrate your graduation," Mason said loudly. "Scott, Ryan," he motioned for them as they came out with a few rolling trays of dinner and a pale with cold beer in it. I turned and walked away from the table, heading over to the gun range.

I glanced back as they started eating and drinking. Looking over at the exit sign that hovered one door to my left. I walked over to it, and pressed the bar down, opening the door. The door closed behind me as in front of me was a flight of stairs to another door at the top. I ran up the stairs, and then pressed the door handle, exiting to the roof access. Inhaling fresh air, making my way over to the wall across from the door, looking up at the sky where the sun was setting. I closed my eyes, letting the night in July shower my memory of Liz and I. Her birthday celebration to my conversation with mom on the porch.

Creaks fled from behind me as I glanced over my shoulder, seeing the door open. Mason walked over to me. "You could get sick," he said as he pointed back inside. "Let's go celebrate."

Chuckling at his genuine side, I turned around to face him. "You go on, celebrate all you want," I smiled. "I'm staying right here." I looked up as the stars settled in the sky above our heads.

"You know that we worked it out," he said as he moved closer to me. His arms wrapped around my waist, catching my attention. "Jackson isn't going to treat you like that anymore."

Shaking my head as I chuckled, turning away from him, facing the city overlook. He came up behind me, wrapping his arms around my stomach. The moment took me by surprise, and I gasped at his touch. He nuzzled his face in my hair by my neck. "Let's go celebrate your completion," he whispered as his hot breath against the chilled evening sent shivers down my spine. I unwrapped his arms and pulled away from him.

"I don't want to celebrate," I said taking a step away from him.

He smiled as he put his hands in his coat pockets. "What is it that you want?"

I looked down from the stars and locked eyes with him. He walked over to me, backing me against the wall. I felt his hand grab my waist, and then the other slowly moving my hair off my face. He leaned into me, pressing his body against me. I felt a trembling sensation rush over me again. "Stacy, what is it that you want?" He asked as he whispered his hot breath into my ear.

My mouth dried up as a lump formed in my throat. He leaned closer to my neck, edging the anticipation on as he always does. I grabbed his coat jacket, sending him a wave of shock. He moved his hand behind my neck, lips close to mine. "I want you," I said as I felt myself leap forward. He moved in on my reaction and kissed me. I gripped his jacket tight as he pulled me in closer.

Then suddenly he pulled away from me, turning himself away. Breathless, I used both hands to push my hair back as I realized we kissed again. I watched as he put his hand to his mouth, wiping away our shared moment. "I can't do this with you," he said not looking at me.

I looked around, and then back at him, taking a step towards him. "You kissed me just as much as I did with you," I snapped. I turned away from him as mixed emotions rushed over me. "Do we have to be on the edge of being caught for you to love me?" I asked.

"It's too dangerous," he said glancing over his shoulder at me.

I took a step forward, grabbing his arm. "You already brought me here," I said as our gazes met. "Don't do this to me now."

He looked away and turned around to me. He put his hand on my cheek as he moved the other around my back. "I'm not going to do this to you," he said as our lips almost met again. "I'm your boss, that's it."

I felt the breath of his words shower me. My body wanted to react in the way he did moments ago. Forcing myself to hold back as he let go of me. I watched as he walked away from me again. Anger built as every part of confusion with him rolled through me as I knew I wanted him; my body and soul craved him. The fight for self-control was about to play an ultimate tow on my life. Letting out a deep breath, I looked up at the stars once again and walked back to the roof access door.

Rejoining them inside, Mason had joined Ryan and Scott at a couple chairs in the corner, sipping on a beer. I went over and grabbed a beer from the ice pale. Jackson approaching my position. I kept my eyes locked on him as he reached around me, grabbing a beer. "Sorry," he said, and then turned around. I watched as he walked over to where Thomas sat with Kyle and James. I glanced around the room, seeing Preston by the gun range.

I walked over to the gun range, opening my beer, and then taking a few sips. "You're going to get yourself hurt," Preston said as he loaded the clip.

"Already there," I said, and then took another sip.

He shook his head. "I'm not talking about romance," he said. "You mess up with the wrong person around, and then you won't be able to wait for Mason to bail you out."

"I'm screwed," I said glancing back at Mason who locked eyes on me for a moment. He broke the stare as he sipped his beer and looked back at Scott. I watched as Preston shot the target. I sat my beer down and picked up a small handgun, loaded the clip, and then got in line to shoot. "I think I'm in love with a killer."

"Aren't we all killers now?" Preston asked glancing at me.

I nodded. "Silencers," I corrected.

I sat the gun down and chugged the remainder of the beer. "You want one?" I asked.

Preston nodded as he reloaded the clip. I walked across the room, grabbed two beers, and walked back to Preston's location. He sat the gun down on the table beside him, grabbed the beer and opened it. I opened mine, and then we tapped our beers and drank. Typically, I could drink at least four beers before feeling a buzz, that night felt awfully strange after the second beer. Preston went to grab another for us as I didn't refuse. Drinking was one of the best ways to forget things or at least temporarily. Throwing the beer back as I guzzled it, feeling more buzzed than the one before it.

We moved over to the water trough, laughing as we sat there. I watched as it felt like I saw double of everything. "It's normal to see two, right?" I laughed.

Preston laughed too. "Totally." We laughed as we finished another round.

"You two want another?" Ryan asked as he popped the tops off the lids. I held my hand out unable to grab the beer. He put it in my hand, and I tipped it back. All three started laughing as Preston and I started to get up. Preston stumbled five steps and dropped to the ground. Bursting out in a deeper laugh, I held on to the side of the water trough, finishing the final of the beer.

I felt a hand slide across my back remembering that I didn't even want to celebrate this stupid career. "You need to sober up," a voice whispered.

"You need to sober up," I said looking over my shoulder.

I heard a few people laughing. "She wants to be left alone," a voice said. "Leave her here by the water trough."

"She's done," the voice said as the room spun. An arm slipped under mine, holding me as we tried to stand. Dropping the beer bottle as the room continued to spin, I moved forward, tripped and fell to the ground.

"Leave her there," a voice shouted.

Finding this hilarious at my clumsiness, unable to see clearly, I laughed as the room swirled. "She's done for tonight," the voice sounded sternly. It was Mason, I felt relieved and started laughing more at him showing his gentlemen side as I tried to keep my eyes open. He pulled me up, tightly gripping me as I stood, bent over as the room wasn't calming down.

"Alright boss," the other voice said. "We'll make sure she gets to bed."

"Move out of the way," the stern voice of Mason.

I laughed and copied his deep stern voice. "Move out of the way," I mocked with laughter. Mason tried to take a step, I fell again to the ground, laughing harder than the last time.

"Just go on," the other voice that I couldn't make out said. "We'll get her to bed."

Uncontrollably laughing, I hadn't felt this way in months. I shifted over to my side, seeing three of everything. Mason in his black leather jacket where the others didn't wear jackets all the time, threw a punch, and another person landed on the ground. A burst of laughter erupted from my stomach as Mason came over to me quickly, picking me up and throwing me over his shoulder. Suddenly I stopped laughing as the spinning began to feel nauseating. He hurriedly to a room away from the others and sat me down on the ground. Looking around as I realized we were in the shower room, grabbing my head as my head started to pound.

"You need to sober up," Mason said sternly. I heard the sound of water running, and then he picked me up and moved me under the water. The cold water shocked me at first. I screamed as if I were I agony, but only from the shock. He put his hand over my mouth, and then I looked at him as we both were being drenched under this ice-cold shower. The shock of the ice water drawing away the spinning of the room as I focused on him.

He kept his eyes on the corner of the shower, pressing my mouth closed. Moving my hands to his hand over my mouth, I watched as he looked into my eyes. Everything else around me disappeared as I moved my hand to his chin, and then lunged forward, kissing him. He kissed me back, rubbing my back, and then turning me and pressing me to the back of the shower.

I felt his hand move from my back up as the other moved the front of my shirt up and over my head. The intensity grew as we both were triggered, and I moved my hands just as fast to pull his coat off. He helped shimmy it off, and then I started tugging at his shirt. He kept kissing me, letting our tongues explore each other. Realizing how much I wanted this moment and enjoying where it was headed as I knew he could say he didn't want me but his hands said otherwise. He moved from my lips to my ear, and then down my neck. I started to unbutton his pants, and then it was like reality shocked him and he grabbed my hands. Breathless, I moved my hands back to the back of the shower as he moved away from me, turning the shower off. I was in my bra and pants, looking at his shirtless body of abs.

He took a step back as I pushed the hair out of my face. "What," I stuttered. "What is it?"

He turned his back towards me. "Are you sobered up?" He asked in an angry tone.

I nodded. "Yes," I said realizing that I pushed too far. I put my arms to cover my cleavage. "Mason, I-."

"Get your shirt back on," he said picking up our wet clothes. I snatched my soaked shirt and attempted to put on the best I could do. He put his shirt and coat back on, not looking at me but glanced to locate my hand. I grabbed his hand as he led me out of the shower room. The others passed out or sat down letting the drunk phase brush over.

Mason led me to the door to the garage. He opened the passenger door, and then buckled me in. My vision of spinning and seeing multiples was gone as my confused mind attempted to sort out what just happened. Mason got in the driver's seat and rushed me out of there. The nauseas feeling crept back in with his speed but I held it together. The car moments later suddenly stopped, Mason got out of the car and rushed around to the passenger side. He picked me up out of the car and carried me. I couldn't tell where he brought me as dark spots covered my vision, but he put me down on a bed. My eyes rolled back and everything went dark.

*****

The scent of grease from sizzling eggs entered my nostrils, waking me up. I opened my eyes to see the ceiling of my apartment, sitting up as I clutched the bed sheets, looking down and seeing I was naked. Embarrassed with myself from allowing it to go as far as not even remembering anything, then the memories flooded of our heated moment in the shower. *Shit!* I moved the sheets back and slipped out from the sheets into my night robe that lay on my side table. Shaking my head in disappointment with myself as I tied it. Regaining my composure, I walked over to the kitchen area with the breakfast bar. Mason turned around to see me awake.

"Good morning," he said sliding two sunny side up eggs onto a plate and placing it in front of me.

"Did we," I paused as my cheeks flooded red and suddenly the awkwardness flooded me.

"No," he interrupted saving my breath. I sighed a breath of relief as he turned around, moving his plate over to be directly in front of me. "You did work hard on stripping the both of us," he said as soon as I put a spoonful in my mouth, almost spitting it everywhere.

He chuckled as he poked at his plate. I grabbed a napkin, wiped my mouth, and took a small bite looking away for a moment. "We need to set boundaries," he said.

"You mean you want to place a boundary over me, but I get to just accept your mixed emotions," I said poking at the eggs on my plate.

"You remember the last night in the bar together?" He asked.

I nodded as I looked up into his gaze. "Do you remember what I told you?"

"Soberminded," I said knowing where the conversation was leading.

Mason took another bite as we held a moment of silence between us. "You're no good to me drunk," he said.

"For someone who doesn't want me," I said stabbing another part of the egg. "You sure are protective of me."

He took a deep breath. "I know I'm no good for you," he said as we met gazes.

"That's you falsely telling yourself," I said as I stood up from the barstool and walked around the counter. I moved his hand from the counter to my hip. He turned, putting his focus on me, and then moved his hand to my chin. "You know deep down that you belong with me."

He cupped my chin with his hands. I slid my hands to the knot in my robe, unfastening it. Swiftly grabbing my robe, he kept it closed, not revealing my body. "I'm not about to lead you wrong again," he said tying a knot in the robe. "I know what's best for you.

If you have any sense, then you will know to back down."

I pulled away from him and turned away. "If you set a boundary," I said glancing over my shoulder at him. "Then I must set one too."

He nodded. I moved around the counter to the front of my plate. "You can't stare into my eyes with those," he stopped. "No staring."

"No invading my personal space," I said as our gazes met, and then we looked away from each other.

"No more getting drunk," he said.

"No more leading me on," I said.

"You must trust me even when you don't feel it's for your own good," he said.

"You can't touch me anywhere," I said looking down at my plate.

He took a deep breath, and then spoke softly, "you must obey every rule." The words stung at the release of his tongue. I looked up at him as I wanted him to go into details but had a feeling I knew what was about to be said. "Scott mentioned of your search for answers."

Shifting my eyes down at the plate in front of me. "How did you get involved?" I asked not looking up at him.

"It's my secret that I won't be sharing with you at this breakfast," he said grabbing my plate. "Get dressed as we need to make it back to the warehouse."

"And how are we supposed to act?" I asked.

"Like I'm your boss," he sternly stated.

He cleaned up the dishes as I went over to my wardrobe and pulled out clothes. I found some blue jeans and a red button up blouse, pulled on my sneakers, and then went to the restroom where I fixed and styled my hair. We left my apartment and headed to the warehouse blocks away. When we got there, I followed behind Mason not looking much at the others as we entered.

Preston stood with Kyle by the table. Jackson and Thomas stood near the shooting range. Scott talked with Henderson by a door. James and Ryan weren't in sight. Mason walked up to Scott and Henderson with me at his heels. I kept my arms around my chest as it felt that rumors were already stirring in the room. Slightly embarrassed as last night's events popped into my mind, unsure who was trying to convince Mason that they would ensure I got to bed safely.

I finally picked up the nerve and made my way over to Preston. Kyle walked over to Mason, Scott and Henderson. "Are you okay?" Preston asked as he stood up straight to face me.

I nodded. "Why wouldn't I be?" I asked.

"You didn't hear," Preston said glancing over my shoulder, and then back at me. "Ryan and James both got the hell beat out of them from Mason. We all got pretty messed up drunk, but they apparently had other motives in mind."

An unsettled feeling rose inside of me, heating my face at the thoughts of a dangerous position I put myself in last night, I turned around to look over at Mason. Mason was discussing a heated conversation as I could see his expression wasn't at all happy with circumstances. I looked back at Preston. "Mason didn't hurt me," I said swiping my hair behind my ears. "He brought me somewhere safe for the night."

"Better be glad you didn't have to sober up here," Preston said as he took a seat at the table.

"Where are Ryan and James?" I asked looking around to see if I saw them anywhere in the arena.

Preston shrugged his shoulders. "Possibly in body bags," he said throwing his hands up.

Mason whistled as we all jerked our heads in his direction. He motioned for all of us to come to him. Preston got up from the chair as we made our way over to him. Preston and I exchanged looks as we stopped and stared at Mason. He had pagers in his hands and handed the first to Jackson. "These are your work phones," Mason said handing Thomas his next. "You hear it go off; you better drop everything that you're doing and come running. A location will be sent for a meeting with a handler. You complete the job, and then you get paid."

"Speaking of pay," Jackson interrupted.

Scott walked up behind Mason, handing Jackson an envelope. Jackson peeked inside and nodded. "Like I said we don't let you do free work around here," Mason said handing Preston a pager. Scott handed Thomas his folder, and then Preston his folder. Mason stopped in front of me. "You going to answer this pager faster than you called me?" He asked holding the pager out in front of me.

"You going to make me wait a lifetime," I said taking the pager.

A smirk slipped across his face as Scott reached around Mason, quickly he formed a line with his lips, handing me an envelope. Mason turned as Scott walked away from us. "Watch yourself," Mason said, and then turned away from me. I clutched both the pager and envelope near my stomach.

"You all are free to go back to your normal lives until the time comes," Mason continued. "You speak of anything about this place and like we've stated before," he paused. "You will end up in a body bag."

Jackson and Thomas nodded, and then were the first two to leave. Preston glanced at me. "I guess I will be seeing you around," he said tapping my shoulder with his envelope. "Be careful out there."

I nodded, "you too." Preston turned around and left behind Jackson and Thomas. I glanced over at Mason who had turned away from us and went back towards Henderson with Scott and Kyle. I wanted to stay but knew better than to do so. The tension between the four of them felt like a warning that if I stayed around I would be witnessing more than I needed too. I turned around and walked out the door behind the others. They were already out of sight of the warehouse as I made my walk back to my apartment.

Chapter Seven

I GOT BACK TO MY APARTMENT, putting the pager down on the countertop, taking the envelope to my bedroom, sitting down on the bed and opening it. Dumping its contents out onto the bed seeing four stacks of hundreds as I counted ten thousand dollars. My mouth dropped in shock that the job paid this well. I looked at the money, and then looked out my apartment window as the shock was overwhelming. *This can't be real.*

After several moments of allowing the shock to cease, I got a mailing envelope and sorted out a thousand dollars, addressing it to my mom. I wrote a note for her. I split the rest of my money, paying my rent a year in advance, and then paid for a few burner phones. Investing in a bank security box and placed money inside it with the flash drive I had of files of that corporation. *Collateral.*

I made a purchase of my own equipment for IT work, running codes and setting up black websites.

After a few days, keeping the pager on my belt in case it went off, I finally got the courage to call mom. "Hey mom," I said as she picked up the phone not allowing her to speak first.

"Stacy," she said with a sigh of relief. "I literally have been worried sick about you."

"You don't have to worry about me," I said calmly. "I'm back from my trip."

"You scared me," she said taking another deep breath.

"I know," I said. "I'm sorry for doing that. I had important work things. You know, city life mom."

A moment of silence between us, and then I felt guilty as I knew my web of lies felt like they grew enormously. "Mom," I said in seriousness. "I sent you a package. Can you put it in a safe place for me?" I asked as the silence made me uncomfortable.

"You remember what I told you back in July," she said with a serious tone. "You get yourself into any trouble and you come home."

I chuckled. "I'm not in any trouble," I said sitting down on my bed. "Quite the opposite."

She sighed. "Stace, you best not be lying. I know you think this computer stuff is worth big money, but I feel it's going to cost you more than its worth."

"How's Liz doing?" I asked changing the topic.

Mom held her breath a second, and then spoke, "she's managing with school. Medical school isn't for the faint."

"She's tough," I smiled. "I know she'll make you proud."

"I'm proud of both my girls," mom said. "Is something on your mind, Stace?"

"No ma," I said. "Just good to hear your voice for longer than ten seconds."

"You coming to see me at Thanksgiving?" She asked. "We all would love to see you, spend time with you."

"I don't know ma," I said. "Work's been taking up a lot of my spare time right now."

"A job isn't life," mom said. "Remember that! You can always find work; you can't replace time."

I felt the prickling of tears at my eyes as I rubbed them. The emotional mess that I was putting myself in by not seeing my family started to feel as if I were shredding apart. "Ma, I got to get back to work," I said. "I'll let you know about Thanksgiving."

"Stace, remember your roots," she said. "Love you."

"Love you too," I said, and then disconnected the line. I tossed the phone down on the bed beside me as I wiped my face off from its dampness. I sat up on the bed, looking down at the pager, and then thought of the conversation between mom and me. Knowing that her warning, *remember your roots,* would disapprove of my ongoing lifestyle. Getting up from the bed, pacing back and forth, and decided to go the next best place in life. I grabbed my apartment key, and then the burner phone that I contacted mom on and left the apartment.

I made my way around the block and headed inside the bar. I took a seat at the bar. "Hey stranger," Wade said with a smile. "You want your usual?"

"Nice to see you too, Wade," I smiled. "I'll take six rounds."

"Six?" Wade asked arching an eyebrow.

I nodded as I pulled money out of my wallet. "Pour me six shots," I said putting the cash down on the bar. Hesitant at first, he collected the money, pulled out the glasses and turned the bottles upside down and filling the glasses.

"You on duty tonight?" He asked as he flipped the bottles back over.

I shook my head, "not that I'm aware." I took the first shot in my hand.

Wade smiled as he poured himself a shot and took one with me. "Well, here's to freedom," he said.

I slammed the first glass down absorbing the burn and grabbed the next one. I threw the remaining five back with no hesitation, ignoring Mason's boundaries. The heat of the alcohol rose my body temperature as I looked around the bar. The music had become louder with the crowd, turning back around to Wade. "Pour me four more," I said putting more money down.

"You should probably take it slower," Wade said as he leaned over the bar. "You never know when that call will come."

"You're my bartender," I said putting my hands down in front of me. "Not my dad."

Wade gave a nod, understanding his place, and lined up the four glasses. He poured the content, and I took the shots, not feeling the alcohol burn. The buzz was reappearing inside of me as I made my way over to the dance floor. Remembering the nights at the bar back in North Carolina, dancing with strangers, getting drunk and flirting with other men. A young man came up to me, started dancing with me, and then put his hands on my hips.

I turned my back to him as we both moved our hips with the music. "You ready to ditch this place?" He asked in my ear.

The buzz of the alcohol synchronized with the beat from the music as I moved my hips. I faced the young man, placing my hand on his shoulder. "No," I said firmly continuing to dance.

Allowing the past to revitalize inside of me as I danced and others joining behind me, around me. A sense of happiness rushing over me as this familiarness brought me pleasure. I made my way back over to the bar. "Wade," I said as I flopped down in the chair. "Give me four more shots."

"You're close to being over your own limit," Wade said.

I waved a finger in the air. "Not my dad, remember," I said as I turned around to face the dance floor. My new friends were still dancing and drinking. I reached in my pocket and pulled out cash, dropping it on the bar. I turned back around to face Wade who shook his head. He placed the glasses in a line, staring at them as he stared down at them. "Pour the shots," I said slamming my hand down as I realized his hesitation.

He flipped the bottle over and poured the shots. I reached for the first glass, and he grabbed the top of my hand. "You don't want to get yourself hurt," he said. "Just leave them here for another person."

I swiped my hand out from his, toasting my shot at him. "Thank you," I said, and then flung back the shot. Another buzz rolled through as I slid the glass over to Wade, reaching for another glass. He walked away shaking his head as if he were disappointed with me. I took the next shot, sitting the glass down and turning around. I could feel all of what I felt days ago from one-to-many beers.

Beep... Beep... Beep... Beep... I looked down at the pager on my pants as the sound erupted. *You got to be kidding me.* I turned around as I had two shots left. Glancing between the two shots and the pager, recalling Mason's warning with the pagers. I grabbed the pager off my pants and placed it beside the two shots; it went off again. Realizing I was in no shape to meet up with them, knowing that if I didn't that I may not be able to stay alive for disobeying one of the rules. I rolled my eyes as this night just got a bit more challenging.

Wade came back to where I sat. "You never know when they will call," he said. "You best give the number paging you a call."

I shook my head, waved my hand in the air to wave him away, contemplating on what to do. Looking at the two shots that I desperately wanted to take and pass out from this night. Instead, I grabbed the pager and stumbled to my feet and made my way to the exit. I knocked into a few people as I stumbled out of the bar. A hand slipped under my arm as I made it outside, looking at who grabbed me, seeing Wade.

"Look," he said. "You show up in this condition," he hesitated. "I just know you may want to sleep this off for a few hours."

I pulled my arm away from him. "Bartender," I slurred. "Not my dad."

"You best be finding your way home," Wade said as I stumbled off from his grip. I waved my hand in the air as I walked down the street.

I kept close to the wall as the pager went off again, annoyed by the beeps that erupted from it. Looking up the address that scrolled through its screen, having double vision seeing the information. Pulling up maps on the burner phone and struggling to input the address.

Every wrong call that I made tonight pulsated through my body as my fingers weren't cooperating. Heading to the bus stop and waiting for it to arrive, leaning on a streetlight post. I stumbled onto the bus, putting my head against the window as I watched us travel in the direction of the maps on the phone. Closing my eyes weren't an option because missing the correct stop would delay my arrival to their location. We finally arrived close enough that I stumbled to my feet, fumbling the phone and pager in my hand as I got off the bus.

Looking down at the phone and heading in the direction that I needed. I picked up my pace as I struggled to put the pager back on my pants. Arriving at a building, feeling nauseas from the double vision. I leaned over and forced my hand in my throat to throw up. Allowing the hurl to finish as my body felt better, I stood up straight to regain my posture.

I looked over my phone and saw I had another block to go. Picking up my pace, feeling the sweat form on my body as I jogged. I got to the building feeling extremely exhausted from the weight of the alcohol. I got to the door at the side of the building. I twisted the knob, falling inside the building. I stumbled to my feet as I looked around, not seeing anything with the low-lit lighting.

"Stacy," Preston's voice said as I stumbled into a chair. I fell to the ground, unable to get up this time.

I heard someone else chuckling. "She's wasted," Thomas laughed. "Guess you'll be sitting this one out."

I rolled onto my knees, stumbling to get up. The low lighting and an awful buzzing noise sounded. "Enough," I heard a deep voice shout. I looked around as the images were coming clear with Preston and Thomas standing near me. I looked around to my right, seeing Ryan walking up into the lit area. Half of his face was blue and purple. I fell back down on my bottom.

"She's too drunk," Thomas said. "She'll just get us all caught."

I glanced over at Preston, who appeared jumpy as he wasn't sure whether to jump to my side or stay put. A hand slid under my arm and was pulled to my feet. Ryan dropped my arm as I stood there, seeing the room sway a little. "She'll be sober in time of need," Ryan snarled. "We're heading out tonight via subway, then going to market plaza. We have two targets, husband and wife. They do have children which from my intel will be gone this weekend," Ryan stated. "So, the only target is the husband and wife."

"Where are we pulling this off at?" Thomas asked.

"Their home," Ryan snapped. "Let's head out." He came over to me and grabbed my arm, dragging me along. My legs wobbly as if they were going to give way. He slowed down, turning around to face me. "What did Mason tell you?"

I couldn't find the words to speak as my mouth was dry. He turned around, dragging me along. We got to the subway cart where he shoved me down in the seat and sat down beside me. I felt the swaying of the cart, nauseas feeling arose. "I think I'm going to be sick," I whimpered.

"You throw up on me, and I swear-."

"I will sit beside her," Preston interrupted. "Ryan, I will sit beside her." I looked at Ryan, who glared at me, and then stood up as Preston took a seat beside me. "Put your head between your legs," he whispered as he stroked my back.

I did as he said, closing my eyes. The nausea feeling subsided for the moment. Our subway came to a stop, Ryan grabbed my arm and pulled me to my feet. We exited the subway and headed to the Market place. I started to feel my legs not wobbling as much. Ryan dragged me along as I could feel his anger tension with each tug and jerk. We got to the apartment building where Thomas entered first, and then Ryan and me, and finally Preston. Ryan shoved me on the floor next to a wall. I rolled into the wall, and then back onto my knees. I stood up as I held onto the wall.

"Bathroom is in there," Ryan snapped. "Get sober up!"

I turned to my left, seeing the door cracked open with the bathroom. I went inside and closed the door behind me. I splashed cold water on my face and sat down on the toilet lid. Placing my face in the palms of my hands as I sat and waited for the alcohol to subside.

Knock. Knock. I looked up as Preston entered with a bottle of water, medicine, and a sandwich. "This should help," he said kneeling in front of me. I took the medicine, sipped on the water, and then ate the sandwich.

"I wasn't meaning to get wasted," I said after I chewed a bite of the sandwich.

Preston shrugged his shoulder. "Not like we're not young and stupid. We all did sign up for a job that ends with one route out."

I nodded as I took another bite of the sandwich. I finished eating and drinking the water. "You need to rest some, it will help ease off the alcohol."

I nodded. He helped me to my feet and we exited the bathroom. He led me to a room with two cots. Thomas had already claimed one. I went to the opposite one and lay down. "Get some rest," Preston said. "We'll switch shifts in a couple of hours."

Preston left the room as I glanced over at Thomas. He was curled up looking at me. I rolled over onto my back and put my hand to my forehead. "You weren't the only one to get drunk tonight," Thomas said with a sigh.

"You too?" I asked glancing over at him.

He nodded. "I was almost home to drink another before bed, had a lady walking with me and everything."

"So, what did you do with your date?"

"Ditched her at the bus stop as I high tailed on to it," he laughed. "Bet I won't be able to make that up to her."

I chuckled at the comment. "Our lives are truly screwed up," I snorted.

"Shhhh…." Ryan shouted from the other room. "You two idiots will be the reason I turn on this entire operation." We both glanced at each other, and then I looked back at the ceiling and closed my eyes.

I felt a nudge on my arm, shaking it off at first, and then a harder nudge. I opened my eyes, seeing Preston standing over me. "You got to get up," he said. I rubbed my face and sat up. The aftermath of a hangover headache rushed over me. He handed me another bottle of water and medicine. "I got to get some rest. Apparently, we're hitting their place tonight."

I nodded. I got up from the cot, looking over at Ryan who was snoring where Thomas lay beforehand. Walking to the door as Preston lay down, looking back over my shoulder as he got comfortable in the bed. I went through with the bottle of water in hand. We were in an apartment with a living area, kitchen and a single bathroom. Thomas staked out by the window, munching on a small bag of chips.

"Hungry?" He asked holding out the chips towards me.

I waved it off as I walked over to the other window. "Which house is it?" I asked looking at the rows of houses.

"The three twelve," Thomas said.

I looked as it was just breaking sunrise. "Any information on who they are?"

"Just that their targets," Thomas stated. A simple answer which was all he ever provided.

I rolled my eyes as I glanced around the apartment. Spotting an envelope on the table in front of the couch. "This the profile?" I asked taking a seat and opening the envelope.

"Ryan stated we shouldn't dig too much into it. Payout is a hundred grand each," Thomas said as chips crunched in his mouth. The sound was quite irritating and horrific.

"You're not curious at all?" I asked glancing up at him.

He looked back at me. "It's not our place to dig," he said bluntly. "I'm just here to collect a paycheck."

I started looking over the files, viewing the images of the man and woman. They were accounting representatives for a major firm in California. I looked over as the details didn't state their reasoning of the hit. I saw a family Christmas photo of the two with their four children. I put down the folder immediately as it felt heart wrenching. I stood up and turned away from the file, walking towards the kitchen area. Thomas kept his eyes on me.

"Women," he scuffed. "Too emotional."

I nodded. "It's the best quality of us," I said as I opened the refrigerator door. There was half a gallon of milk and a case of water. "I don't see much to eat."

"Chips," Thomas said as he walked over to the kitchen area and opened a cabinet. "We have chips."

I nodded as it didn't feel appeasing to me. "I'm going to take a stroll," I said heading towards the apartment door.

Thomas walked back over to the window. "Ryan stated to stay put," he scuffed.

"Ryan is sleeping," I said glancing at the room where snores erupted.

"Your funeral," Thomas said.

I nodded as I opened the door and slowly closed it behind me. Walking down the hallway towards the staircase, keeping my head down and hands in my pocket. I went out the back door of the complex and headed to the street of chaos. Blending in the crowd, heading to a small diner. I looked over their menu, ordering a few breakfast plates, and then a latte for myself.

I sat near a window, browsing out as the streets remained chaotic. Glancing around the diner, seeing a teenager with a gray laptop and stickers all over it. *What a shame!* I looked away as the thought of killing a perfectly structured device with stickers sickened me. It hit me like a light bulb as I thought of entering the firm's database. I sighed at the thought of Mason and Ryan's warning, and then walked over to the teenager with pods in his ears, hood over his head. I sat down across from him.

"Can I help you?" He asked looking up from his laptop and pulling the pods out of his ears.

"How much for your laptop?" I asked.

"Not for sale," he said shaking his head.

I glanced around to see if anyone was watching, no one had their eyes on us. Placing my hand on the laptop, closing its lid. "How much for me to rent it?" I asked. "I just need it for fifteen minutes, top."

The boy looked up as if he was confused and sat back in his seat. He slid it over to me. "Fine, fifteen minutes," he sighed.

I nodded. I grabbed the laptop and got up from the seat. "I'll be back," I said as I moved over to the restaurant's to-go area. I unplugged their router and directly connected it into the laptop. I opened the laptop, minimizing the kid's gaming sites and pulling into the network of the restaurant. I quickly rerouted to nearby servers, finding house three twelve's network. I logged into it and quickly accessed their files in the network. I saw a flash drive on the side of the kid's laptop. I erased his data and quickly downloaded the file to the flash drive. I logged out, erased the trails, and then discarded the flash drive, shoving it into my pocket.

I unhooked the network, plugging the restaurant's network back into their router and closed the laptop. I pulled out two-hundred-dollar bills and brought the kid's laptop back to him. I placed the money on top of it. "Thanks," I said.

"Where's my drive?" He asked as I turned away.

I glanced over my shoulder. "Sorry kid," I said. "I'm sure you have more than enough money there to buy you a few of them."

"Ma'am," a waitress stated. I turned away from the kid to look at her. She had two bags with trays and a latte in her hand. I took the bags and latte.

"Thanks again," I called out as I walked out of the diner. Making my way back to the apartment, I sat the bags down on the counter as Thomas came over to see what I had brought in. The aroma of eggs, bacon, sausage, pancakes, gravy and biscuits filled the air. Ryan was quick to appear in the room as I took a tray and my latte, walking away from the others.

"You weren't supposed to leave," he snarled.

I shrugged my shoulders. "I am starving," I said and took a seat next to the window.

"Thanks for the grub," Thomas said as he grabbed a tray.

Ryan walked over to the trays of food, looked through them, and then grabbed one. I sipped on my latte, looking out the window as we watched the family leave their home. Preston woke up a couple of hours later, grabbing the last tray of food and devouring it. We cleaned up our trash and watched as the family returned.

"You said they would be alone," I commented as we watched them enter the home.

"We wouldn't go anywhere near that place till after midnight," Ryan snapped as he sipped on water.

"Well," Thomas said. "As fun as it has been staring at a house," he paused as he stretched. "I'm going to get some rest."

"You too," Ryan said motioning his hand at me.

I looked around the room, and then back at the home. "I'm good," I said.

"Well, if you aren't going to rest," Ryan stated as he walked over towards me. I shifted slightly to face him and glance at their home. "Then I'm going to get another few hours rest."

He walked past me and stopped. "Don't leave the apartment," Ryan sternly stated. "I'm not messing around."

I nodded, glancing over my shoulder at him. He walked on to the room with two beds. Preston walked up, propping himself on the opposite side of the windowsill.

"You definitely know how to put a twist in things," Preston chuckled.

I nodded. "You have to make life interesting at times," I stated as I folded my arms. I watched as the mother left with three children.

"I guess she's taking them to their places away from home," Preston stated.

"You going to catch some shut eye?" I asked glancing over at him.

"Yeah," he said rubbing his eyes. "I'm going to take the couch."

I nodded. He put his hand on my shoulder and gave it a slight squeeze. I looked up at him as our gazes met, and then he walked past me. He went over to the couch and lay down. I paced across the room, grabbing a bottle of water, and headed back to the window where I propped an arm on the top of the sill. I sipped on the water and watched as a couple of hours passed. I would pace around the room, constantly glancing out the window to keep watch of the couple's house.

The lights in their home went out, looking down at the clock. It was half past ten. I walked over to the cabinet, taking a bag of cheesy chips and inhaling the aroma as I ate a bag. Pacing around the boring apartment that had nothing but cheap magazines of women and cars. Snores sounded throughout the apartment as another hour passed. Glancing as the street became silent. I heard a noise of someone getting up from their bed in the other room.

I looked over to see Ryan walking through. "How long has their lights been out?" He asked walking over to me.

"Over an hour," I said crossing my arms.

He nodded. "Get the others up," he ordered.

I uncrossed my arms, and then went over to Preston first, nudging him. He finally woke up after several nudges. He got up from the couch and went to wake Thomas. Ryan pulled out a suitcase and opened it up on the floor. It had several guns and clips. He handed me a gun and clip. I loaded the gun, placing it in between my back skin and pants. Thomas took his next, and then Preston got the final gun and clip from Ryan who stood up as he looked at each one of us.

"The guns are not for use unless you absolutely have no other choice," he said. "The noise of the gun will arouse neighbors which is something we avoid at all costs."

"What's the plan on killing them?" Thomas asked.

Ryan picked up another small bag and unzipped it. "We have things to smother and make it look as an overdose. We will plant the evidence in their bathroom and bedroom. Thomas and Preston will take the lead as Stacy will be our stake out. You see anyone or hear anything, you notify us immediately. I will help you plant the evidence," Ryan stated. "This should be clear and concise." We all nodded as he grabbed the small bag, and then we headed out of the apartment.

Chapter Eight

LEADING US OUT, I went first down the stairs, out the front, pulling a coat around me and placing my hands in my pockets. There weren't even sounds of dogs barking in this part of town, the streets were quiet, no movement. Keeping my pace as I made my way over to their house, peeking in the windows, no movement. I looked back around the corner as Ryan and Preston were walking casually down the street towards me.

Thomas came up the stairs out of nowhere, and kneeled down in front of the door, pulling out a few tools and working the lock. He picked the lock and opened the door, stepping to the side as to let me in first. I looked around as we entered, still no movement. We made our way through the first floor to the back door and unlocked it. I heard a small alarm, and then quickly went over through their kitchen to an office on the right of their kitchen.

"Who tripped the alarm?" Ryan snapped.

Logging in their computer system as I remembered where they hid their codes, hacking into the software, and silenced the alarm in under thirty seconds. "It's disabled," I said as I walked past them to the stairs. I felt a hand slip under my arm and push me to the wall of the staircase.

"No," Ryan snapped. "You stay down here and keep a lookout."

He let go of my arm and continued up the stairs. Thomas followed him and Preston, who gave me a slight look of guilt. I glanced out the windows of the front door and headed back to the kitchen to the small office. As the others were creaking along the second floor, I hacked into the family's computer database. I saw a picture of their family, four children. Heartbroken as the kids would soon be without parents. If there was a way I could stop it, I would, but I knew that if I overstepped or didn't listen then I would be killed alongside them. Ryan was already on edge with me showing up drunk as I was last night. I glanced around at the papers on the desk as the database on their computer didn't have anything different than I already downloaded. I quickly and quietly shuffled papers, seeing invoices, general ledger documents.

I looked over the numbers as I knew they must have done something pretty bad to be a target on a hit list. Siffling through the paperwork, seeing miscellaneous charges. I saw great entry amounts, larger than their expenses at times. I took my phone out and snapped a few photos of the information as I wanted to investigate it further when not around the others. These people were being killed over a price. The curiosity arose as I kept snapping pictures.

The floor above me sounded like footsteps running, alarmed as they should be almost finished with the parents. I got up from the chair, pulling my gun out from behind me, and slowly ascending the staircase. At the top of the stairs, seeing multiple doors, one to my far left shut appearing to be over where I was at downstairs. Slowly, I inched down the railing to the door, keeping my eyes on that door. I heard a noise to my right and glanced over.

Preston walked out of the room to my right as Ryan and Thomas were still in there. "What are you doing?" Preston asked.

"That far door just closed," I whispered.

Preston reached behind him to grab his gun. "Preston," Ryan said in low loud tone. I kept slowly walking down the hallway.

"Go on," I whispered. "I will check it out." Preston and I exchanged looks, and then he went back into the room with the others. I kept a slow but steady pace as I went down to the final door. Placing my shaking hand on the knob, twisting it open, pushing it wide open as I looked around at a small light up disco with stars slowly swarmed the room with a lullaby tune.

The thought occurred to me as I lowered my gun. Earlier the mom had three of the four children leave with her. I gasped as I looked around at the beautifully decorated room of a child. *No, no, no!* I closed the door behind me as I paced in a small circle realizing this was a room of a child. A child was still there as they murdered their parents in the other room.

A small whimper arose, and I stopped in my tracks. I looked around the room, looking down under the bed, and then over at the closet door that was cracked. Opening the door, seeing a small brown-haired little girl in a gown with her face red and wet. A petrified feeling arose over me as I glanced back at the door that led to the hallway. She started to cry out.

I quickly put my hand over her mouth. "Shhh..." I said as I held her close to me. "Not a sound." A rushing flood of pulsations stirred my mind and chest as I felt a sweat breakout over me. The little girl looked up at me as I looked at her beautiful brown eyes. The prickling of tears attacked my eyes as I wasn't sure how I was going to get her out of here. Sounds of movement erupted outside the door. I slowly shifted myself to in front of her. "I need you to stay here," I whispered. "Don't cry, don't go outside of this room." I tried to remain as calm as I could with the circumstances that were in front of me.

She nodded as I slowly moved my hand from her mouth. "I need you to be strong and stay hidden," I said as I got up and slowly shut her closet door. Turning off the light up stars and lullaby tunes. I quickly walked backwards, opening the door, and slowly closing it behind me.

I turned around to see Ryan behind me. I jumped as his presence of being there scared me. "Everything clear?" He asked.

Sweat rolled off my forehead. I nodded, "yeah, false alarm."

"Good," he said staring me in the eyes. I kept my hand gripped firmly on the doorknob behind me. "Let's go our job here is done."

I nodded. He stared a few more seconds as neither of us broke eye contact. Finally, he took a step back and turned around. A breath of relief escaped my lips as I glanced back at the door behind me. I let go of the knob and walked down the hallway, following them downstairs.

"Change of plans," Ryan said as he went into the kitchen turning the gas stove burners on. "We burn the entire home."

"Why?" I asked as Preston, Thomas, and I stood in the kitchen doorway.

"They want all evidence of this family's work destroyed," Ryan said as he started putting cleaning supplies in the microwave.

Preston glanced at me. "Did you find something?" He asked lowly.

I glanced over at Ryan, and then Thomas exited the back door. Ryan already had gasoline cans placed outside of their home. They returned with gasoline cans in each hand as they went into the small office, pouring gasoline all over the desks, walls, and computer.

"There's a child," I whispered.

Preston turned sideways to face the stairs, and then back at me. "What are we going to do?" He asked as the strong smell of propane and gasoline filled the air.

I shook my head as my mind was racing against time and ideas. "I'm going to save the girl," I whispered.

"What do you need from me," Preston whispered as Ryan poured the last bit of gasoline out.

I shook my head at Preston. Ryan and Thomas came over to us. "Let's go," Ryan stated as he tossed the jug by the staircase.

"Why go through all that work to set up a scene if you're changing plans?" I asked as he looked over at me.

He walked over to the microwave, putting a timer on it as it started. "Because it's what the boss man said to do. Now let's go before we're burned alive," Ryan shouted as he went towards the back door. Preston followed, glancing at me as Thomas exited behind Ryan.

"You keep him off me," I whispered as I glanced at the popping microwave with one minute left on the timer. Following them outside, Ryan ran with Thomas on his heels down the sidewalk. Preston picked up his pace to catch up with them. as I turned around.

"Stacy," Ryan shouted. Running back inside the house that was drenched in gasoline and the smell of propane. I dashed up through the kitchen as time was running out. Seeing out the window, Preston side tackled Ryan who was running back towards the house. Running up the stairs, stumbling on a few, quickly retaliating to get to the girl. Moving around the railing as I rushed to the last door on the left. I shot through the door and ran to the closet. The little girl screamed out as I scared her from my fast reaction. I grabbed the comforter off her bed as I wrapped her in it and picked her up with no time of talking calmly.

Running out of her room, realizing the time was about out, making my way to the parents room, seeing the overhang roof, I pulled out my gun and shot the glass. Taking the butt of the gun and pounding the rest of the glass out, the timer dinged as I jumped out the window. Falling onto the overpass, flying out with the explosion, releasing the girl as I landed on my back in the street. The girl rolled out of the comforter as it took a moment for my breath to come back inside of me.

Gasping as I rolled over in the street to my hands and knees, the girl screamed with tears as she saw her home engulfed in flames. Lifting myself to my knees, looking around the thick smoke, seeing Ryan, Thomas, and Preston on the other side. Ryan grabbed his gun as I swept the girl up and turned around, running up the street. I turned the corner as the girl screamed.

"You got to be quiet," I yelled breathlessly as I carried her. My entire body pained from the fall, fighting the agony to keep my strength. We rounded a corner, hitting a street with moving vehicles, afraid of drawing attention to us. I ran up the sidewalk in terror that we were going to be killed right here in the middle of the street. Taking a sharp left, putting her down to catch my breath. My throat feeling as it were going to close, sweat pouring, placing the gun behind me as the girl cried. I grabbed her wrist and pulled her as we ran another alleyway. She had tears rolling down her cheeks, she was barefooted, in her night gown.

I pulled her over to the side and hugged her. "You're okay," I said patting her back. I kneeled down in front of her to get eye level with her. "Listen to me," I said stroking her arms. "I'm going to get you to a hospital," I paused to catch my breath. "You can't say a word about what you saw tonight. To no one," I demanded. Her lip puckered out as she tears rolled down. "Can you be brave for me a little longer?" I asked knowing that I was putting a lot of pressure on this young girl.

She nodded and wrapped her arms around me. I stroked her back, allowing the moment of a hug temporarily comfort us, and stood up. I peeked around the corner to see which way would be the best route. I glanced seeing cars one way, and then another street had some walking traffic, but not enough to hide us. I kneeled back down to her. "You ready?" I asked as I took my thumbs and wiped her damp face.

She nodded as I picked her up, gripping her tightly in my arms as I carried her down the street with the cars, glancing as we looked around each corner. I went up another street, and then down another block. We got to a little neighborhood with black picket fences. "My aunt lives here," she said pointing to one of the buildings. I looked up at the house and back at the little girl.

"Your aunt lives here?" I asked looking it over and around us.

She nodded. I sat her down on the pavement as she curled her toes. I looked around to see if anyone was around us. No one in sight, taking a breath to gain my composure, and unlatched the gate. Taking a few steps towards their house, keeping on the sidewalk, and stopped, kneeling down once more to face the girl.

I licked my lips as I looked around us again. "Can you please promise me that you won't speak of what happened tonight?" I asked holding her face in my hands.

She touched my cheek. "You're a pretty girl," she said, and then looked at the door of her aunt's home.

"You saw a fire break out and you got out of the house," I said as I focused her face on me. "You saw a fire break out and you got out of the house," I repeated.

She nodded. I wrapped my arms around her tiny neck. She embraced me back and shivers rolled through my spine. "Goodbye, pretty girl," she said as we let go of each other. I watched as she walked up the sidewalk to the door. As she reached the top step, I quickly back stepped out onto the street, ducking behind a red brick pillar. I heard her push the button and a doorbell sounded.

Glancing around the corner, looking to see lights immediately flashed on and the door opened. A woman quickly picked up the little girl, hugging her, asking her questions. A man came down a couple of steps, looking left and right to see if he saw anyone. They all went back inside as I heard the man state, "I'm going to call the police." I crept out from behind the pillar and ran back in the direction of the streets I toured.

I wrapped my arms around me as the chill weather rose, pulling my jacket tightly. I got back on the street with the traffic of cars and scarce sidewalks. Emotions unraveled as I wasn't sure what to think about the little girl, the fire, and now the chance that I would be killed. Tires squealed behind me, turning to see a car drive up. The door opened and someone came up from behind me, shoving me into the car.

I looked out as the door closed, seeing Jackson walk away from the car. I turned looking over at Kyle, and then glancing at the driver, Scott. Mason wasn't with them, a sense of panic fled through me as my breathing hardened. I pulled myself to the door, grabbing the latch, it wouldn't open. Kyle glanced at me and pulled out a gun from his pocket. I gulped as my hands slowly rose in the air. "Hand yours in," his tone serious with his eyes narrowed as he held out his other hand towards me.

I had one hand up while slowly reaching behind me, pulling out the gun and placed it shakingly in Kyle's hand. His gun pointed at me as he inspected my gun and placed it inside his holster. I kept both my hands up as I glanced at the rearview mirror, seeing Scott fully focused on the road ahead. I looked back at Kyle who relaxed himself, keeping the gun pointed at me.

The ride was short to an abandoned building. Scott got out first, opening my door, and then grabbing my arm. I walked as his firm grip hurt each step. Kyle walked behind us, keeping the gun pointed at me as we went inside the building. Scott sat me down in a chair under a light. I kept my hands up as I felt the fear for my life with Mason nowhere in sight.

I heard a few more enter the room, yelling. I looked to see James had a hold of Preston and swung him down in front of me. "Preston," I shouted as I leaped forward. Kyle grabbed my arm and swung me back into the chair.

Preston had blood dripping down the side of his face. Kyle kept a hold of my arm, shifting back in the chair slightly. He released the grip of my arm and walked around Preston to where Scott and James stood. "So," Scott said to James. "He ran too?"

"He attacked Ryan," James said pulling out a pack of cigarettes.

Scott sighed as he rubbed his hand across his face. "Where's Mason and Henderson?" He asked.

Kyle spat to his left, a blotch of brown and black hit the cement floor. "Mason had a scope out up state," Kyle said. "Told us to handle it."

Scott rubbed the back of his head as he turned away from us. I felt so much tension and feared what they were going to say with Mason not being here. "Tie them both up," Scott said. "Let's leave them here till Mason returns."

"Mason would dispose of them," James said. "Once you've gone rogue, you don't get any more chances. Stacy's been on thin ice since her arrival back."

Scott looked over at James, and then at Kyle. "Do either of you want to dispose of them?"

They both shook their heads. "Not our tariff," Kyle stated. "Besides Mason left you in charge."

"Exactly," Scott said. "Tie them up and leave them both here."

A door swung open from behind me. I turned to look, seeing Ryan storming through with Jackson and Thomas behind him. Ryan went straight for Preston who was on his knees and forehead on the ground. I shot up from the chair and stepped up as Ryan neared him. Anger boiling his face, Ryan reached out to grab me. Scott intercepted, pushing himself between Ryan and me.

"We done made a call," Scott said putting his hands out in front of Ryan.

"Good," Ryan stated staring at me. "I'll help dispose of these two."

"Not the call," Scott stated as they inched closer to us. I looked around as James and Kyle stayed back, one flipping a coin. Preston stayed on the ground, tears rolling down his face. I looked past Ryan seeing Thomas and Jackson cutting up.

The rage boiling in me as the two of them always ensured to laugh at us if we made a mistake. A mistake was thinking I could live with the guilt of this job. I walked over to Ryan, ready to take myself against the biggest person here, pushing Scott out of the way. Scott wedging between the two of us. "You want me," I said throwing my hand up as the anger raged through me. They all wanted me dead and here was there chance because I knew my decisions tonight were not the plan. "I'm right here."

"Stacy, get back," Scott yelled. I shoved Ryan back as he looked at me. He went to swing his arm. Scott grabbed it mid swing, shoving Ryan to the ground. Scott quickly maneuvered wedging his knee into Ryan. I reacted quickly, grabbing Scott from behind and moving him off Ryan. It was my turn as I moved myself to shove him to the side. Ryan pushed back on his hands and jumped up to his feet in a swift motion.

"Stacy," Preston yelled as I ran towards Ryan balling up my fist, ready for the fight. Moving to tackle him as I knew that would be my better angle, I threw my arms around his stomach as I tried to ram him backwards. He shifted some weight back, falling into

Thomas. Ryan grabbed my waist to shove me back as I continued to fight to bring him to the ground. He brought his knee up, kicking my side. Pain emerged as my breath escaped, I gasped and loosened my grip as he tossed me to his left, rolling onto the floor, and then hitting a pillar with my back facing his direction.

Unable to breathe, as I rolled over to my knees, sweat dripping finally breathing small short breaths, looking up as Ryan made way back over to me. I glanced to my left, seeing Scott eye me, and then rushed towards Ryan, side tackling. They both rolled over to the ground. Jackson and Thomas stumbling out of the way. My body ached more now than when I fell out of the second story window.

Scott got up from the ground, pulling his gun out of his holster and aiming it at Ryan. "That's enough," Scott yelled.

Falling backwards as my body was ready to collapse, unable to catch a deep breath, panting. I moved to position my back to the pillar, groaning in pain as I watched. Ryan threw his hands up, anger all over his red face. "Now, you, Thomas, and Jackson get back to the warehouse," Scott said. "Kyle drive them there. James, you're with me." Scott pulled the keys out of his coat pocket and tossed them to Kyle. Scott took a few steps back as Kyle helped Ryan off the ground.

My hands shook as they touched the floor beside me, salt burning my eyes, the four of them left. Scott put his gun back in his holster as James walked over to them. "You still want them tied up?" James asked keeping his body positioned towards Preston and me. Scott kept his stance towards the door.

"No," Scott said. "They won't get far if they do try and run."

The agonizing pain erupted abruptly, panting more as I wrapped my arms around my stomach. Looking up at the ceiling, I groaned in pain, struggling to breathe. Preston groaned as well as he fell over to his side. Scott propped himself near the pillar facing the door. James took a seat in the chair, eyes glancing between both Preston and me.

"Well," James said. "Ryan sure got to beat the hell of these two."

"Can it, James," Scott snapped.

James shrugged his shoulder as he moved his chair to a position where he could see both of us clearly. After several hours, I finally closed my eyes, sweat dripping down my face. The breathing still hurt with each breath, but the pain had become manageable if I didn't move a muscle. I opened my eyes to see Preston finally able to sit himself up, moved over towards me, propping himself to my left.

"Did you save her?" He asked lowly.

James and Scott were talking with each other at this point. I glanced over at Preston. "Ryan bust your face up," I said as I looked back over at Scott and James.

"When I side tackled him," he said. "He beat me up good, trying to go back in after you. I held him down for a few moments, then Thomas jumped in."

I chuckled. *Ouch!* I grimaced in pain as I touched my stomach. "It doesn't hurt if I don't move," I whispered.

"Bet you wish you hadn't of fell two stories," Preston chuckled.

I nodded. "The girl is safe," I whispered looking down at my ripped jeans. My knees had blood dripping off them. "That's what mattered to me."

Preston leaned his head over towards mine. I slightly shifted my head towards his head. "If we end up dying," he said. "I'm just glad it was over one great cause."

I closed my eyes as the thought of doing one good deed felt amazingly better than what we were doing for them. The pain simmered as I contemplated the thought of my reaction when I found that girl, how panicked I was to hide her from them. Fearing for her life over mine in the moment, freaking out to save her and convincing another teammate to turn against the odds.

It felt like an eternity that we sat there, waiting for Mason's arrival. I'm unsure if Mason would allow me to survive this round. A part of me was devastated as the fear of my expiration fell on the rise. I knew Preston feared for his life as he had since the first day we met. It was something they continuously preached that any moment, a mistake, could be the cause of our last breath.

The door swung open, and we all jerked our heads in its direction. Mason stormed in first with the others following behind him. I shot my head up from leaning over on Preston as Mason went to him first. I slowly rose, pulling myself up as Mason grabbed Preston by the shirt collar.

"Mason, stop," I yelled as I turned to face them ignoring the pain. I put my hand on Mason's shoulder of the hand that had Preston pressed against the pillar. Shifting my body towards them, wedging myself in between them. A hand slipped around my stomach, pulling me away from them resisting with kicking and hitting. Thrown to the ground, knocked out of breath again, I rolled over to my side.

"Someone better start talking," Mason shouted as he let Preston go. He walked over towards me, looking at me as I gasped and struggled to breathe. I looked up as Mason eyed each person in this room. "Ryan," Mason shouted pointing his finger across the room.

"It was supposed to be a simple drug overdose set up," Ryan stated. "Your girl there was our stakeout. She screwed it up."

"I want details not comments," Mason demanded.

"Anyways, she was supposed to be the one to listen out for anything. She did come up to the second floor. Preston met her at the top of the stairs. According to him, she went to check things out." Ryan stopped talking for a moment as he made his way towards Mason. "She was in there for several minutes, door was closed."

"Was there someone in there?" Mason asked looking over at me.

I dropped my head, pressing my fists on the ground as I moved onto my knees. I sat up, keeping my eyes lowered. "Yes," I said.

The sound of a gun being pulled out was heard. I looked up to see Kyle standing over me. "Stand down," Mason demanded. I watched as Kyle's eyes narrowed at Mason, and looked back at me. He moved his gun down to his side.

"Who was it?" Mason asked very sternly. I looked over at him, and then around the room as eyes were on me. "Who was it?" He raised his voice.

"The youngest daughter," I cried dropping my head as tears surfaced. I moved my hands to my face as I sobbed.

Mason sighed a breath of disappointment. "Ryan, what happened next?" Mason demanded.

"Well, she came out of the room and advised me that no one was there. We made our way downstairs, I advised it had been a change of plans. I turned on the burners, put things in the microwave. Thomas helped pour gasoline in their office. Everything was going according to plan." I looked up to see Ryan had shuffled himself over towards Preston. "We get out of the house, and then I look back to see her running back inside. I went to go after her, and this idiot side tackles me."

"You side tackled your handler?" Mason asked looking over at Preston.

Preston nodded. Mason ran his hand over his mouth as he looked at Ryan, me, and then Preston.

"Anyways, we have a brawl in the street while she's in the house," Ryan continued. "Next thing I know, I hear the gun going off, and then she jumps out the second-floor window with her arms wrapped around a comforter. She falls on the first floor's overhang, and then rolls off onto the ground, letting go of the wrapped blanket." Ryan stopped for a moment. "A child was screaming as she had unraveled from the comforter."

I glanced over at Mason as tears streamed my face. He kept stroking his face as he wasn't sure how to handle this mess. "I went to pull my gun, when hero their side tackled me again. She grabbed the child and ran."

"The child wasn't with her when we picked her up," Kyle said shifting his weight, moving the gun by his side.

"Stacy, where's the child?" Mason asked.

I shook my head, looking down at the ground. Mason walked over to me and grabbed my arms. "Where is the girl?" Mason raised his voice as he shook my arms. I kept my eyes looking at the ground. He let go of my arms, pulling his hand to my chin, forcing it up to look him in the eyes. "Where is she?"

"Over my dead body," I said through gritted teeth.

Mason shoved me back as he stood up. He turned away from me as I rebalanced myself to my knees that hurt. Mason turned around, pulling the gun from his holster, and then shoving the barrel at my neck as he put his hand behind my neck, gripping my hair, shrieking from the pain. "Where is she?" He yelled.

I looked him in the eyes as he looked back into mine. His face had pain all over it with fear of this moment. He didn't want to shoot me but was willing to do so to get the answers. "Mason," Scott spoke up.

"Tell me where she's at," Mason demanded gripping my hair tighter. Another shriek as a rush of panic flooded most of the room. Then as Preston had said, if dying over one good deed was how we were to end, then I was ready for it. I closed my eyes, taking my breath in as I knew his anger was boiling.

"Mason, drop her," Scott said.

I opened my eyes to see Scott had a hand on Mason's shoulder. Mason's hand with the gun shook, sweat dripping off his face, teeth gritted as I could tell it was about to be my last moment alive. I felt no more pain as I stared in his eyes. "Just tell me where she's at," he said calmer as he tried to beg for the answer. I could tell this was killing him.

"She's safe," I said. He pulled the gun away from my neck and let go of the grip of my hair. A roar of anger raged from his throat as he stepped back putting his hands down by his sides. I watched as Scott patted Mason on the shoulder.

Mason looked back at me, and then around the room. "Find the girl," he said.

"NO!" I screamed moving to my feet.

Mason grabbed my throat pushing me back as I stumbled back into another pillar. "Then tell me where she's at?" He demanded. I gasped as his grip felt firm against my windpipe. He eased the grip as I put my hands around his wrist. He got close to my eyes. "Where is she?"

"Trust me," I gasped.

Shaking his head, staring into my eyes, and finally letting go of my throat. I dropped down a few inches, gasping again for air as my hands grabbed above my knees. "I can't just trust you," he screamed.

"You have too," I said after catching my breath. "You have to know that I put her in a safe place, and that she isn't going to talk about that night."

Mason let out another bellowing scream as he put his hands on top of his head. "Ryan dig up anything you can on that family," Mason shouted.

I stood up straight as he turned back around to me. "Mason," Scott said putting his hand on Mason's shoulder. "What do you want to do with these two?"

Mason glanced over at Preston, and then at me. He lowered his eyes as he turned sideways and looked away from me. "Dispose of them," he snarled.

"You coward," I screamed.

A swift movement shifted the air beside me as I looked to my left, Kyle raised his gun at me. My heart fluttered into a million beats, breaths became short and looked back at Mason. He turned around to face me. Kyle had his hand on the trigger, aiming it at my head. Mason stepped forward, putting his hand out. They exchanged looks, Kyle lowered the gun. Mason came up to me, pinning me to the pillar as he stared into my soul. A familiar stance with him that once had me unravel felt alarming as I called him out.

A pain rupturing as my back hit the pillar, a groan escaped my throat. I stared into Mason's eyes as lifted his gun to my neck. Our gaze equally matched, my heart beating out of my chest, and then the tears slowly escaping the eye lids. I took a deep inhale as I was ready to accept the consequence.

"What if the girl is too young," Scott commented, interrupting Mason from pulling the trigger. "She may not give anyone any inclination that they were there."

Mason broke our gaze as he glanced over his shoulder at Scott. "Mason," Scott said. "Ryan screwed this up by not ensuring all things were cleared. He can go to the station and dig up anything on the family, statements, and all." Mason loosened his grip as he moved the gun from my chin. "If the story checks out clear, then no harm was done."

"You want her to walk after all the hell's she put us through," Kyle spoke up in disgust. "I'm ready to shoot her myself."

"Mason," Scott said as he patted his shoulder. Mason took a step back from me, moving the gun away from under my chin.

"Go check it out," Mason demanded. "If the story checks out, then this falls back on you." Mason pointed at Ryan.

A loud breath escaped me as I bent over forward and threw up. Ryan and James left the room. Everyone else stayed with us. I finished vomiting and wiped my mouth, propping myself back on the pillar. "You're not out of the woods yet," Mason said.

I put my hands on my knees as I looked up. Scott stood sideways, whispering into Mason's ear. A wave of shock rush through me as the pain was back more intensely than before as well as the continuous span of them delaying my death. I moved away from the pillar, over towards the center of the floor as I sat down, exhausted and in excruciating pain. I closed my eyes.

Chapter Nine

WHISPERS ERUPTING THE ROOM, air shifting with movement, I opened my eyes, feeling the pain radiating through my body as I rolled over to my side, and sat up. Looking around the room, Preston by the other pillar across the room. Thomas and Jackson near the door, propped up against the wall. Jackson had his arms crossed with a look of disgust on his face. Mason sat in the chair that Kyle sat earlier, looking between Preston and myself. Kyle and Scott stood near Preston, whispering to each other. Mason looked down at his watch.

"Any update?" Mason asked as he looked over at Scott.

Scott pulled out his phone and shook his head. Mason got up from the chair and paced around the room. The door near Thomas and Jackson swung open as Mason stopped and looked in that direction. I looked as well knowing that it was the news my life now depended on. James came through the door first, then Ryan slowly made his way inside.

"She made the right call," James said handing the paperwork off to Mason. "The little girl stated a fire broke out, she left the house and walked to her aunt and uncle's home."

Mason flipped through the paper as Ryan came up to their sides. "It doesn't make what she did any better," Ryan stated with anger in his tone. "She showed up stumbling at the meet location, then does this," Ryan stopped. "Mason, she's a threat to us."

Mason shook his head as he pushed the paperwork into Ryan's chest. "She made the right call. You should have staked the scene better. A life that wasn't being paid out wasn't taken, nor were we turned in. Take the win, learn from it," Mason said as he poked Ryan's chest.

"So, she gets away with it," Ryan stated with anger in his tone.

"Scott," Mason said turning to look at him. "Get Preston back to the warehouse. Get him the help he needs." Mason came over to me. I jumped slightly as he leaned down and scooped me up. He turned around with me in his arms to face Ryan. "Ryan, she got the hell beat out of her. Take it as her punishment and move on." The anxiousness and fear that swarmed my body dispersed as his comfort and touch felt like protection around me. My initial reaction of fearing that my expiration date had approached disappeared. I felt lightheaded as he carried me out of the building, tucking my head into his chest as the dizziness shook my sight, and then complete darkness flooded me.

*****

The air shifting around me, a touch on my arm, keeping my eyes closed as a clearing of the throat sounded. "Henderson," Mason said as he stroked my hair behind my ear.

"She's risky for sure," Henderson stated. I couldn't tell with my eyes shut where he had brought me but felt the mattress beneath me and the pillow. It felt like the bunk room at the warehouse. "She's bullheaded like you."

"I need to ask a favor," Mason said as he stroked my head. "I know we've never done it in the past."

Henderson sighed, "I have a feeling I know where this is leading."

"This isn't the world for her," Mason said shifting away from my body. I felt his hand leave my forehead, keeping my eyes closed.

"You know how the others will feel about it," Henderson said lowly.

Mason grumbled under his breath. "They've all treated her poorly. She's proved from day one that she can pull this off," Mason stated. "I just rather her get out while she's alive."

"You think she will just walk away?" Henderson asked.

Mason shifted as I felt the wind of his movement next to me. "If she wants to live, I think she will walk away."

I heard what sounded like a pat on the shoulder. "Then move her out," Henderson said. "Give her the option, and if she leaves for good then we will let her go." A shift in the air sounded as if he was leaving. "Mason," Henderson paused, footsteps had stopped.

"Just understand that this is the one and only time I will ever give you this pass."

The footsteps faded as it sounded like Henderson left. Mason sighed, stroking my hair again. I didn't want to open my eyes immediately as the conversation struck hard in my chest. Mason had stuck out for me, following through on his words from the beginning, *trust me*. He was giving me a chance to survive outside of this bondage that they drilled in us. The thought of walking away and not having to kill another soul sent warm fuzzy feelings through my body. Then, they were crushed as the thought of losing Mason forever rushed in. If I left this world, his world, then I knew for sure that I wouldn't ever be his soulmate.

Their conversation weighed hard on me as this was about to be a very difficult choice. I wasn't fond of the work that they did, but I was in love with Mason. I knew that he had feelings about me as he broke his own rule by kissing me. We nearly became intimate with each other. Overall, I knew he was struggling with me being here when he held the gun to my throat for answers. He screamed as a part of him didn't want to kill me. Placing him on the verge of having to pull the trigger against me, something that appeared to trouble him.

Mason kissed the top of my forehead, making the hair stand, goosebumps appearing on my body. I kept my eyes closed as the pain arose, causing me to feel exhausted again. Staying completely still and not give off that I heard their conversation while pretending to still be unconscious. I fell back asleep after several moments of exhaustion flooded through me.

*****

Shifting under a comforter that covered my body, I opened my eyes, looking around the room. In my apartment bedroom, I rolled over to my side, pain emerging with every movement. I slowly sat up, feeling the pain rush into action as every bone in my body ached. Looking down to see I was in my blue tank and pant pajamas. Placing my feet on the floor, cold hardwood floor, sending chills up my feet and into my legs. I looked around, seeing Mason walking into my room.

"You're awake," he exclaimed as he looked me over.

I nodded as I glanced over at the clock. "How long have I slept?" I asked looking over at him.

"A few days," he said as he put out his hands in front of me. I felt embarrassed as I've never slept for a few days unless I was sick with the flu. My cheeks flushed red as I took his hands and stood up. "You were knocked around pretty good."

"Yes," I said feeling every muscle and bone covered in soreness. "I guess jumping out of a two-story house, and then getting beat up-."

"Let's just focus on getting you better," Mason interrupted as we walked into the living area. "I'm planning to help ensure you get recovered."

I shook my head as I walked over to the windowsill, peeking out to see the busy and chaotic streets below. "I don't want you to help," I said. "I got myself into this mess."

"You had help," Mason said as he moved over to the window. "I need to talk with you about some things." I remembered the conversation I overheard with Henderson and him. My heart fluttered as I wasn't ready to have this conversation, wanting to process now that I've rested. "Stacy," he said grabbing my hand. I looked up at him as our gaze met. His face hurt as it appeared his thoughts were harming him.

"I'm not ready to talk," I said breaking away from his gaze. Turning away from him, I slowly paced towards the kitchen area.

Mason let out a breath behind me as he followed, I went to scavenge the fridge. I saw a yogurt container and pulled it out, grabbing a spoon from the drawer. I peeled back the top and ate. Mason propped himself against the stove as he watched me eat. "When will be a good time to discuss matters with you?" He asked.

I shrugged my shoulders. "I just woke up after being out for several days," I said in between bites. "Just let me have some time." I watched as he moved from the stove over to me. The memory of him holding my hair back and a gun to my chin flashed through me. Jumping back, I dropped the yogurt container and spoon. We both looked down at the spilled contents, stepping around the counter, brushing my hair back.

Mason leaned down and picked them off the ground. Turning away, fear creeping inside of me as my breathing hardened at the thought him being around me flooded my mind. "I," I stuttered as I crossed my arms, bringing my hand to my mouth. "Can you leave?" I asked turning around to watch as he lay the items on the island countertop.

He glanced down at them, and then at me. "I can give you some space," he said lowly. "A week at most, and then I will need to talk things over with you."

I nodded as I bit my fingernails. He walked around the counter towards the front door of the apartment and stopped as he put his hand on the doorknob. Looking over his shoulder, "I know you're going to have all the memories of that night flood you. You're going to get scared.' Mason spoke clearly and without hesitation. "Just do me a favor," he paused. "Don't run until I get the chance to talk with you."

I nodded. "Okay," I commented as I leaned further back into the island counter.

He looked back at the door, hesitating for a brief moment, and then opened the door and exit. The door closed quickly behind him as I rushed over to it, locking the deadbolt and other lock. Moving back, brushing my hair as my breathing hardened. I no longer felt the soreness that consumed my body, but the fear of what he put me through. Panting, struggling to breath, picking my fingertips through my hair as I paced around the apartment.

Emotions flooded me, memories flashed, the impact of each hit as I paced throughout my apartment. Questioning how I even slept for several days knowing he was ready to dispose of me. My airway tightened as I fell to my knees onto the hardwood floor, tears streaming, and then the pain of it all rushing through me. Tears falling, unable to breathe, I curled up in the fetal position on the floor.

It felt like an eternity on the floor as I sat there for an entire twenty-four hours, not passing out. The devastation of the thoughts tried to consume every breath of mine. Realizing the rabbit hole my body was quickly buried in. Then, like the subway carts screeching by the platform, the thought of his hesitation with shooting me flooded my mind. The look in his eyes as if he was begging me to tell him. I could see the pressure he had of doing his primary job shred his soul.

His pain changed my perspective entirely as I sat up on the floor. I noticed his pattern of reacting to my soul in fear of both of our lives. He feared my life the day at the bus station when that security guard was almost around the corner. It was the moment he took my being into consideration. The moment that all the other anticipations of my body begging for him to kiss me unfolded. At the celebration, a few wanted to take advantage, but he kept telling me to sober up. He fought them off and stood in the cold shower with me. Leading to another kiss after hours earlier telling me that we were no good for each other. Finally, securing his thoughts of our relationship was when he screamed in front of everyone as he didn't want to shoot me. He almost allowed Kyle to shoot me, turning away just so he wouldn't have to see it.

Pulling myself up from the ground, I went to grab clothes for a long hot shower to process. I took a long hot shower, allowing the thoughts of his weakness that showed how much he cared and loved me run through my mind. After showering, I put on a regular shirt and sweatpants. I ate and lay down on my bed. Thinking of Mason in a positive way as I knew he was as much in love with me as I with him.

The week passed, I kept myself inside the apartment and allowed emotions to flow out whether it was anxiousness, fear, or the complete opposite comfort of Mason being there for me. Recovering from the pain, I ate and worked on stretches to help with the soreness. I cleaned up, finding my clothes from that night, and hiding the flash drive in a drawer. Refusing to contact mom, not wanting to breakdown over the phone, not wanting her to rush to my aid as she's always done in the past. My emotions were still a mess, and I wasn't about to use the comfort of her voice to allow myself to break apart any more than necessary.

I dressed for the day, eating a light breakfast, drinking coffee, and then working on stretches. It was a little after eight in the morning. *Knock. Knock.* I stopped stretching and walked over to the door. Taking a breath, placing my hand on the deadbolt, knowing it was time to face him. I unlocked the latches and opened the door. Mason stood in the hallway as I stepped to the side for him to come in. He walked in, looking around the room as I closed the door behind him, keeping my eyes on the door. I turned around and took a step towards him, and then turned to the kitchen, looking down at the counter.

"How are you holding up?" He asked once inside the apartment.

I took a moment to gain composure as heaviness weighed in from all that he's done. "I'm doing the best that I can under the circumstances," I said as I sat down at the island counter.

He took a step over towards me, propping his arm up on the island countertop. "You ready to talk?" He asked.

I interlocked my fingers and bit my lip. "Can I have another week?" I asked slowly.

He looked around the apartment, and then I felt his eyes were on me. Glancing over, our gazes met, he moved his left hand to touch my face. I flinched as I quickly broke the gaze, looking back down at my fingers. He moved his hand away from me. "Are you sure that I can't talk now?" He asked sounding desperate.

I shook my head as I kept my eyes locked on my hands. "I want more time," I said. "I need more time to process."

He shifted his weight. "I told you that I'm no good for you," he said lowly.

"Mason," I snapped. "Please give me the time that I need."

He went silent, shifting himself to prop his elbows on the counter. "Just don't take too long," he sighed, pulling himself off the counter. Shifting off the stool, I walked to the door and opened it, he left without saying another word.

Another week passed, giving me the time that I needed to process the triggering events. Knowing it was time that I needed to talk with Mason, and I knew my space that he was graciously giving me was narrowing. Each day feeling stronger, less sore, and contemplating my thoughts of the conversation I knew he wanted to have with me. His words, *I'm no good for you,* impacted greater every second that I felt my life was on the line.

Early in the morning, I dressed in jeans and a comfy sweater when a knock at the door sent rattles through the apartment. The window was closed, it was time to talk, I took a deep breath as I unlocked the latches and opened the door. Mason stood there for a moment, looking over me as I kept my eyes lowered. "Are you ready to talk?" He asked.

I moved over to the side and nodded. He entered the apartment as I closed the door behind him. Turning around to face him, he glanced around the room and turned around to face me. I glanced for a moment up and down to his hands in his pockets, and shifted myself over to the seating area, sitting down on the small chair by the window. He propped himself next to the windowsill, facing me in silence.

Silence filled the apartment, caused anxious thoughts to invade, coughing to clear the uneasiness. I pushed my hair behind my ears while leaning forward in the chair, propping my arms on my legs, and then interlocking my fingers. I kept my eyes lowered.

"I tried to warn you," Mason began. "Of how dangerous I am."

I nodded, keeping my head lowered.

"The work we do isn't for anyone that's weak," Mason continued. "It pays well. Regardless of how inhumane you may feel it causes."

I took a deep breath. "I'm not killing a child for you," I interrupted, speaking lowly. "I've played by all your rules, but this is my personal one."

"You got lucky with her," Mason said shifting his body to be more angled onto the windowsill, moving his hands from his pockets to across his chest.

I shook my head, keeping my eyes lowered. "You were ready to kill me," I said lowly as my throat started to feel dry. "Did you kill Preston?"

"No," Mason responded. "You both work harder than the other two. When they cleared the statements, we got you both help." He went silent for a moment. "I noticed you haven't checked in with your family in a couple of weeks."

I glanced up at him as he shifted his head to look out the window. "I was afraid to call them," I said looking back down at my hands.

"You feel you would say something?" Mason asked.

The question sounded alarming with his tone. My eyes shot up to meet his gaze. "I'm afraid that I will breakdown on the phone with them," I admitted. A sense of relief barreled through me as I looked away from his stare.

"What if I give you an out?" He asked.

I kept silent as I already knew the question from their conversation at the warehouse. "Say I take it," I said keeping my eyes down. "What does that mean for you and me?"

He snorted. "If you take the out," he said shifting his body to take a step towards me. I looked up as he walked around my chair, keeping his eyes on the ground. "Then you don't have to worry about seeing me again."

I looked back at my hands as I began to fidget. "My mom asked me a couple of weeks ago," I paused. "Before the job." I swallowed a lump that hardened my throat. "If I would visit them for Thanksgiving." He stopped pacing around my chair as he squatted down in front of me, looking up into my eyes. "I don't want to formerly say that I'm out," I said. "I just want some time to process."

"You understand that this is a one-time opportunity for you to walk away," he stated as our gazes met. I looked into his green eyes, feeling the pain that burned in both of us.

I licked my lips as I stared at him and nodded.

He stood up and held his hands out to me. I took them as I stood up to my feet, keeping my eyes lowered. He pulled me in and embraced me. The motion sent shockwaves through me as I wrapped my arms around him. "You have till December first," he whispered into my ear. "You don't come back here and find me, then I will know what you chose."

I felt tears prick at my eyes as the weight of this decision felt heavy. I took in the comfort of his embrace, inhaling his scent, and realizing that I knew my body didn't want to let go of him. He pulled away from me as he shifted his hands to my arms and squared his face to mine. I looked away as I knew what those beautiful eyes would do if I stared too long.

He moved his right hand from my arm to my chin. The sensation of his touch fluttered my skin as I moved my eyes to look back into his eyes. I grabbed his wrist, pulling his hand away from me, and turned quickly to pull myself away from the love spell he's instilled in me. "I have one question," I said as I took a few steps away from him. I turned my body, folding my arms across my chest, as I looked up at him. "How did you become part of the Silencers?"

He slightly turned away, taking his hand to the back of his neck, and then looked away. He took a brief moment and looked over at me. "You sure you want to know?" He asked as our gaze met.

I nodded as I shifted my weight. He put his hand down and turned around to face the window. "My mother died at the hands of my father," he said lowly.

"He was abusive towards us both, but in the end his temper overpowered her. He ended up snapping her neck. I witnessed the entire fight as I was only four years old at the time." He stopped as he glanced over at me and looked back out the window. "Instead of calling the cops, he moved her body to the stairs, breaking one of her high heels that was on her feet. After he set up the scene, he took me out for ice cream."

I shifted myself back to the chair as I sat down, feeling mixed emotions as his story saddened my heart. "Being four years old at the time and not knowing any better, I enjoyed the ice cream. After our outing we went back home where we found her body as he framed it." He stopped again as he took a moment, processing the words. "He put me down, running to her and called 911."

I shook my head as I felt sorry for him, witnessing the murder to framing the scene. "The cops showed up as he moved me to the kitchen with him. He gave me more ice cream as a way of keeping me distracted. If I was older and knew better, then I more than likely would have been killed with her. After the cops did a small investigation, ultimately ruling it as a fatal accident of her breaking her neck over a high heel that broke as she walked down the stairs. I never told anyone about that night," he paused. "Until now."

Swallowing another large lump that formed in my throat as I looked up at him. He turned to meet my gaze and shifted himself to prop against the wall facing me. "Years later," he began as we kept our eyes locked. "I found out the reasoning of their fight that ended my mother's life." He shifted his arms to fold them across his chest as he took a deep breath. "She found out about his secretive life as a professional killer. She had discovered his stash of money and old assignments." He took another deep breath. "My father was a detective, so at first, she thought it was cases from work until one of the files showed a family she recognized. She discovered the father of the family of three was a person she went to high school with in which she had attended his funeral months prior." The terror of his story sent chills running down my spine as I interlocked my fingers, feeling my heartbeat slightly faster than moments prior. Beads of sweat formed on my forehead, feeling uncomfortable. He took a deep breath and walked over to me. I looked up at him as the fear of him sharing this dark secret roused my anxiety with his presence. "Do you want me to continue?" He asked as he touched my chin.

Another hard swallow and slightly nodding. He moved his hand from my chin, turning to walk to his left, my right as he paced around the chair I sat in. I kept my eyes on him as he put his hands in his black leather jacket. "A few months after her funeral, we moved out of the house. We downgraded to an apartment, slightly bigger than here. He would only allow one person to watch me, a man that he trusted from his operation. As I got older," he paused. "I started to be more observant. Around the age of fourteen, he brought me with him to a job. At the age of sixteen, I became a recruit of their team after training alongside of him for two years."

"Did you have any other option?" I asked as he stopped in front of me.

He looked away from me as he walked back over to the window. "I was never given another option," he said propping his arm up on the window, pressing his head forward. "I've been in this line of work for over half of my life."

I looked down at the ground as I fidgeted with my fingers, taking another deep breath. "Do you ever wish that you had another option?" I asked.

He turned around to look at me as I jerked my eyes from the ground to him. "I can't wish for something that I couldn't get," he sternly stated.

I looked down as the message was clear that he was giving me an option that he never received. He was giving me an out, a possibility of living a different lifestyle from his life. Walking over to me, my eyes shot up as I stood, putting my hands down by my side. He slipped his left hand into the right side of his jacket. Anxious thoughts rushed in as I held my breath for a moment at the thought that he may pull out a gun that fled through my mind. Pulling out an envelope, exhaling, he held it out to me. I breathed, putting my hands up to retrieve it.

"I hope whatever you decide makes you happy," he said as he placed the envelope in my hands. The words stung like a shot of alcohol flooding my throat. He broke our gaze as he walked past me. A deep breath slipped as it felt a piece of my soul was leaving with him. I turned my head and watched as he didn't look back and left the apartment. The door closed and tears flowed down my cheeks as I gasped.

Chapter Ten

Processing his offer, his secret, and then how I felt towards him. I took the envelope and spread its contents out onto my bed, counting out six grand. I shook my head as the blood money felt wrong in so many ways. Separating a thousand out for myself as spending money, the rest I split between my apartment, bank security box, and then a portion to go to the ranch.

After placing each in separate envelopes of my own, I got out the flash drive from the job that provided me this money. Plugged it into my laptop, looking through the accounts. I took my phone and downloaded the images to the flash drive. After realizing their intel was about to go public in the next tax year, I knew why this couple was murdered. Properly discarding the drive, clearing my trail on my laptop, and then placing it in my olive-green laptop sack with the envelopes and my cellphone. I deleted the images off the phone, factory setting its content, and then packed a suitcase.

Placing the envelope and flash drives into the bank's security deposit box. After the bank, I made my way to the bus station and purchased my ticket to go home. Emotions were high as I knew I now had money stashed in a few places, like mom taught me growing up, *never put all your eggs in one basket*. Adrenaline of leaving New York dissipated while on the bus, I thought of Mason. His words, *I was never given another option* lingered my thoughts. The statement made me think that he didn't want this position at all. He was bonded to it by his father, or he would have been killed.

The thought of never meeting him felt like daggers stabbing my heart. Knowing he had dug his hooks deep when my sympathy for him trembled my body. Thoughts of how we met at the bar, the way he looked, his voice, all sending me to another world. Biting my fingernails as I looked out the bus window. The thought of how he found me after that man attempted to steal my bag, pressing me into the wall, hypnotizing my brain as it then transitioned to the taxi ride back to the warehouse. "I don't kiss women that aren't mine," he said. "The only way that they're mine is if we were married. I just met you and won't be marrying you."

Numbed, as the moment of us nearly being caught by the security guard forcing him to react in the one rule he set for himself. He kissed me. *He loves you!* I flashed to the scene of the most traumatizing night of my life, leaving me still sore from muscles to heartache as he was ready to kill me. My body broke out in sweat as I remembered his eyes staring into mine with the barrel of the gun at my throat, seconds away from being blown to smithereens.

The bus stopped, I quickly snapped to reality, looking around at everyone standing up. I looked out the window as we were in North Carolina. I took a few deep breaths, pulling my composure together by placing my laptop bag over my shoulder, and then got up and departed with the crowd. As I exited the bus, I saw a neighbor of mom's getting in his white pickup. I grabbed my suitcase and hurried towards him.

Paul was an older man that lived near mom and dad's ranch. He was married to Irlene who both loved to farm vegetables and sell them at the farmers' market on the weekends. "Paul," I called out as he opened the door to his white truck. He turned around and looked in my direction.

"Stacy," he said as he took a moment to realize who I was and let go of his door. I stopped with my suitcase a few feet from him. "I see city life has taken you out pretty hard. You look a bit rough with your face bruised."

I smiled. "I fell down some stairs a couple of weeks ago at work," I said. "You know being graceful nelly."

He chuckled wiping his forehead. "You heading home?" He asked.

"Can I get a ride to the ranch, please?" I asked smiling at him.

He smiled and nodded. "Your folks didn't know you were coming in?" He asked as he walked over to grab my suitcase.

"I thought I would surprise them," I said.

He nodded as he picked up my suitcase and put it in the bed of his truck. I walked around to the passenger side, getting into the truck. The hour ride to the ranch was talking about how he had a pretty decent year with produce and sales. He talked about Irlene. They had been married for forty-five years and never had any kids. We got to the driveway of the ranch. "Can you drop me off here?" I asked.

He pulled the truck slightly into the driveway, off the main road. "I can take you up to the house," he said as he glanced down the mile long driveway.

"I want it to be a surprise," I said opening the door, placing my laptop bag over my shoulder. "Thank you for the ride."

"Anytime girl," he smiled. I pulled my suitcase out of the bed of his truck. He waved as he drove off.

I stood there watching him drive away, turned to the driveway, looking down towards the house. I took a deep breath, inhaling the aroma of the sweet nature that didn't reek of city sewers. I closed my eyes, allowing the birds that sounded peaceful soaring in the sky to flood my ears. The silence of people talking, horns beeping, and chaos brought joy to my soul.

I opened my eyes, dragging my suitcase along as I walked down the gravel road. Anxiously, I arrived, unknowing what I was going to say to mom or Liz when they saw me. I haven't called in over two weeks. I saw the white two-story house nearing as I was a few yards from the porch. The front door swung open as mom came running down the steps. I dropped my suitcase running towards her. She had tears streaming her face as she swooped her arms around me tightly. "Stacy," she squealed through streaming tears. "You're alive!" She pulled away, grabbing my face, clutching me as she moved her lips to kiss my cheeks. I grabbed her wrists as tears rolled down my cheeks. She moved her hands back around my body, a pain shot through me as I was healing from the wars of the job.

"Ow," I said as she loosened her grip.

She moved her hands back to my face, pulling back. "What happened to you?" She asked demanding answers.

I wiped my face as I looked away from her eyes. "I fell at work," I said looking back into her eyes. Her tears rolled as she wiped my face. "I tripped going down the stairs of my office's building. I ended up in the hospital for a bit."

"Why didn't you call me?" She asked as her expression went to as mom's do when worried. "I would have drove all night to get there."

"Ma," I said pulling away from her. "I'm fine."

"You don't look it," she said pulling her hands to my shoulders. "You look like you've taken a beaten."

"With stairs," I lied. An enormous web of lies that I fed grew larger as I knew my life would be at stake if I told the truth. "I took a beaten from stairs," I said staring into her eyes.

She rubbed my shoulders and cried. I pulled my arms around her as I went in for another embrace, letting the comfort of her touch flood over me. I knew in that moment the choice that weighed heavy was much heavier as this visit was going to shred my soul into a million more pieces. Mom wrapped her arms around my neck, kissing my cheek for several minutes. I breathed her scent in as tears pricked my eyes.

"Stacy," Liz yelled from behind mom.

Mom let go of me as she turned, Liz running down the steps. Liz ran over to me, throwing her arms around me. I nearly fell backwards, catching my balance, as the roar of pains rushed through me. "Stacy, I've missed you," Liz cried.

I embraced her and patted her back. "You're hugging me too tight," I gasped. She let go of me as she grabbed my hand, looking between mom and me.

"Are you staying for a while?" She asked as she nearly jumped up and down.

I glanced between the two and nodded. Mom clapped her hands together, a smile swept across her face as she looked up as if thanking the good lord above for sending her daughter home. Liz squealed as she hugged me again. I patted her back, breaking away as the pain shot through me. Liz ran past me to my suitcase and picked it up as mom lightly put her hand on my back. We all walked up the steps and into the house.

Once inside, shaken by how much I missed just stepping foot in the door. Mom went towards the kitchen as Liz ran my suitcase upstairs. I clutched my laptop bag that hung on my shoulder as I looked around the house, feeling the familiar, comforting presence. *This isn't going to be easy.* I made my way into the kitchen and sat down at the table while mom got cups from the cupboard and brought them over to the table. She smiled at me as she went back to the fridge to get tea.

Liz took a seat beside me as she had a smile as big as Texas across her face. Mom sat down at the table with us. We drank tea as I listened to Liz talk about school. She talked about a guy at the hospital that had worked at on the weekends. He was a few years older than her and worked in general surgery. Mom talked about how her and dad had been selling off the cattle they kept and discussed that they would be selling off the horses next.

Dad came in moments later. He was so happy to see me as I stood to receive his embrace. He couldn't talk, I felt a sense of relief as it was already hard enough lying to mom and Liz about my life upstate. I only talked about what I had lied to mom on the phone these past several months. She asked about the mystery man that I had mentioned the one time to her. A smile rushed over my face as it was after I met Mason for the first time. We talked for several hours and excused myself to head up stairs for bed.

I went to my old room, seeing it the way I left it. A few posters on the wall of some laptop coding sayings, cleaned and tidy bedroom. Liz had left my suitcase at the foot of my bed that sat next to a huge window that overlooked the field behind the house. I sat down on the bed, putting my laptop bag beside the head of the bed, and then pulled off my shoes. Glancing out the window, smiling at the beauty of this life, I took a moment to allow it to flood my soul. Reminding me of my simple life here at home. It was less complicated than finding work in the city, being crowded with noises, and then secretly taking on a job that wasn't meant for a person like me. Taking a deep breath in as I lay down on my back, looking up at the ceiling and closed my eyes. That night was the end of November fifteenth.

The next few days, I helped dad with the farm, collecting eggs from the chicken coop, milking the two dairy cows they had left, and feeding the horses. Mom stayed inside mostly, tidying up the house while Liz went to school. We would all sit at the table at supper time, talking and laughing. Each second spent there burdened me more as the thoughts of Mason lingered in my free moments.

It was November twenty-second; Thanksgiving was quickly approaching as well as December first. After doing the chores, I sat on the porch swing, letting the moments that were breath taking with Mason to heart wrenching flood my soul. The moment of the gun to my throat, and then his scream as pain of heart ache radiates through me. My forehead broke out into a sweat, my breathing hardened.

"Stacy," mom said sitting down next to me on the swing. I jerked as my mind came back to the ranch. I looked around as it felt like a simmering hot smoldering day had consumed my lungs. "What's going on with you?" She asked as I slowed my breathing down.

I shook my head, moving my hand to my mouth as I started biting on my thumb nail. "I'm fine," I said. "Just had flashback of the fall," I said looking out at the driveway.

"How did you say you fell?" She asked as she put her arm over my shoulders.

I rolled my eyes as the hovering mother returned. "Ma," I said feeling annoyed. "Just let it rest. I tripped over my own two feet is all."

She took a deep breath in as she shook my shoulders slightly. "Are you moving back in?" She asked quickly changing the subject.

Pain striking through me as I quickly got to my feet. I moved over to the porch rail, leaning onto it, and folding my arms over it. I heard as she got to her feet and walked over to me. "You keeping it a secret too?" She asked. I jerked my head over to look at her as if she had already found out about everything. I tried to keep a straight face as I didn't want to give an inclination in case she didn't know about my secret life in the work I had obtained. She looked at me sternly. "You didn't tell us about the fall, or that you were coming here," she said as if I didn't know what she was referring to.

I looked back out towards the driveway. "Yes," I sighed. "I rather keep it to myself."

Glancing over at her as she put her hand on her hip. "You've changed," she said as her lips pressed together. "I'm not sure whether to love it or dislike it."

Her words tore through me as I looked away. I knew I had changed, being forced into deadly circumstances tends to change people. "Ma," I said trying to change the topic. "Can you teach me how to make your famous cobbler?" I asked as I looked back over at her.

She smiled as she nodded. Walking towards the front door as I stood up straight and followed her inside the house. We went to the kitchen where she brought out her own scrapbook looking cloth binder. She opened it up as she talked about it being her personal cookbook. Flipping through and pointing out different recipes and explaining who gave them to her, she finally reached the cobbler recipe. We went to make it together, spending time and talking about Thanksgiving. She was excited to have all of us together and even talked about Liz bringing her fella.

Staying busy assisting her in cooking that the thoughts of Mason subsided for the present time. I showered and went to my room. Looking at my laptop bag, snatching it up, I pulled out my phone as if I were going to see if I had a message or missed call. Rolling my eyes at the thought of being a guy to message me as if we were in high school. I tossed my phone on the bed as looked in my bag, seeing the envelope I had brought to give to mom for the ranch. Closing my laptop bag, sitting it back down on the floor as I shifted to plant my feet on the ground.

The bedroom door opened, I quickly shot my eyes up, seeing Liz in her button up blouse, jeans, and boots. "You want to hit the bar tonight?" She asked as she entered the room.

A smile crossed my face. "Let me change into something compatible," I said as I got off the bed.

She squealed with a jump as she closed the door behind her. I changed into my pink and black plaided button-up blouse, jeans, and boots. Leaving the room, finding her on the porch, we took her silver Nissan to the bar we were at back in July. We got inside the bar and sat at the bar. Brian, the bartender, gave me a hug as he hadn't seen me in months. "You want double shots?" He asked with a huge smile.

I nodded as Liz held up two fingers. He nodded as he pulled out four shot glasses and poured the shots. He slid them towards us. Liz grabbed hers up and held it in the air towards me. I grabbed one of mine and held it next to hers.

"To having the best sister in the world," she said and tapped my glass. She flung her head back as she took the shot.

I hesitated as the thoughts of Mason flooded through my mind. "I need you soberminded," he said. I sat my glass down and looked around the room.

Jumping from the grab of my shoulder, turning to see Liz. "Hey, you okay?" She asked as a look of concern flooded her face.

I glanced around the room again, not seeing Mason anywhere in sight. I looked back at her. "Yeah, I'm fine," I said pushing my hair back behind my ears. I looked back down at my hand holding the shot on the bar countertop.

The flashback of his touch flooded me as I felt his hand touch mine. "Put that shot down and follow me," he said staring intensely into my eyes. I jerked as Liz shook me again. My mind swarming as the thoughts of the night of graduation flooded me. "You need to sober up," Mason said. My mind flashed to the bathroom where he ran cold water over us in the shower room. The kiss as he leaned into me, pressing me in the back of the shower. I gasped as the thoughts flooded. Liz shook me again, and I snapped back to reality.

"Stace," she said shaking me.

I put the shot down, letting go of the glass. "I'm fine," I said flailing my arm to knock her hand off my shoulder. I looked around as the noise of the music heightened. People dancing with other people flashing my mind of that night. I had eight shots flooded into my vision. I remembered the guys I danced with, then I stumbled over to the bar. Wade arguing with me. Another sensation erupted as Liz had both hands on my shoulders, standing in front of me.

"Stace," she said in a panicked tone.

My sight came back to her. I shook off the memories, and stood up, pulling her arms off of me. I walked past her as I headed for the exit. Going to the car, trying to open the door, but unable to as another memory flashed over me. Jackson had shoved me into the car with Kyle and Scott. I put my hands to my temples as I brushed my fingertips through my hair, sweat dripping, breathing hardened.

Liz ran up to me as she tried to grab my shoulder. I jerked back from her as I paced in a circle. Mason's words, "Dispose of them" rushed over me as my knees buckled. His gun to my throat and his stare. *Oh God!* I watched as he feared for my life, pulling away and bellowing out a scream.

Liz grabbed my arms as I fell to my knees. "Stace," she said in a panic tone. "Stace, what is going on?"

Tears running down, breathing shallow, emotions flooding through me, pressing my fingertips to my scalp, letting out a small scream under my breath. Liz embraced me as she held me tightly as I sobbed. "You're okay," she said loudly. "You're okay!" She held me tightly as I held back any longer.

Struggling to stop crying, but unable to as the thought of Mason for the final time flashed across my mind. "I hope that whatever you choose makes you happy," he said. I moved my hands from my scalp to wrapping around Liz's body as I held her tightly as she did me. My sobbing lightened as I gritted my teeth, trying to block the thoughts.

She pulled away from me, grabbing my trembling face, body shivering. "Let's go home," she said as our eyes were locked. I nodded, and she nodded as I calmed down. She reached in her pocket, grabbing her keys and unlocking the door. I crawled into the passenger seat, buckling up as she ran around to the driver's side. She got in and looked over at me. I kept my eyes out the passenger window, putting my fingers in my mouth as I bit my nails. "Do you want to talk about it?" She asked before cranking the car.

"Just get us safely back to the ranch," I said wiping my face with the sleeve of my shirt.

She cranked the car and drove us back to the ranch. We got there, mom was sitting on the porch swing wrapped in a blanket. I looked at Liz, as she looked over at me. "Just keep what happened quiet, please," I begged as I put my hand on the door handle.

She dropped her head as she felt a burden was placed on her heart. I could see the emotions that tore my sister's personality. She was always the one to keep things tucked inside her heart, rupturing her inside out. "Tell us what's going on with you," she said as she shot her eyes back up. "You don't even act the same as you did before you left."

"Drop it, Liz," I snapped. "My problems only."

"We're family," she cried. "Your problems! My problems! Our problems!"

I huffed as I opened the door. "I mean it," I snapped as anger of the interrogation from her began. Rushing out of the car, looking up to see mom had got up from the porch swing and walked down the steps towards us. I glared at Liz as she got out of the car. She slammed her door shut and hurried past mom with no words.

"Stacy," mom said as I approached the steps. "What happened?"

I stopped at the bottom step, looking at it. "I just wasn't feeling up to it," I said trying to hide the frustration in my voice.

Mom exhaled loudly as she let out anger of her own. "What mess are you tangled in?" She asked.

I shook my head. "None, now drop it," I said as I hurried up the steps. She reached her hand out and grabbed my arm. She gripped my arm as if I were a child. "Ma," I said not able to look at her. "Just drop it."

"What is going on with you?" She asked as I could hear tears forming in her voice. "You come home looked as if you were beaten to death. You won't talk much. Then, when we ask you if you've come home to stay, you change the topics."

I pulled my arm away from her as I looked in her eyes. Water filled them as her voice started to tremble. I looked away as I shifted to the other side of the step's handrails. "Look," I said licking my lips. "I'm not in any trouble. I just have a lot to process." I kept my eyes glancing between her and the ground. "Coming home was very tough. I miss being here, but I also have things at work to think about."

"Are you in trouble?" Mom asked again as she took a step towards me.

I gripped my hands behind me on the handrail. "No, ma," I said. "I'm not in trouble."

"You know where your roots are grounded," she said as she wiped her face. "If you're unsure where about something-."

"Ma," I interrupted. I looked up at her as she wiped her face again. "I'm staying through Thanksgiving," I said. "Just let it rest."

She let out a deep breath as she came over and hugged me. Releasing the rail, accepting her embrace as I wrapped my arms around her. She kissed my cheek and held me tightly. "I mean it Stacy," she said into my ear. "If you're in any trouble, you stay here."

Silent. I let the thoughts of her comfort flood me as the thoughts of Mason also swept in. Her embrace reminded me of his embrace, and the touch felt similar to, I felt a piece of him connect to my soul. Mom let go of me as I did her in return. She turned back towards the house and walked inside as I took a second to realize the similarities in the sensation.

Shaking it off, heading inside, I ran upstairs, and went to my room. I closed the door behind me, propping myself against it, feeling nauseas as the two worlds that both swarmed my soul felt like a raging war on the inside. Sitting down, running my hands through my hair, breathing heavily as the thoughts weighed on me.

Chapter Eleven

THANKSGIVING DAY. Dad tended the animals early, assisting with as much as he allowed, and then headed inside to help mom and Liz with cooking. Since the night of the bar, Liz has distanced herself from me. She wouldn't talk much to me as she felt the burden of keeping what happened tucked away ripped her heart to shreds. Mom didn't attempt to get anymore answers out of me either. She kept her questions to only things of the present time being at the ranch.

We ate early afternoon, as soon as Liz's boyfriend, Eric, had finally arrived. He talked a lot with mom, and they all laughed. Staying quiet, I watched Liz constantly touching Eric's shoulder. She laughed with him, and they would stare at each other as if a spark illuminated between them. Each looked at the other as if they were made for each other's soulmate. Their gestures pricked at my own heart as I constantly thought of Mason and me staring into each other. It was like our souls had fused together, creating this spark between us.

We finished eating, I collected the plates and washed dishes. Keeping quiet and distanced as mom, dad, Liz, and Eric went to the living area. I could hear their laughs echo through the house. A part of me wanted what they had, the joys of being under this roof with the people they loved and felt tied to. I thought of Mason's secret of how he became part of the silencers. The devastating loss of his mother's death, *I wasn't ever given the choice* echoed in my ears. I finished tidying up the kitchen and grabbed my winter coat, walking out to the front porch. I sat down on the swing, looking across the driveway, the barn, and then back to the ground beneath me.

I leaned forward, resting my elbows on my knees, and pressing my forehead to my hands. The creak of the screen door opened and closed. I kept my head down as I had my own mind battling. "You didn't have to clean up everything by yourself," mom said as she walked across the porch.

I kept my head down, hoping she would go back to entertaining with the others. She leaned against the railing as I heard her boots stop. "Ma, I just want to be alone," I said.

"Why are you fighting all alone?" She asked firmly. She always sounded firm when she wanted to have a serious talk. "You know where the roots are grounded."

I sighed as I pulled myself off my knees, crossing my arms over my chest. "I know where the shovel is at too," I snapped. "My roots have been plucked from the ground."

She chuckled as she walked over to me and sat down. "That's the best thing about seeds then," she said as she patted my leg.

I rolled my eyes as I felt another life lesson was about to be dropped on this porch. "Those have been burned," I snapped as I felt anger towards her words.

"Stace," she said calmly. "You can pluck the roots up, burn the seeds, but you won't ever get it completely out of your heart." I huffed as I knew she was gearing up. "So," she paused. "Why don't you tell me about the new seeds you've planted in New York." The words threw me off as I looked over at her with confusion. "Well," she said. "You apparently have a battle you don't need to fight alone. You can pluck roots, burn seeds all day, but I know you." She wrapped her arm around my shoulder as she stared into my eyes. "What root have you planted in New York that has you at war with rather to stay here or go running back there?"

I looked away as the conversation that she led started to clear up. "Ma," I said lowly. "I don't want to talk about it."

She leaned her head over onto my shoulder. "Is it the mystery man you only allowed to come up a handful of times?" I sighed as a burning fire started inside of me. I fumbled with my hands in my lap as I kept my eyes out towards the driveway. "You know it's okay to fall for someone," she edged on. "It's not okay having a war inside yourself that makes you fall apart."

I coughed to clear my throat that began to feel on fire. "Can you tell me about you and dad?" I asked her to detour the conversation away from me.

"What do you want to know?" She asked.

A weight lifted immediately. "Was he a good guy?" I asked. "Was he like a prince from those fairytales we grew up hearing about?"

She laughed in my ear. "Gracious, no." She let out a few more laughs as she got her composure together. "Your father was the worst kid in school. He was a football player, bully, and anything but good. He had me in tears from childhood playgrounds to young adult."

"Well, how did you know he was your soulmate?" I asked.

She sighed. "He may have been as mean as a rattlesnake, but there was something inside of him that I knew was the best thing anyone ever could want." She moved her head off my shoulder as I glanced over at her. "I knew his heart was good."

I chuckled as I looked away from her. "You may have to do some explaining," I laughed. "You said he had you in tears all the time."

"You can stare inside someone's soul and know whether they're good or bad Stace," she said with her voice as clear as the night sky. "You look into their eyes and immediately you can tell whether they're good or bad."

"That doesn't make any sense," I said fumbling my fingers. "You said dad was a bully."

She nodded. "The worst of their kind too," she commented. "It wasn't until one day at a high school rally that I realized he wasn't what we thought." She stopped as if she were allowing the memory to flood her eyes. "I was behind the bleachers as the players were about to go out. I wasn't into sitting in the bleachers with the other students. Well, that day in particular, I wasn't alone. I heard some voices and looked, I saw your dad taking off his nice name branded, high dollar shoes. Confused at first as why he was behind bleachers, taking off his shoes, when in moments he should be rushing out of the locker room with the other players." She stopped and took a breath. "He got his shoes off and handed them to another student. This student was one of the poorest students in our class. The student cried as he handed his shoes to your dad. Your dad put them on with no hesitation as the other student broke down in tears, unable to put these nice brand-new shoes on. He tried to refuse them, shakingly trying to give them back. Your dad helped him put the shoes on this boy's feet. He looked the boy in his eyes and said something I will never forget."

Shifting to look mom in the eyes as she continued. "Life isn't about fame, but about being there for someone else." The words were confusing as I looked away from her. "I saw in your dad's eyes that day he put on the duck taped shoes of this poor fella and wore them with pride as he stormed out onto the field with the other football players that day. Your dad, mean as a rattlesnake every day, showed compassion to this person. He let his fame as a player march the field with those raggedy shoes be the face as others didn't look at his shoes. They were celebrating his fame that day with the other players."

"He showed compassion," I said lowly as the memory of Mason with the gun to my throat, ready to kill me, swarm my mind. Standing up from the porch swing, letting myself stare off the porch to the night sky filled with stars be a moment marked. "Thank you," I said turning around to face her. "Thank you for sharing that with me."

She smiled as she stood up. We embraced each other as she kissed my cheek. "Remember where your roots are grounded and take it with you to wherever you decide to plant your seeds," she whispered.

Pulling away, I made my way back upstairs to my room. Pacing around the room as I thought of everything, the impact of being home with family versus being with Mason. Our stares, compensating my feelings, and then the one stare that had me questioning everything. Mom's words about her knowing how dad was the right choice for her weighing in. I knew her choice of a man showing compassion to Mason being a silencer had no comparison except for one thing.

The very one thing that sent chills down my spine, heat to my cheeks, and took my breath away. It was cold if I chose the route of being with him. I would have to commit my life to him. Allow his world of pain and devastation overcome my world of living the simple southern dream. The ache was real as I sat down on the bed, looking around the room that I once found as a safe haven.

I flopped back on the bed as the shattering of my world collapsed. Knowing deep down, tucked inside me, what to choose regardless of how it was going to affect my livelihood. The thoughts stole my breath as I gasped and tears flowed from my eyes. I stayed in my room the rest of the evening, letting my body finish its fight as I knew what choice I've decided.

The next day, November twenty-ninth, I got up early and grabbed the envelope from my laptop bag. Tucking it in my back jean pocket, pulling my shirt over it as I made my way downstairs. Liz and mom were in the kitchen. Mom had her hands at work making gravy. Liz leaned against the sink; arms crossed as she watched mom.

"Mom," Liz said as they hadn't noticed me entering the room yet. "I'm going to go to Eric's family's house for the day. I won't be home till dark."

"Be careful," mom said as she glanced over at her.

Entering the kitchen, they both glanced over at me. Liz walked out of the room, keeping her eyes lowered. Her tension clearly known as she left the house. Mom finished the gravy. I walked over towards her as she turned around, wiping her hands on her apron. "Good morning," she said smiling at me.

"I need to talk to you," I said glancing back towards the front door, and back at her.

Her smile shifted to a tight line lip as she motioned her hand towards the table. We sat down at the table together. "I sent you a package, a month or so ago," I said rubbing my hands through my hair. "What did you do with it?"

She sat back in her chair. "I did as you stated, put it in a safe place," she said. "I locked it up in your dad's safe."

I nodded as I reached behind my back and pulled the envelope out of my pocket. She put her hand to her mouth as she grabbed the envelope, peeking inside it. "Stacy," she hissed.

"Ma, it's not what you think," I exclaimed.

She slapped her hand on the table. "What I think is you have yourself in trouble," she raised her voice in a tone of anger.

"It's money I earned from my job," I said putting my hands out in front of me. "Just trust me when I say I need you too."

"Gracious no," mom snapped. "This is twice!" She stood up, pacing a few steps away from the table. "How'd you earn it?"

I shook my head as I looked over at her. Seeing the anger raging inside of her. "I will bring it to the cops," she shouted.

I stood up. "You bring it to the cops, then kiss your life goodbye," I snapped. "I earned this money fair, and if you try to think or say otherwise-."

"Don't you threaten me," she snapped as she pointed her finger.

"Just know that I earned it," I said shaking off the edge this tension roused. "Ma, I need you to understand something."

She looked at me as if she was ready to get a belt after me. "I'm going back upstate," I said.

"Oh," she yelled. "No, you're staying home."

I shook my head. "For the first time in my life," I said as I put my hands down by my side. "I finally feel something that I've never had here. I have something there that I can't let slip away."

"Stacy," mom said through gritted teeth. Tears in her eyes as they started streaming her cheeks.

"You have to understand something," I explained. "That you may not get a phone call from me, you can't call the cops to go looking for me." She gasped as she sobbed. "You know that when you get one of these envelopes that I'm safe."

"Stacy, no," she cried wiping her face, putting her hand on her hip. "You can't do this to us."

"Ma, I love you with everything that I own," I said as I took a step forward. "But I know where my place stands." She shook her head, sobbing. "I need you to trust me."

I embraced her as she grabbed a hold of me. She gripped as if she wouldn't release me. It was heart shattering as I knew this wasn't what she wanted me to choose. And knew if she knew what monster I was going to become, she would have probably killed me with her bare hands to prevent it going any further than her house. She loved me as a mother's heart forever tied around their offsprings. I pulled away from her grip. "I love you, ma," I said as I backed out of the room. "I will always love you till the day I die."

She grabbed onto the table as she sat down in the chair. Placing her head in her hands as she sobbed. Slowly backing out of the room to the hallway and ran upstairs. I grabbed my laptop bag, threw my things in my suitcase, and grabbed it up. I rushed downstairs as I glanced in the kitchen at my mom who had bowed her head with her hands firmly interlocked. I knew what she started to do, and then I rushed out the door.

I saw Liz's car still in the driveway as she came out of the barn. "You leaving?" She asked as she approached me.

"Can I ask a favor of you?" I asked.

She shrugged her shoulders. "We're family, so I suppose," she grumbled.

"I need a ride to the bus station," I said as the adrenaline pumped through me.

She looked up at the house and back at me. "You coming back anytime soon?" She asked.

"Liz," I said breathlessly. "You know that twinkle you have for Eric?"

She nodded as she crossed her arms across her chest.

"It's time for me to go back where mine's at," I said as my heartbeat fluttered out of my chest.

She sighed as she came over and picked up my suitcase. "Get in," she mumbled. Placing the suitcase in the backseat, I got in the passenger side as she climbed into the driver's side. She drove me to the bus station, getting out of the car with me as we arrived. I purchased my ticket and met her in the waiting area of the bus I was to board. Liz hugged me tightly. "You be safe up there," she said squeezing me.

I nodded. "You take care of our parents down here," I said.

She let go of me as I pulled away, grabbing my suitcase. "I'm glad you still wear that," she said pointing at my neck. I grabbed the gold cross in my hand.

"I don't take it off," I said with a smile.

"Kick ass in New York," she said as she walked back, blowing kisses in the air.

"Finish medical school," I yelled back. She threw her thumbs up as she smiled and waved. I handed my suitcase to the attendant and boarded the bus. I took one last look as Liz waited for my bus to leave. I waved again and got seated on the bus.

The ride back North had several stops, bus switches, and then traffic. I spent twenty-four hours between buses. It was now November thirtieth at eleven in the morning when I arrived to the city. I got on the subway and headed to my apartment. I put my bags away and left the apartment. I looked at the time as it was early afternoon. I have less than twelve hours to find Mason.

I walked around the block to the bar. Wade shook my hand. "You drinking tonight?" He asked.

I shook my head. "You know if he's been around?" I asked.

Wade shrugged his shoulders. "It's been a week," he said as he took a towel and dried some cups. "I heard he was on a business trip."

"Where is he?" I asked putting both my hands on the bar.

Wade shrugged. "Go find out where you know to do so," he said as he swung the towel over his shoulder.

I hit my palm on the bar as I turned around, leaving the bar, and taking the hour walk to the warehouse. I got to the warehouse and felt nauseas. Anxiously ready to grab the doorknob, and hesitated. I thought about what could possibly happen if Mason wasn't around, and these others took it upon themselves to dispose of me before his arrival.

My body debated the worst-case scenarios, and I finally twisted the knob and entered. The room was dark with the center lit. I walked in, looking around to see if I saw anyone there. I didn't hear anyone as I went towards the center of the room. "Mason," I called out.

I heard a sound that alarmed every hair on my body as the sounds echoed through the warehouse. I looked in the direction to my left as I saw the two attack dogs. *Shit!* I glanced to see the guns table across the room. Aggressive growls and barks roared the warehouse watching me. Putting my hands out, slowly stepping back. They took a few steps towards me, beating their paws on the cement floor, showing their teeth, and then another growl ruptured from their throats.

In sync, they both started their way towards me. Dashing towards the gun table, I glanced back as one leaped. Ducking, it missed me, going over my head to looking back at the other. I turned to my right, heading towards the shower room door. Glancing over my shoulder as I ran, the one about at my back. I turned as it leaped, kicking my leg out. I hit the dog as it fell to its side, falling in a squatted position.

The second dog leaped, I rolled out of the way, pulling my sleeve to take my coat off. Removing my coat off as the first dog back on its feet, making its way back towards me. Spinning my coat with both hands, making it into a tight rope. The dog leaped towards me as I wrapped it around its neck, falling to the ground, gripping for life to it. The second dog came after my ankle. I locked my feet around its neck.

Both dogs now fighting for their lives as they tried to get out of my grips. An opening of a door ruptured through the warehouse, looking over towards its direction, Scott came out of the room with the lockers and table. He looked over the scene and quickly yelled something. Both dogs stopped fighting as they heard his command. I let the one at my feet loose first, and the unraveled my coat from the second. The dogs got up, shaking their heads, and trotted over to Scott. He said something else to them in a different language. The dogs sat down beside him.

I gasped as I put my head back against the floor. He walked over to me. "Stacy," he said holding his hand out. "Do you have a death wish?"

I laughed as I grabbed his hand. I looked around as the dogs stayed seated where they were commanded to do so, away from me. "Where's Mason?" I asked. "I have to see him."

"He's not here," Scott said rubbing the back of his neck.

I rubbed my right hand through my hair as I held my coat with my left hand. "Where is he?" I asked. "I need to talk with him right now," I said.

"He went on another job," Scott said. "They probably will be back in a few hours. Is he expecting you?"

Scott looked over at the dogs, and back at me. "You probably need to stay here till he gets back."

"Was the job close?" I asked shaking off the still rushing adrenaline.

He nodded. "I can't give you any details," he admitted.

"Bring me to him," I said. "I have till December first which is less than twelve hours."

Scott looked down at his watch. "Geez, you're going to get us both killed," he said and motioned for me to follow him. He jogged towards the door that led to the garage area. I stayed on his heels as he unlocked the car doors. Jumping in the passenger seat, he cranked the car, and I saw it was already five o'clock.

He pulled out of the garage and drove fast down the road.

I kept one hand on the dash, and then the other on the handle above my head. Nauseated with the ride as we drove around curves, into traffic. Hours passed, not feeling like I was going to make it to him. "You have to hurry?" I yelled in panic as it was nearing eleven o'clock.

"You want to drive?" Scott asked as he rounded another curve. He got onto a main highway and exited to a city.

"Where are they?" I asked as gripping the handle above my head.

"A hotel near-." The car came to a complete stop as we were in another stand still traffic. He reached down and pulled his phone off his clip. "Take this and run like your life depends on it. He should be on the tenth floor, room ten fifteen.

Pulling open the door, dashing out of the car, looking at the phone's tracking system. I slammed the door shut as I took off running ahead, shoving people out of my way. The adrenaline kicking in as I knew each minute that passed by only made it closer to time being up. Mason was going to think I chose the ranch. I ran as fast as I could, breaking through crowds, shoving myself past people who stopped to wait at traffic lights. I missed being hit by seconds as brakes squealed, and shouting from the people erupted in cars.

I looked down at the phone, one block to go, eleven forty-five. All that crossed my mind as I ran was the sound of a ticking clock. My lungs were on fire as I made the final turn, coming to a sudden stop in front of the hotel. I swiped my hair to adjust the windblown look as I entered behind a couple who were dressed in casual clothing. I put the phone to my ear as I entered, acting as if I already had a room key, and then headed for the elevator. It was eleven fifty-one.

Pressing the elevator button to see if it would speed it up as it climbed to the tenth floor. I moved my hands, above my head, interlocking my fingers as I pressed them on top of my head. I wasn't sure what to think anymore as I knew everything felt so rushed with exertion. The elevator beeped as we passed the eighth floor, and then the ninth. I removed my hands from the top of my head as I got ready for the doors to open on the tenth floor.

It was eleven fifty-three. I felt my breathing hardened as the doors opened. I walked off the elevator, looking up at the plaque to see which direction I needed to go. turned left and quickened my steps as I counted the doors down to ten fifteen. Stopped in front of the door, sweat dripping down my face, and realized I had no way of entering except through knocking.

I closed my eyes as I debated whether to knock. If I knock and whomever was the next hit opened it, then I have screwed up this entire job. If Mason was in there, he wouldn't answer the door. Shifting my weight between my feet, time was gone, I moved my hand up to knock on the door. The door opened, I moved my hand in front of me as Mason turned his body, looking up at me in complete shock.

I pushed him back into the room. He reacted quickly pulling me to him as he shut the door behind him, pressing my back against the wall by the door, looking down at me. Breathless, I stared into his eyes.

He moved his left hand behind my neck, gripping my hair lightly. "Sta-."

"I choose you," I interrupted grabbing onto his jacket. "I choose your world if it means that I get to be with you."

"My world doesn't come with me as your partner," he said staring into my eyes. Melting in his arms as I wanted nothing else than to be with him.

I licked my lips as I kept a firm grip on his jacket. "Then teach me," I gasped.

He leaned his head onto my right ear, putting his hand around my back. "You understand what you chose," he said breathing hot air into my ear.

The familiar lump in my throat that he forced every time we were back in this corner. "I want you to teach me how to become part of your world," I said. "I know that you're afraid of me getting killed in it." He breathed hard as he pressed his head on the wall by my ear. "I also know that you want me here with you. So," I paused as I moved my hand to his chin. He moved his hand from the back of my neck to my hand on his chin as he turned his head to where our foreheads were pressed against each other, both of our foreheads accumulated sweat. "Teach me how to survive your world."

He moved his arms around my back as he pressed me into him, embracing me as his lips pressed hard onto my forehead. The beating of my chest with his as he held onto me. Breathing hard, I wanted to kiss him. His entire body shook as I wrapped my arms around him. I couldn't tell if he was crying, but I knew I made the right decision as this comforted my soul.

Our hearts synchronized, bodies trembled as we held each other.

He loosened his grip as he pulled back away from me. I let go of him as he turned away from me. "You're choosing me," he said lowly. "I gave you an out, and you chose me."

"Mason," I said reaching out to grab him.

He put his hand out to stop me. He shook his head as he took his other hand and wiped his face. "No," he sternly said. "You don't get a say from here out. You do exactly what I tell you to do."

I took a step back as I watched him. He kept his hand out at me and his head turned away from me. I started to open my mouth but immediately closed it as I felt the terrible taste of what he warned me consumed my taste buds. He stated that I could be in his world, but I wouldn't be a part of him. I knew when he couldn't look at me that it was one of the rules he had set. We aren't to stare into each other's eyes. I took a deep breath in as he gained his composure. He moved his hand from his face. "We get back to the warehouse and not a word to no one. You keep your mouth shut, and then anything that gets handed to me," he paused. "You go directly with me to do the job. You do everything that I tell you to do with no questions at all."

Silent, I swallowed the next hard lump that had formed in my throat. "You know you will have a lot wanting to target you. You let them speak freely, but you keep your mouth shut. You say anything at all, about the deal, this conversation," he paused. "If a peep comes out of your mouth, you will be gone before you can say oops."

I held my stance as he kept his hand out towards me. "When I feel that you reached a level where you can advance, I will let you know."

He put his hand down as he took a deep breath and rubbed both hands through his hair. "How did you locate me?" He asked as he glanced over at me.

I grabbed the phone from my back pocket and handed it to him. He looked over it, knowing from the second I handed it to him whose phone it was that I had in my possession. Sliding it into his coat pocket, he put his hand on the doorknob. "Let's go," he said not looking back at me as he opened the door. I followed behind him as I felt every fear-stricken nerve send lightning waves over my entire body.

I knew from the beginning that he was going to be my deepest darkest devastation. I also knew that in this moment that he led me down the hallway to the elevator that I had never felt more confident than I did right now beside him. Behind him on the elevator as he kept his face forward, not saying a word to me as we descended. We got outside the hotel where Scott had the rear passenger door open for us as he stood outside of it. Mason stepped to the opposite side as I without hesitation slid into the car first. Mason followed behind me, and the door shut. I kept my hands in my lap as Mason kept to the other side of the car. I didn't even glance at his direction but felt the very thing that lured me to him. It burned inside of me from the moment I first met him at the bar.

Chapter Twelve

WE ARRIVED AT THE WAREHOUSE, Scott got out first, and then Mason. I glanced at him slightly as he turned to exit the car, he didn't look back at me. Pulling my handle, got out, followed behind them inside. Scott walked in first, then Mason with me behind. Mason went over to the table they served food and sat down, grabbing a cold one from the metal bucket with beer and ice on the table.

Ryan sat across from Mason, Kyle to his left, James to Kyle's left, Preston sat a few seats down at the other end with Thomas and Jackson. They all wore their jackets and had beers in their hands.

"What is she doing here?" Ryan asked as the tension already felt uneasy. I stood at the wall behind Mason, propping myself against it, keeping my head lowered. Mason wasn't lying about this being my last chance. I pulled my coat around me and slid my hands into my pockets.

"She will be with me for now on," Mason said. "So, if you have a problem with it then let's go settle it out right now." Ryan sipped on a cold one as he glared at me. Preston stood up from his chair, grabbing an extra beer and walked over to me. He propped against the wall next to me and held the extra beer out to me.

The thoughts of the night with Liz ruptured as I shook my head at him. He shrugged his shoulders, and walked back over to the table, took a seat. Each had different looks as they glanced at me, then looked at Mason. The tension felt mixed with anger. Scott took a seat next to Mason. Silent, I remained propped against the wall.

Over the next few weeks, I had come each day and trained with the others. We read up on different techniques the handlers have used, read case files, and handled a few jobs. Mason kept me with him on each of his jobs. He had Jackson join us several times as I kept silent, not speaking to either of them and only following his directions.

When I left the warehouse, after being paid, purchased several flash drives. Stashing them in my laptop bag and brought them with me to job. Mason primarily assigned me to stakeout and not actually killing which turned in my favor as I would take pictures, copy files to my drives, using my computer to finish the transfers, and then clearing my trails. Staying hidden as Mason and the others would complete the job at hand.

After each mission, I would go back to my apartment and review the information. I transferred pictures, and then did drops several days after being paid to my bank security box. I sent the letters to mom, only calling her every few days. I kept the same burner phone and attempted to keep conversations short. I informed her to watch for packages over the next several days after a job was finished. Our conversations always ended with *know where your roots are grounded.*

Annoyed as I knew what I had signed up for by choosing him. We weren't intimate partners as he stopped pinning me in tight spaces. He quit staring at me as he would only inform me of the job, and my part in it. Conversations were short and when finished he walked away from me. I held my tongue as I was afraid to talk with him. I only talked with mom, but not of missions or work. I asked about her recipes, and I checked in on Liz. After ending the calls, I would stay in my apartment, not exploring bars or riding subways. Isolating myself to the darkness where I wouldn't be seen.

It was a month after committing myself to Mason's team of silencers that we all were at the warehouse. I had been reviewing their past hit jobs with Preston, keeping silent. Preston attempted to have conversations with me, but I would bury my eyes into the material. The door from the garage sounded, everyone's attention jumped in reaction. A man in regular clothes, long brown coat, and a brown hat walked in. I put the folder I was reviewing down as Preston stood up.

Mason walked over to the man as I closed my folder. Mason held out his hand to shake the man's hand. "Detective Jones," Mason said as they shook hands. Preston and I exchanged looks, since Mason was so calm with a detective, and got up from our seats. "What brings you here?"

The man looked around the room. "I heard you were back in business a few months ago," the man said with an accent unfamiliar. "I had my hands tied into some cases down south to make my way out here."

Mason nodded as he moved his hands back to his pockets. "Henderson isn't here, but let's go talk in the office," Mason said as he glanced around at all of us. I looked to my right, seeing Thomas and Jackson staring as they were in a corner watching the detective. Jackson's expression of interest heightened my senses as I watched him cross his arms.

I looked back over at the detective and Mason. "I see you have some new recruits," Detective Jones said as he took a step towards me. "And this must be the pretty girl."

My body jumped in reaction as I immediately feared that the little girl I saved had surfaced his attention. He pulled out a paper from his pocket, and handed it over to Mason. "The aunt brought it to the desk last week," Detective Jones said. "The aunt had spoken with me directly about it."

Mason looked over the paper and glanced over at me. He looked back at Detective Jones. "What did the child say?" Mason asked as they looked at each other.

My heart rapidly beating as sweat drew on my forehead. "She wouldn't tell her aunt who it was," Detective Jones said. "She just calls her pretty girl. I helped dismiss it with the aunt."

"How so?" Mason asked as he handed the paper over to Scott who walked up.

"Told her some kids draw angels," Detective Jones said. "Maybe the girl thought this was her guardian angel. The aunt took the bait. I asked her if I could keep the image in case something come of it later on."

"Did the aunt accept your response?" Mason asked as he crossed his arms across his chest, shifting his weight on both feet as if he were anxious over the situation.

"It's been two weeks, and she hasn't come back by the station," Detective Jones said. "You can keep that image as a once grace period."

Mason nodded and patted the detective's back as he led them to the office. Scott followed behind him. Ryan came over to us. "Best be careful," Ryan said through gritted teeth. "You won't always have someone covering up your tracks."

He walked past us as he went over towards Thomas and Jackson. I gasped as the anxiousness of this detective's words settle down. I turned back to the chair, sitting back down at the table. "We both got lucky," Preston said as he started to shuffle papers around.

Keeping my head down as I fumbled my fingers in my lap. After several moments, Mason, Scott, and Detective Jones came out of the office heading towards the garage. I watched Mason and Scott shook hands with Detective Jones. He glanced over at me, tilting his hat, and winked as he turned to exit the door to the garage. Scott and Mason shared a brief conversation, and then Mason walked over to where Preston and I sat.

My throat dry as I looked back down at my fidgeting, shaking hands. Preston glanced over at me as Mason stopped behind my chair. "Stacy," he said lowly. "Let's go talk."

I gulped as I looked over at Preston with a feared expression. I got up from the chair and turned around and walked with Mason to the door with the exit. We went up the staircase to the roof access. I stopped and looked out towards the city as he stood next to me, putting his hands in his pockets. I licked my dried lips as I moved my hands to my coat pockets.

"You must be on someone's good graces," Mason said. I glanced over at his face that stared out the same direction I looked. "You got lucky with this one. She hasn't talked, but it doesn't mean if you pull that stunt again that the next person will be silent."

I looked down at the ground as tears prickled my eyes. "Go home for the night. We will regroup tomorrow," he said ending the conversation.

I wiped my eyes as I turned around to head back to the door to go back into the warehouse. I hurried down the steps and walked across the arena to the other side of the warehouse, exiting the building. I walked to my apartment, closing and locking myself inside. Propped against the door as I felt the fear that struck through me as lightning touched earth. Sliding down onto the floor, I pulled my knees to my chest and wrapped my arms around them.

Three months later, we completed three high paying hits. We were at the warehouse, Mason had us gathered in a circle. "We're moving James, Ryan, and Thomas to Southwest states. Henderson has a location set up for you. Scott, Kyle, you're taking Preston to the

Southeast. Jackson you will stay with me and Stacy. We have a few big clients needing multiple work," Mason said as he paced around in circle.

The sound of my phone's ringer went off. I jumped as I never got any calls, pulling it out my back pocket, itt was the ranch. *Mom.* I silenced it quickly, looking back up. Mason had positioned himself in front of me. "Do we have a problem here?" He asked as we stared into each other's eyes. I shook my head as the ringer went off again. A rush of fear flooded me as I saw all eyes were on me. I dropped the phone on the ground, crushing it under my foot. Mason looked a bit shocked with my reaction and turned away from me.

"These jobs aren't all hit cases like we usually get," Mason continued. "Some are some protection work, odd and end jobs, but paying jobs."

Jackson cleared his throat. "Yeah, um, boss man," Jackson called out. "We didn't sign up to be some person's bodyguard."

Mason paced over to Jackson, getting in his face. "You do as you're assigned, and no questions ask," Mason said through gritted teeth. "You do whatever job we tell you to do."

Jackson swallowed hard as Mason backed off. He glanced around the room. "Head out immediately," he shouted. My body trembled as his angry tone echoed the room. Everyone scattered as I stood silent, looking down at the crushed phone, I reached down and picked up the pieces, and threw it away in the trashcan.

We all left out, Mason put Jackson on stakeout as we were assigned a hit case. Anxiously, I hadn't executed a hit since the graduation case. We were located in North New York, staking out a business PR Representative. It was a lady who had alarming emails in her case file that were sent to local reporters. She had leaked some personal matters of a family-owned business and was following up on payout to the sources that she gave information too.

She lived alone, thankfully, as I wasn't sure if I could handle another hit on a family. I was to disguise as a waitress at a fancy restaurant where her latest email indicated she was meeting another reporter. The information she had to share on the business must have been bad enough for them to silence this meeting. Mason was going to be attending as a patron eating out. I already stashed my laptop bag in the back with other waiters and waitresses.

Her reservation was closing in as I prepared my tray like the others and followed their step out. I got eyes on the target as she arrived early, seated at a high cocktail table in the back, looking at the city's finest view. She had black hair that hung down her shoulders as she wore a black business suit, with a light blue button up and black heels. Diamond earrings with a matching necklace and bright red lipstick. Dressed for a special occasion like others there.

Jackson positioned as another patron by the opposite end of Mason's location. Both were able to view the target and watch me. I was to take the order and drug the drink. I went over to the lady's table, Veronica, was her name on the case file. "Good evening," I said as I placed a napkin in front of her. "What drink may I interest you in tonight?"

"Dirty martini," she said looking around the room. She locked eyes on someone across the room.

"I'm meeting a friend soon, so you can keep them coming." She glanced back at me and shifted her sight again.

"Is he a gentleman that you're serving as well?" She asked as she glanced at me, looking over to her right. I glanced over as I saw her staring at Mason.

We both looked back at each other. I smiled at her as I wasn't sure how to respond. "Please order him a whisky, put it on my tab," she winked at me, and looked over at him. I glanced to see him staring at her.

I walked away as I went over to the bar to provide them with her drinks that were ordered. I waited patiently as the bartender poured both drinks and handed them to me. I placed them on a tray, pulling a small bottle from my pocket of the formulated drug. I quickly poured its contents in her dirty martini and swirled the toothpick with olives to mix it. Picking up the tray and walking over to her table first, she had been going back and forth smiling at him, and then looking away. I sat down her drink and walked over to his table across the room.

He looked up at me as I sat his whisky down in front of him. "The nice lady ordered you a whisky," I said as our gazes met. He looked back towards Veronica, holding his glass up with a smile.

"Whisky, such a killer," he whispered. I walked away towards her table. I saw her purse hanging over the back of her chair as she started sipping on her martini. I snatched it off the back, tucking it behind my tray I turned sideways. Walking where the waitstaff lockers were located. I placed the tray down on the bench beside me, keeping her purse clutched as I dug out my laptop bag. I quickly pulled her phone out of her purse, connecting the cord from laptop to it.

I typed quickly copying her data over to my secure file on my laptop to transfer later. I glanced as noises were breaking out in the kitchen. The bar that signified its transferring reached a hundred. I unplugged the cord, shoving my laptop back in my bag, and then closing it in the locker. I placed her phone back in her purse, grabbing the tray up, and going back out to the bar. As the bartender was busy mixing drinks, I pulled the small bottle that I had emptied in her first glass out of my apron pocket, sliding it into his pocket as I shifted the tray to hit his opposite arm.

"Sorry," I said as he looked at me. "Make another dirty martini please." He rolled his eyes and got to work as I went out of the bar, hiding her purse under my apron. I walked over to her table, carefully sliding her purse over her chair.

Veronica had finished the first glass. "You better have my next one ready soon," she slurred. I picked up her glass and walked back to the bartender as I placed the empty glass in a bin. He handed me another dirty martini that I walked back over to her. She held onto the table, looking as her eyes weren't able to focus.

"Your dirty martini," I said sitting it next to her hand.

I quickly walked away, heading towards Mason's direction, and then turning sharply left. I picked up a few dirty plates, and then a shattering noise broke out. I glanced as Veronica fell from the table, knocking her dirty martini to the floor with her. A chaotic murmur fled through as people jumped up to her aid. I headed toward the back, sitting the plates down, and then going to grab my bag. Taking off the apron, I unbuttoned my blouse, switching over to a red blouse. I put my bag over my shoulder as I unpinned my hair, shoving the clip in my pocket. I slipped out the side of the kitchen, blending in with the bystanders, and then making my exit.

I got out of the building and headed for the subway. I got to its platform, seeing Mason and Jackson's arrival as we all three entered different doors into the same cart. I sat down on the bench as Mason and Jackson stood at opposite ends of the cart. I kept my eyes on the ground in front of me, not speaking a word to anyone, or glancing in anyone's direction.

After the hit, we did a few days in different locations, scoping out some people. Mason collected data, pictures, and then we headed back to the warehouse. I didn't pull my laptop out in front of them, and I stayed out of their way. We got back to the warehouse where I changed into a black tank top and olive green pants and sneakers. I pulled a coat over me and swung my laptop bag on my shoulder. Mason stopped me before leaving. "Great work out there," he commented as he didn't stare at me. "You want to stay a while to rest off the heist?"

I shook my head, keeping my eyes lowered. "I rather rest alone," I said lowly.

He nodded and shifted out of my way. I left the warehouse and walked to the apartment. I locked it up as I sat my laptop bag on my island countertop. Pulling out the laptop, opening it up, and then plugging in a flash drive. I synched the data from the secure file to the flash drive. Veronica had information regarding the business pharmaceuticals, and then also what the research of their testing phase discovered. I read through the material, and then took out the drive, deleting the trail on my laptop. I placed the drive in my bag and closed up my laptop.

I knew that I was breaking Mason's rule of not looking into the job, but it was the only way I could participate in finding his out. I wanted to give him the choice that he gave me months ago. I fixed, ate a sandwich, and then went to my bed. I lay down on it, thinking of Mason. The burning desire that consumed me every unspoken moment as I wasn't able to talk with him. I was training to do his job, be as good as him, losing myself in the process.

He wouldn't talk with me much, but when he did, he kept it strictly about the jobs. He didn't touch me like he used to that caused every hair on my body to rise. I missed the sensation as it was the drive that fueled me into choosing his life. I chose his world to be with him, and I knew when he told me that I wasn't going to be his lifelong partner it shattered me. The way he reacted that day, hugging me, pressing his lips to my forehead. I knew that this space he's forced between us was only temporary.

Six months passed since my return, Mason was meeting with all of us again. Jackson had finally learned to keep his mouth shut during these meetings. My black tank top that exposed my chest with the golden cross. I had felt a sensation to clutch it and wrapped my left hand around it. "We have new jobs," Mason started. "We need these to go smoothly. No mess ups from handlers or others." He looked over at me. "Handlers ensure to stake out completely, no rest until all factors of possible mistakes are accounted for. Ensure not to kill anyone that isn't our target. Keep the killings suicidal and regardless of what new intel is brought forth, don't cause any huge scenes." Mason had turned as he talked with all of us.

The feeling of the cross on my chest nauseated me as I clutched it. Mason assigned work. "Scott and Preston will be with Ryan, Kyle and Jackson. Thomas and James are with Stacy and me." My hair on the back of my neck stood as he continued to talk. "These are high payout jobs, lots of factors are in play as the security teams they have for these families are much greater than we've encountered before." My body broke out into a cold sweat, my breathing harden at his word *families.* I lowered my eyes as I tried to shake the feeling.

Suddenly my thoughts went to the little girl I rescued. I remembered the tension I felt after I saved her life, haunting my existence. "Just make sure we keep it clean," Mason said. "Any mishaps cause tensions as it raises the press interest."

The room swayed as if it were going to spin as he continued to talk. I couldn't no longer hear his words as I tightly gripped my fingers on the necklace. "Stacy, are you coming back?" Liz's voice echoed.

I looked around the room as the group had scattered. Mason talked with Jackson as I still couldn't hear them. Numbed as Liz's voice echoed again, "your problems, my problems, we all deal with it as we're a family."

My eyes were scattering as I could feel the spinning as her words echoed. "Stacy, are you coming back home?" I blinked as I focused back to the warehouse. Mason stood in front of me. I jumped as I didn't notice him shifting himself in front of me.

Our eyes met; he moved his hand to my necklace as I released it with a jump from his reaction. His hand barely grazes my chest. "Is this a problem for you?" He asked looking at the cross that sat above my breasts.

I cleared my throat as I licked my lips. "What?" I asked as I took a second pause. "The cross or your hand on my chest?"

His eyes shot up from the necklace as we stared into each other for a moment. The feeling I craved to return burning through my veins as I arched an eyebrow in curiosity of what he had to say next to me. He let go of the necklace, taking a step back from me. A breath slipped as he turned and walked away from me. I looked around and noticed Jackson had his eyes on me from across the room. He had Thomas standing in front of him, facing him, but he wasn't looking at Thomas. I looked away as I walked off from the center of the room.

Mason called the first team to leave, gathering us at the door. "Stacy, you stay behind," he said as he tapped James on the shoulder.

"Mason," James said. "This is a four-person job."

"Not anymore," Mason snapped. "Stacy, you go back home. I will reach out to you when we're back."

James looked confused as he glanced at me and walked off. Thomas followed behind James. I clutched my jacket as Mason turned away. "Wait," I said reaching for him. He turned around to look at me, and then we both quickly looked away from each other.

He put his hands out in front of me. "Just trust me on this one," he whispered. "Stay behind and don't do anything reckless."

"I didn't mean to joke with you earlier," I said as I started to bite my lower lip.

He shook his head as he turned away. "I'll reach out to you," he said, and walked away quickly. I felt a shattering sensation as I watched him leave, clutching my stomach. I stood silent for a few moments and then took a step as if I were going to run after him. Then his words that took control of my life that his new rule engraved inside of me. *You do exactly what I say with no questions.*

I kicked the ground as I turned away from the door. Walking over to the table and sat down. I didn't leave the warehouse as I waited for their return. Working on target practicing; read over chemicals and drugs they used for their hits. A few days passed as I never went back to the apartment. I fell asleep in the chair with my head lying on my arms that rested on the table.

A nudge that shook me awake, startled me as I looked up. Mason stood next to me. "You stayed here?" He asked.

I looked around as others were filing in, going to the bunkrooms. I stood up and faced him. "I didn't have nowhere else to be," I said looking down. He was a foot away from me, not touching me, but just standing there. I thought of his stance, wanting his hand to touch the back of my neck. I looked up at him.

"Go home," he said as slight smirk expression crossed his lips. "We'll see you back tomorrow." He took a step back as he stared into my eyes and then turned away from me. The burning desire that I desperately needed, walked behind him. I took a deep breath and then turned around, walking towards the warehouse exit, seeing Jackson by the door.

"You look," he said as he stepped out in front of me with his hand out to stop me. "Sad like a lost puppy." I kept my eyes down as he shifted himself in front of me. "I bet it sucks watching the one thing you did all this for turn away from you." I turned my head away from him as he stepped closer to me. "You don't talk anymore; he must have silenced you." He grabbed my chin forcing my head back to look him in the eyes.

A coughing noise as in someone clearing their throat broke out from behind me. Jackson looked over my shoulder and then let go of my chin. He stepped out of the way as he put one arm behind him, and then the other out as if he was bowing for me to leave. I didn't even turn around as I knew who cleared their throat. I walked out the warehouse door and then headed in the direction of my apartment.

Jackson was arrogant but also spoke true words. Since I decided to enter Mason's world it's like he wedged a stone brick cemented filled wall between us. He no longer touched me like he did that day I chose him. He didn't stare for more than a few seconds into my eyes as I could see the lust that burned inside of me, also burned inside of him. I knew when he stated that I must follow his exact commands that I had lost my power to make him fall in love with me.

I was surviving his world because he forced himself to look away. He's training me to be him, to be a silencer. My body fell down on the bed as tears of losing him rushed down my cheeks. He warned me that I wasn't choosing him. I was ignorant and wanted him, the way he made me feel, sending me into another world with his stares. The way he kissed me, leaving me breathless. Torn as the shredded devastations of his world seeped through me.

I desperately wanted to call home, but I hadn't spoken to my family since before crushing my phone under my foot. Never replaced it with another as I didn't want suspicion of mom calling me rattle the others. I watched how they all looked at me, waiting for me to make another mistake that keeping in touch with my family would only cause tragedy for them. I put my hand on my necklace as the feeling of it wanting me to connect heightened. I placed my other hand on my stomach and looked up at the ceiling of my apartment and then closed my eyes.

Chapter Thirteen

IT WAS THE NIGHT of November twenty-eighth; we were at the warehouse. Preston and I had stayed around the target shooting area. Mason, Scott, Ryan were by the table that we ate at. Kyle, James were collecting items as we had been assigned our assignments. Thomas and Jackson always stood in the corner, never really practicing or engaging with the others until time. In the process of reloading my gun, Preston shot a few rounds. I looked up, he had hit the head, shoulder, and then off target.

"Ah," he snorted. "This gun has to be off."

I smirked as I looked back down at the gun in my hand.

"Only thing off is your aim," Jackson said walking up to us. I glanced over as he slowly made his way over to me. "Like yours," he said.

I stayed silent as he came closer to me. I loaded the clip. "I haven't seen you and Mason googling eyes lately. You still trying to bark up that tree, or have you finally put that dog to rest?"

I slid the clip into the handgun, keeping my eyes on it as Jackson inched closer. "Are you finally ready to spread them legs into new territory?"

"Jackson, leave her alone," Preston snapped.

Jackson laughed. "You her new boyfriend now?"

I instantly turned my wrist, plunging the barrel of the gun to his pants with my hand on the trigger. Jackson looked down at me with no hesitation, as he kept his hands to his sides. We looked into each other's eyes as his facial expression tightened, exposing his cheekbones. "We've been doing this for over a year," I said. "You always try making smart remarks. You should know by now that when a specific item, such as my gun here," I glanced as I pressed it a little closer to his manhood. He kept his lined lips and exposed cheekbones as it appeared he swallowed a lump that now had formed in his throat. "That either one or two things happens." I stopped as I glanced down at the gun, and then back into his eyes. "One, you will either start singing like a canary and begging for mercy on the little thing that seems bigger than your actual head." I stopped as I felt the room had shifted. Glancing around, the others had come over towards us. "Because if you were using the correct one, then you wouldn't be in this predicament. Two, is my personal favorite," I paused as I smiled. "Two is you shut the hell up. And to be honest, this is my favorite of the scenarios as it finally gives the ringing in my ears a break from your pathetic voice that sounds so desperate." His mouth tightened as he kept still like a statue. "You say I look desperate yet I'm not the one with a gun pressed against me. You want to start keeping that mouth shut around me," I said. "Next time, I may not be so graceful."

He took a step back, keeping his hands away from his side, eyes locked on me. He took a few more steps back and turned around, walking off. He shoved Thomas as he tried to speak up. I turned around and sat the gun down on the table between Preston and me. Preston and I exchanged looks, and then he positioned himself back and began shooting at the target.

"Teams need to move out in thirty," Mason yelled. I kept my eyes down at the gun on the table. A shift of air and heard feet scattering, glancing over my shoulder to see Mason standing there. "You good?" He asked.

I nodded. "Never better," I said as I turned and walked away. Collecting my laptop bag and jacket.

We were assigned a man and lady within the IT department of another corporation. I done my usual downloading of files, and getting it stashed away before anyone caught guard. After the job was finished, appearing as a late-night office fire, Mason suggested we celebrate. When we returned to the hotel, a long red dress and black heels were in my room on the bed. I had slipped on the dress, seeing the back was out to the bottom of my spine. I took off my bra, put on the heels, and then fixed my hair, leaving it down, parting it, and clipping back a few inches with a gold clip.

After I looked at myself in the mirror, amazed at the beautiful dress that complimented every curve of my body. I smiled as it reminded me of the second phase of our training when I picked up a red cocktail dress and wore sneakers with it. I grabbed my black clutch and took the elevator downstairs. Inside the hotel's bar, Preston and Scott sat by the bar. I decided to let them know I was there but would be at a table near the music.

Walking over and standing next to a tall cocktail table that was meant to stand around for conversation. After a few moments, taking in the scene of people drinking in nice formal dresses and suits. I saw women flirting with men, music playing as some danced together. I smelled the alcohol aroma as people passed by my table. A little out of place as I hadn't been to a bar since Liz took me. I've completely quit drinking as the haunting of my own decisions when I drink seemed careless. I was ready to move on past that stage in my life.

"I know you usually like shots," Mason said approaching behind me. "But I got us whisky." He sat a glass down by my hand that was on the table, curled into a small fist.

I looked over my shoulder at him in a black tuxedo with a red tie. "Thank you," I smiled. I kept my hand away from the glass.

"You're not interested in it?" He asked as he put his glass to his lips.

I glanced down at it and back at him. "I prefer to stay sober," I said.

"You act as if you drink all the time," he said taking a sip. He shifted himself to put both arms on the table with the glass in hand. A look on his face as if he were thinking hard on something. "I haven't seen you take a sip of alcohol in-."

"I don't drink anymore," I interrupted looking down at my hands.

He exhaled as if the conversation had gone a direction he didn't expect. "When did you decide to quit?"

I giggled. "It's an interesting story," I said as I interlocked my fingers, keeping my eyes on them.

"Tonight is us all celebrating," he said. "So, I have time for an interesting story." His tone was light but joyful. It sounded much like the tone when we first met, and he spoke to the bartender. I gasped as I tried to snap out of the fantasy that we'd become more than silencer partners.

"I quit drinking because of you," I said. "When I went back home, my younger sister, Liz, she wanted me to go to a bar. We went together and ordered drinks. However, when I touched the glass every moment that's happened from the time before you brought me to the warehouse to the assignment that almost ended my life I couldn't touch it." I stopped as I glanced over at him. "It was the moment that put me in tears about you. I decided at that moment to become soberminded," I said as we stared into each other's eyes. A lump hardened as the twinkle in his green eyes appeared. I didn't want to look away, luring me in. Irresissting to make a move, something I haven't done in a year.

He broke the stare as he stood up straight, clearing his throat, and then kicking back his glass. "When you came back to me a year ago," he whispered as he shifted closer to me. "You thought that it would be for me only."

I shook my head as I looked down in embarrassment. "I know you brought me into your world, and I knew that I wanted to be with you."

"Are you happy with the choice you made?"

I cleared my throat like the question was a double-edged sword. Looking back into his eyes, he shifted himself an inch from my right side, putting his left hand on his hip. "I knew that making this choice wasn't going to be easy," I whispered. "I'm not fond of the work."

"Then why did you choose to come back?" He asked as he leaned in.

I looked away, swallowing the new lump that had formed in my throat. "Because I knew that I wanted you," I whispered in embarrassment. "I wanted whatever it took to be with you."

He cleared his throat as he moved his hand onto my bare skin back above my waist. Shifting his other hand to graze my interlocked arms. Every hair on my body rose as his pressed against mine. Shocked by the gesture, I looked into his eyes. "Will you be happy with just me alone?"

My mouth dried up as we stared into each other's gazes. The room suddenly quiet as I couldn't process the emotions that were unfolding. "What?" I managed to gasp.

"Will you be happy if my world that you've entered includes me as yours only?" He asked.

My mouth dropped as I was stunned at his words. He was proposing to me in an odd way. I knew this had been the moment I craved for a year, wanting him, our bodies touching, kissing. I wanted him. A shockwave rolled through me as we intensely stared at each other. Then, the thought reappeared to me of the way home from the second phase of training.

My memory flashed back to the scene where as breathless as I was now, him next to me in the cab and whispered, "I don't kiss women who aren't mine." I snapped back to us staring intensely at each other as the bar reappeared around us.

"Mason, are you wanting to be with me?" I asked.

He smiled as he moved into my ear. "I don't want to just be with you," he whispered as his hot breath sent chills down my spine. "I want you to be mine." Inhaling abruptly, I pulled back to look into his eyes. He wasn't joking with me, and I could feel it from the stares. He moved his hand on my back as I turned to face him. "Are you okay to be part of my world with just me in it?" He asked again.

The words of just him held at the edge of my tongue. I felt as if it were something more to his phrase *just me in it*. Searching into his eyes as he and I stared. Unable to speak as I didn't want anything else more than this moment, but it was like everything from my childhood was out the window. My mom always told us growing up, a good man would ask your father first and then kneel on one knee to propose. I didn't see me saying this to Mason as his world was completely different. He was raised in a world of pain, death, and for him to be asking me to be his was unordinary.

I licked my lips to bring back moisture that had escaped me from this exhilarating moment. "Yes," I whispered.

His face lit up as he shifted his hand from my interlocked hands to the glass. He picked up the glass, turned it up, and then sat it back down. My breathing heightened as I wasn't sure what to expect next. He motioned me to follow him. We walked over to the bar where Scott and Preston sat.

"Scott," Mason said as I glanced between them. A rush of adrenaline as I wasn't sure what we were going to tell the others. "You and Preston head back tonight. Let Henderson know that we are staying out here another week," Mason said.

"Another week?" Scott asked arching an eyebrow.

"No questions," Mason said as he patted him on the shoulder. "We will be back in a week."

Preston glanced at me as I shrugged unsure of what to say at that moment. Mason pulled out some money and put his hand on my back as he pushed me towards the bar's exit. Without hesitation as the rush felt like lightning. We left the hotel in a taxi. He didn't touch or move close to me as he gave the driver an address.

We pulled up to what looked like a mansion, except it was a venue. Mason got out of the car and ran around to get the door for me. He held out his hand to me. Taking it with a smile as all of this felt unreal. I kept silent as we made our way inside. We entered the grand hall with white paint, pictures, floral arrangements, breath taking and overwhelming.

"Stay here," he demanded as he let go of my hand.

I looked around, spinning in circles, as I was shocked at the gesture. I clutched my black clutch as I faced a picture of a bride and her husband in their wedding attire. The photo was close in on their kiss with a bouquet.

"Stacy," Mason said behind me. I turned to look as he had stood across the room at a doorway. His hand held out towards me. I walked across the room and placed my hand into his hand. He led me through multiple rooms to a patio that was covered in arrangements. He stopped as we stepped onto the paved rock sidewalk that led to a gazebo. He pulled me to him as we looked into each other's eyes.

A breath escaped my lips as I was taken by shock of his moves of touching me again. He moved his hands to cuff my cheeks as I wrapped my fingers around his wrists. "Stacy, you understand that once we become one, you will never have a chance of getting back to your old life. You understand it's just me?" He asked as we both were breathing hard as if we had just run for our lives.

I blinked as I smiled looking into his eyes. "You are my life," I said.

He pressed his forehead to mine. "Let's get married right now," he said.

I inhaled as we locked eyes on each other. The moment took me away like I was no longer standing, but in the air. Breathless, heart beating out of my chest, and then my body wanting to lunge forward and kiss him but refrained. I nodded as a squeal left my throat. He pulled away from me, moving his hands to my hand as we walked to the gazebo.

Mason paid the man there that evening to wed us. We were placed in specific spots, holding each other's hands. They had two additional people there to witness our vows. I looked around as not a soul here was a person I knew except the man in front of me and that's all I needed. I His hands clasping mine, sweating, but the look in his eyes as we stared. Magical even when it was spontaneous. Everything around us appeared more vibrant than I ever saw. A photographer took pictures of us, my cheeks flushed red, and I kept staring into the one that made me feel even more confident than beforehand.

"Do you take Stacy Edwards to be your beloved wife, to cherish and to hold, for sickness and for health, till death do you part?" The man asked Mason.

"I do," he said with confidence as his hands squeezed mine tighter.

I inhaled another breath as I wanted this ceremony to be over with and us to be kissing. "Do you take Mason Henderson to be your beloved husband, to cherish-."

"I do," I interrupted.

Laughter broke out amongst all of us as Mason's face lit up, shaking slightly at my impatience. "Do you have rings?" The man asked looking at Mason.

Mason let go of my hands as he pulled off his black leather strapped watch. "No, but until I can get you one. I want you to have this," Mason said looking at me. I smiled as I watched him place it on my wrist.

"As the power invested in me, November thirtieth at eleven fifty-seven p.m., I now pronounce you husband and wife," the man said. "You can kiss your bride."

Mason moved forward, grabbing my chin as I grabbed his arms, and we kissed. The kiss felt so different than any other kiss we had ever shared. Mason moved a hand to my back as he dipped me back a little. I grabbed the back of his neck as we continued to kiss. We had a hot minute as the breath was taken from both of us. Mason pulled me back up as we stared into each other's eyes.

Mason thanked the man and additional guests, and then confirmed we would pick up everything in a few days. Mason grabbed my hand, and we went to get a cab. He brought me back to the hotel where he took me to a suite on the tenth floor. He swooped me off my feet as we got off the elevator, smiling and giggling at the romantic gesture. I put my arms around his neck, we shared a kiss, and then he walked down the hall. He opened a room door and carried me inside. He sat me down once the door was shut. I looked around at the California King bed with red and gold satin comforter and sheets.

I walked in, absorbing the room, as I saw a jet tub, a patio with a balcony. "Mason, did you plan this?" I asked turning around to face him.

"I knew I wanted you a year ago," he said. "But I had to make you work for us to stay alive." I faced the bed as he walked up to me, putting his arms around me. I turned my head slightly, he brushed the hair off my shoulder as he kissed my neck. "I had to refrain myself from you as I wanted to take you a year ago to be mine." His tender kiss sending chills down my spine, my lips quivered as I placed my hands on his that were around my stomach. "I love you, Stacy Henderson."

I smiled as the name had a ring to it. He shifted his right hand to my right shoulder, pulling the strap down as he kissed me tenderly from my neck to my shoulder. I breathed hard at the touch. "I love you," I gasped. "Mason Henderson."

He smiled as he pulled my dress down, working both hands, and then turning me to face him. He rubbed his hand on the back of my neck, and we kissed passionately. Every arousal inched its way up as he moved me back, slowly falling back on the bed. I worked my hands to pull his tie off and then unbuttoned his shirt. He moved his hands from my neck, speeding up the process. He pulled my underwear off as I slid up onto the bed kicking my heels off. He climbed over me, exploring with his hands every inch of me as I moved mine across his bare skin. We both were breathing hard as he forced his naked body over me.

The anticipation rose as I could feel his waist moving closer to mine, my legs moving around his hips. I was about to feel the love between married people. I couldn't catch my breath as he kissed me, he moved down to my neck, my head flew back as the arousal escalated. "I have to tell you something," Mason breathed.

I looked down at him as I was getting closer to releasing a built and escalated arousal. "What?" I gasped as I was anxious for the next part and geared for it to happen.

"I had a vasectomy at eighteen," he gasped as he moved his lips to my left ear. "I'm sterile." He forces himself inside of me and a moan slips my throat as I have no time to process his words. My head flung back as the built arousal was relieved. He tightened his arms around me as I put mine on his back. We had multiple rounds, and then finally crashed into each other's arms.

I woke up, opening my eyes, looking at him on his back with his head facing me and eyes closed. I shifted myself under the covers next to his skin. He woke up from the movement, placing an arm behind my head, and then taking another and stroking my hair. I smiled as I looked away from him. "Good morning my beautiful wife," he said, and then leaned over to kiss my lips.

"Good morning, husband," I said as I kissed him. He kept kissing me, moving my hair off my shoulder, and then he moved me onto my back. He was over me again, and the intensity built up. After another shared moment, he sat me up and stroked my hair back.

"You know I'm not ever going to get enough of you," he smiled as he moved his hand behind my neck.

I shifted myself to sit in his lap as he put his hands on my back. "I haven't stopped getting enough of you since the moment we first laid eyes on each other," I said brushing my hands through his hair. He laughed as he pulled me in closer. I put my hands on the back of his neck and kissed him again.

We finally decided to end our moments and call room service. I wrapped up in a white plush robe as Mason put on shorts. We had our food brought out to the patio where we sat beside each other, looking over the view of the beach. We ate and smiled at each other. We laughed and kissed. The moments felt priceless as a new life had begun for us.

We finished eating, Mason had shifted himself to the balcony's fence. "We have to tell the others," I said as I got up and went over to wrap myself around him. He put his right arm around me, kissing my forehead.

"I'm not scared of anyone knowing what we did," he said. "You've committed yourself to them, but you also bound yourself to me."

"In more than one way," I said laying my head on his bare chest.

He squeezed me tighter. "Maybe now that you're officially mine, you want get as much mouth from the others," he said moving his head down. I looked up, meeting our mouths to share another kiss.

I pulled my mouth away from him. "You shock me every moment I'm with you," I said. "The bombshell you dropped on me is something I want to discuss."

He smiled as he put his chin on the top of my head. "Can we not begin our first day in marriage with an argument?"

"You didn't think that was something to mention before you had me wrapped in your bedsheets?"

He chuckled. "I did mention that you will have just me."

I closed my mouth as I pressed my face on his chest. I loved the connection that our skin-to-skin contact created between us. Thinking about the words that had me stumbling with last night and knew he had in his terms explained it the best he could at the time. He wrapped both arms around me as he kissed the top of my head. "This is our honeymoon, what all do you want to do?" He asked.

I laughed at the way he has handled these past twenty-four hours. "I'm sure we can figure something out," I smiled. After another shared moment, we moved inside to get dressed. Mason had our suitcases brought in last night before we got back to the hotel room. I dressed in a white tank top with a light blue button up top and blue jeans. I put on flip flops as we headed down to the beach, strolling hand in hand.

I took in every moment of our honeymoon as we went snorkeling, eating at different restaurants, going to the aquarium. We took a boat tour together and did some hiking. Our honeymoon of loneliness from the warehouse was a great experience. I embraced these moments even Mason appeared to have fun. The best moments of our honeymoon were inside our hotel room. We even stayed in place one entire day as we found ourselves unable to break away from the shared moments we never before got to experience.

At the end of the week, Mason broke the news to me that we had to go back. I was wrapped in our satin comforter sheets. I placed my hand on them as he was up, getting suitcases packed. "Are you going to get dressed?" He asked.

"Is there anyway I can convince you that we need another week?" I asked looking up from the sheets.

He put down the clothing he was attempting to fold and walked over to the bed. He sat down putting his hand on the back of my neck, I moved my hand to his wrist. "I love you," he said as he pressed his forehead to mine. "But if we don't want a fleet coming after us, then we better get back and explain ourselves."

My smile faded away. "Have you ever thought of fleeing?" I asked as I looked down at his chest, avoiding his eyes contact.

"I told you before of my past," he said and kissed my forehead. "I didn't have any other choice. For me to dream of something else is useless." He stopped as he took a deep breath. "There's only one dream I've had since you and I shared our first breathless moment of that bar you remember so vaguely. You stared in my eyes as I told you to put down that shot and follow me." My face lit up as I remembered it.

"I never thought in a million years that a woman as beautiful as you would do it," he said. "Then at my amazement, you followed me, and then you trusted me." I laughed as tears flowed. He took his other hand and tilted my chin up to look him in the eyes. "I have never looked at any other woman like you. I never kissed another woman, and I for sure have never married anyone else."

"Why did you make that silly rule?" I cried.

He exhaled as he wiped my tears away. "It was the one thing I wanted to honor my mother with," he paused. "I wanted to find a woman that looked at me the way she did."

I couldn't hold it back anymore as I moved forward and kissed him. He moved his hands as he kissed me back, our breaths being taken away again. He pulled back as he got up from the bed and looked away.

"No," I said getting up with the sheet wrapped around me. I grabbed his hand, he looked back at me. "You don't get to that anymore."

"Nothing changes when we go back," he said.

"Everything has changed," I said moving myself to be next to him. He wrapped his arms around my back as I looked up at him. His chin moved up to look up at the ceiling as he closed his eyes. "When you said I do, you took me as yours. That means everything changes. I'm as much of yours as you're as much as mine."

He looked down into my eyes as he slightly shook me with emotions. I wrapped my arms around his back letting the sheet be wedged between us. "You can't take it back now," I said. "We had a ceremony and a honeymoon."

He chuckled as he squeezed me tightly. "Are you happy with me?" He asked beside my ear.

I nodded. "I've never been happier in my life," I gasped. He pulled me back, letting the sheet fall as he moved his hands through my hair and kissed me. He picked me up and pulled me back onto the bed, taking his shorts off.

"Then we might as well leave this place where we began," he said as made his way to me. I smiled as I accepted his embrace. We shared another marked moment that put stitches in my heart from the tears that were there beforehand.

I knew being with him I risked everything, including my reason to live as it was taken from me. As a silencer, I no longer had the free life that I once had when growing up. Mason stole it from me as he stole my heart, making me question everything. In this world of questioning, he also gave me confidence that I've never before had in my life. I survived a year from leaving my world of freeness. Accepting him as a reward with this choice was the best decision I ever could have made.

Chapter Fourteen

Mason and I finally left the hotel, stopping by the venue to collect our wedding certificates, photos, and gift the venue provided. We flew back to New York, bringing our luggage to my apartment for the time being as Mason lived at the warehouse. We changed into our usual wear and headed for the warehouse, hand in hand until we reached the door. Mason let go of my hand as instinct. I quickly retaliated, grabbing his hand and clutching it.

"I-."

"You and I are now one," I said. "There's no turning back as we are now one."

He nodded, kissing the top of my head, and then opened the door. We walked into the warehouse as nerves and excitement overwhelmed me. The thought of what may happen to both of us flooded my mind as we walked towards the center of the arena. Henderson and Scott were in the center of the room. Everyone's eyes shot over to us as we walked in. They quickly made their way to the center of the room as we walked up.

Mason kept his hand interlocked with mine, looking over each of their expressions. "Mason," Henderson said as he had his hand to a cigar that was at his mouth. "You took some extra time. What is the reasoning?"

My body suddenly felt hotter as the nerves of everyone staring. Mason stepped back, putting his arm around my back. "We got married," Mason said as we looked into each other's eyes.

Expressions and sighs of all kinds broke out as excitement chattered filled the room. Scott came over first, extending his hand out, and then moving in for a hug. I had stepped back as they came up, congratulating and shaking our hands. This definitely was a shock as they each embraced the news with excitement and not terror.

Jackson had come over, shaking Mason's hand, and looking at me. "Sorry about the other week," he said.

I glanced up at Mason who glanced back at me. I looked over at Jackson. "You're forgiven," I said, and then shook his hand.

"Congrats," he said, and then walked off.

Mason wrapped his arm around me as conversations broke out. We sat down and ate. Mason talked about the last job with Henderson. I stayed by his side as Preston later on made his way to my side. "I was expecting much worse for you," he admitted. "You two are definitely meant for each other."

I smiled as I leaned closer to Mason. "What happened when Scott broke the news?" I asked lowly.

"Henderson didn't react much," Preston whispered. "After a few days, rumors broke out. Scott and I didn't feel it was going to be bad between the two of you. But we definitely didn't expect you both to come home married."

I chuckled as the events that took place over this past week had me in a whirlwind of my own. Mason and the others drank a beer, clinging together. I stayed wrapped in his arm as they all talked among themselves. Jackson and Thomas were the first to leave, not saying much when they left. Henderson was ready to wrap up the party. Mason and I sat down with him in his office of filing cabinets and chairs after everyone else had left.

"You know this doesn't look good, Mason," Henderson snapped. "I never expected you to do something this outrageous."

"We're in love," Mason said. "There's nothing outrageous about it."

"You're getting soft boy," Henderson said as he lit another cigar. "You should have taken her out a long time ago. Now that you two are married and doing these assignments," he stopped as he glanced at me. "It's just riskier."

"We'll continue our work just as before," I spoke up as Mason opened his mouth to speak. "There won't be any difference."

"Best not be," Henderson snapped. "You both will now be paid as one. I will give you the average of what you both would have earned." Immediately, the thought about me sending money to my mom after each assignment sent me to sit back in my seat. "I hope you both understand the choice that you made,"

Henderson said. I kept my back straight as I tried to appear that a problem hadn't emerged, but internally I had a lot of things that Mason didn't know about.

The thoughts of the money stashed in different locations with the flash drives, and then the fear that I may need to confess rose. Mason wasn't aware of these, and it would crush him to find out about it. He devoted his life to the silencers. I'm sure he still felt that it was primarily part of his life as I was the second. I knew I fell in this place when he advised me at the hotel that they would send a fleet after us.

Mason stood up, and I followed his reaction. He shook Henderson's hand, and then I shook his hand. We left and headed for my apartment. After we got there, Mason and I went to bed. I waited till after he was asleep and got up. I slid on my robe and went to find my laptop bag. I went to the kitchen island counter, downloaded the content, and then erased the evidence on my laptop. I placed the flash drive in my laptop bag. After I secured my laptop bag in the closet, I slipped off my robe and then slid back into bed. Mason didn't wake up. I was relieved as I lay there, staring at the ceiling.

I thought of what my mom would think of me being a married woman now. I thought of the things she used to say about marriage. "A lady that is married honors her husband," mom said once as we were in the kitchen together. "You may not always agree, like each other, or even want to be around each other. But, she always honors him." The thought of mom stung my eyes as I wished I could call her up and tell her about the wedding. If only I could tell her about us and how great Mason's to me, after you look under his rap sheet of flaws. The thought of Liz ran through my mind. What would she say to me after a year of no communication.

After dwelling on the ideas and thoughts of calling my family, I decided to think about Mason. He took a leap of faith to ask me for his hand in marriage. Was I happy about the idea of him not being able to produce kids? No. I've enjoyed kids as they always touched my heart, even at home. It wasn't going to be a thing to drive me away from him. We finally established the part in each of our lives that had me sick to the core. We were married, and that I could rest on.

*****

Mason and I had to learn a different way of taking on assignments. We found ourselves in lovestruck paradise as we were next to each other. We had to create a boundary between us as we worked on assignments, saving our intimacy for when we returned. It had become difficult as now when I looked into his eyes, I only felt like pouncing at him every moment we could squeeze in.

The months passed as we learned how to handle being married. Mason and I began more partner assignments than group ones, letting the others take bigger shares. Mason did allow me to handle our money, I separated it and still sent an envelope to mom's ranch. Sneaking downloaded data to flash drives to the security box. Mason kept close to me which in return brought my timeline to collect information shorter.

I didn't tell him about where all the places I stashed our money, except the floorboard of the apartment. He left earlier than me at times which allowed me time to send off money, and then also put things in my security deposit box at the bank. Eventually, I added him as a person to access it, but never officially talked to him about it.

A year married, the assignments were picking up, even becoming internationally. It was something that became alarming to me as we traveled to other countries, being caught in a different country would be worse than the states. Mason assured me that their contacts were legitimate. He flew out a month with Scott and Henderson, leaving Kyle in charge of the states and work. James partnered with me a lot of times as Kyle preferred Preston as Ryan always preferred Jackson and Thomas.

Everyone was able to remain peaceful and no arguments broke out. Kyle even paid us after the arrival of the money. Detective Jones even appeared frequently. His appearance always sending chills down my spine as he was a cop, but he wasn't there to arrest us. Mason referred him as a cleaner for us. I didn't trust him like the rest of them, but after each visit, I caught Jackson being the one to walk him out.

Mason's return from the other country brought back sensation as I feared them being caught. The night of his return, I barely let him walk in as I made him turn around. We went home before he had a chance to debrief everyone. I couldn't allow the feeling to shake until I had him as mine. He didn't refuse as he was very passionate about me. He gave me the urge I longed for, and then afterwards left. I stayed home that night as I hadn't slept a good night's sleep since his departure.

When he returned home, he stripped and then held me close to him.

The next day, we went on a subway to scope out a city as a client had asked us to do so in one of his offices. While on the subway, I saw a lady in a blue dress with a belly that was expecting. I stared for a few moments, allowing my mind to process the very thing I dreamt when younger to have a family like mine. Liz and I joked about it when she turned eighteen. She always stated she would have six children. She wanted three girls and three boys. I laughed as I joked that I would have four girls of my own.

Mason shifted himself next to me as I looked away from the lady. "Are you good?" He whispered in my ear.

I nodded as I picked up my laptop. He interlocked his hand with mine as our subway came to a stop. We exited after the pregnant lady and then departed for the major business. Mason had already had badges made up for us as if we were employees. I was an IT Tech as he was a janitor. We went in at different times to create lack of suspicion. I went to their server room, locating the mainframe, and then hooking up my laptop. Doing a full sweep through each of the employees. Mason had positioned himself to empty trash cans on that floor. He kept an eye on the server room door and would contact me through an earpiece.

I synched to their server, and then inserted a chip into the mainframe, allowing myself access from my laptop. I moved out of the room and then headed back out of the building. Mason changed in a bathroom outside of the server room, and then met me at our meeting location. A restaurant that had seating on their glass covered roof. I opened my laptop up as he ordered us food.

"I saw the look again," he said as I was focused pulling up the company's server.

I glanced over my laptop at Mason, pausing for a brief moment, and then looked back down to locate the employee's information that had been marked for suspicion. "It was not a look," I said.

Mason reached his hand over and lightly grazed my left wrist with his watch. I stopped what I was doing and looked at him. He grabbed my hand as he moved himself closer to me. "Can we talk about it?" He asked.

I closed my laptop lid and moved closer to him. I put my head on his shoulder so that he knew that he had my full attention. "Mason," I started in a whispered voice. "I look because yes once upon my life, I wanted babies."

He moved his hand from my hand to around my shoulders as he leaned in and kissed my cheek. He nuzzled his head back to my ear as he held me closer. "I know you had dreams of a life that was much different than this one," he whispered. His hot breath sending cold chills down my spine as I kept my eyes down. "I chose to become sterile because I didn't want to bring a child into this life."

"You brought me in it," I whispered.

He pressed his forehead against my head as I felt him shake a little. "I chose my soulmate to become part of me. I'm not choosing to bring another soul into a life that I can easily take from them." He moved his other arm around to my leg. "Stacy, it's safe for you and I how we are now. It wouldn't be safe for us if a child was involved. A child could cause a lot of emotions that you and I can't factor in."

"You threw me into a death arena, and then you marry me," I whispered. "I chose you. I'm all for you, but you have to understand that I will look at others. I will look at the other ladies who have a part in their life that I will never experience."

He moved his lips and kissed me below my ear. "Just don't allow that emotion to overbear your judgement," he whispered. Cold shivers as he pulled away from me like it was a warning.

The waitress returned with our meal as we ate in silence. I processed his words as he decided to prevent himself from having another choice as a lifestyle. Contemplating the choices that he made to become a silencer to sterilization as a prevention from him having to force his own child into this world. I felt slightly angry at the selfishness that he made this choice. After we ate, we headed back to the warehouse. I worked on the employee's information, scanning his emails, work notes, and then accessing his personal work laptop. I downloaded the information that our client wanted, printed it off, and then turned it in.

Henderson collected the file. "Did you collect what our client needed?" He asked as he opened the file.

I nodded. "Everything is there," I said as I kept my eyes lowered.

The door opened behind me as I turned to see Mason entering. "Mason, get this to Nelson," Henderson said. "The sooner we give them the data, hopefully the faster the return on an assignment."

I glanced between both of them and then turned to leave the office. "She seems off today," Henderson commented as I started to close the door behind me.

Preston was by the weight area they added in. I walked over to him and sat down by the wall. "You need to talk?" He asked as he put down a weight to attach to the long bar.

I shook my head. "Just processing conversations, data," I paused. "How about you?"

He laughed, "I had a girl give me her number the other night."

I smiled as I looked down at the ground in front of me. "Well, are you going to call her?"

He shook his head. "I wasn't even trying to hook up with anyone," he laughed. "I was just having a drink at a bar."

I laughed as the thought of being a silencer risked so much in life. "How would you handle a girl in this life?" I asked.

He came over to the wall and sat down beside me. "I don't know," he said dripping in sweat. "I've not really thought about it."

I watched as Mason came out of the office across the room. Scott and Ryan approached him shortly as he was making his way over to me. He stopped and started talking with them. "Did you ever want a family?" I asked.

"At one point in my life," he said. "I dreamt of having a family. Since being here, I don't even know how to have a conversation with one. I know they're going to ask what type of work I'm doing," he paused. "How do you tell a person that you're a professional killer?"

We both broke out in laughter. "I would say that would be a conversation killer."

He shrugged. "I've talked with Scott about it. Did you know that he had a family?"

"No," I said glancing over towards their way.

Preston nodded. "He told me that he informed her a long time ago to never ask about his job, or else he wouldn't be able to keep her alive. He gave her money, advised her to tell people that he works in insurance. They have two kids together."

I looked back down at the ground. "Is he the only one with family?"

Preston nodded. "You do realize he's second in command here."

"Yeah," I said. "I've realized."

"You two thinking of having kids?" Preston asked.

I shook my head. "The complete opposite actually," I said as I glanced over at Preston. "Mason fixed that issue on his own before I was ever part of the picture."

"Ouch," Preston said as he rubbed the back of his neck. "What are you wanting?"

I sighed, and then looked away from him. I looked over at Mason who still was talking with Scott and Ryan. "I got what I wanted," I said admiring Mason being the leader.

"You seem like you want more," Preston said.

"We always want more," I said glancing over at him. "I wanted a job, given that. I wanted Mason to be mine. We are married. I want to be free of here, not happening. I want a family," I stopped as I breathed in, looking away from him.

He patted my shoulder. "At least you got a few things on your list crossed off," he said.

"Call the girl," I said as I got up from the floor. "Call her and have a drink with her. Just be creative when you talk about work. You could always say that you work in forensics, or a private investigator."

Preston got off the ground. "I rather just stay hidden a while longer," he said. "Turtle life seems to suit me."

I laughed as I shook my head. I walked away from him, heading to Mason. Mason finished up and then put his arm around me as we left. I glanced around the room, seeing Jackson and Thomas in their usual corner. Jackson had a look on his face as he watched us leave. His looks and stares always creeped me out as it caused terror to rise in my veins. I looked back at Mason, shaking the thoughts, as we left the warehouse.

"Does Jackson and Thomas ever show any," I paused to think of my wording. "Do they ever do anything concerning?"

Mason shook his head as he went to the kitchen. I pulled my coat off and hung it up and then placed my laptop bag on the hook. Mason grabbed items out of the fridge to cook supper. "You read too much into people," he commented. "Their work has been flawless. Ryan has even worked with detective Jones at the station to ensure that all tracks are covered."

"How does that work?" I asked. "The cleaners job."

Mason started turning on the stove as he moved around the kitchen. I walked over to assist him with the cooking. "They all are law enforcement," he said. "If not, then we more than likely would be caught. The cleaners help lure any possible evidence that a suicide or an accidental death looks anything else. They ensure evidence and notes are clear and concise with no questions."

"Has a silencer been caught before?" I asked while I worked with him at supper.

Mason had a look of concern crossed his face. "You have something that I need to worry about?"

"No," I said as I shifted to look him in the eyes. "I'm just curious of things."

He kissed my lips, and then we shifted our focus back to the stove. "We've had a few in the past get caught, carelessness," he said. "They spoke up about the job to the wrong person. Another got caught by not timing himself properly. And another got caught from not doing the legwork before the job."

"What happened once caught?" I asked.

"A lot of things go in factor," Mason said as he started to change the tone of his voice. "If convicted of the potential hit that was to be completed and faces time, well, we have people on the inside of prison to handle their way out."

"Their way out means a body bag," I said as I slowly stirred the soup that we have formed.

Mason wrapped his arm around my back. "You know we don't have to worry about that," he whispered into my ear. "You and I work beautifully together. We don't make mistakes."

I nodded. "Yeah," I said as I looked over at him, turning my head to meet his gaze. "We make a great team."

He smiled as he leaned in to kiss me. I moved my hands from the stove to him as he pushed me back into the island countertop. He picked me up and sat me on the countertop, kissing and pulling our clothes off. After another shared moment, we ate and then went to the bedroom. We were sitting up in bed, just finishing another round.

"I told you I will never get enough of you," he said as he had himself behind me kissing my shoulder. He clutched his hands between my breasts as I had my hands in his hands. He kissed my shoulder and then worked his way up to the side of my neck.

The sound of his phone vibrating on the nightstand pulled him away from my skin as he sighed. He let go of my hand and reached back to grab his phone. "Hello," he said into the phone.

"We got the assignment on that employee," Henderson said on the phone. I could hear as I laid my head back on Mason's chest. "Get it done tonight."

"We'll head out soon," Mason said, and then disconnected the line. He tossed his phone back on the nightstand as he exhaled loudly again. "Work calls," he said as he started to move back away from me. I jumped up and turned myself around, startled by the motion, Mason stopped and looked at me.

"We have some time," I said as I worked my way up to his lips.

He smiled, and then he clutched my hair as we leaned in and kissed. After we finished, we got up and dressed. I grabbed my coat and slipped it on and then pulled my laptop over my head. Mason slid into his leather jacket and then pushed me lightly into the back of the front door of the apartment. He kissed me intensely as I kissed back, allowing our tongues to explore each other's mouth.

"You make this difficult," I hissed as he moved to my neck.

"I'm just letting you know what to expect when we finish the assignment," he whispered as a slight moan roared from my throat. I started breathing hard as my body was craving him again. He kissed tenderly and then pulled away from me. "Let's go," he demanded as his tone went back to seriousness. I exhaled, and then pulled away from the door, letting him out first as I followed, locking up the apartment.

Two and a half years later… Mason and I continued to work small cases together. Occasionally, I would be caught looking at an expecting mom or a mom with children by her side. I had to allow myself to process the emotions and then get back to knowing the choice to be with Mason overruled a family. Preston finally decided to hook up with a girl, but the relationship failed after two months as she wanted a better commitment than someone always running when work called. Jackson, Thomas, and Ryan continued to work cases together as James, Kyle, Scott, and Preston worked on bigger clients' assignments. Everything appeared to have been running smoothly with no fighting or arguing.

Mason and I worked on a lot of assignments, not getting as many cool off days. This caused our intimacy to fade as we were both worn out after cases. Henderson continued to assign one after the other that became frustrating. I knew better than to question, but I wanted to speak up every day. Refraining myself as

Mason assured me things would calm down that it was just a phase.

I kept quiet about the envelope of money sent to mom's and security deposit box of money and flash drives. Staking out more cases prior to the assignments, I was able to download the data faster before the assignment. Since our work was now daily versus weekly, I had to spread out my drop days and mail off days.

I worked on hacking other devices from my cell phone, picking up the skill quickly. Mason didn't bother asking what I was doing, only asked whatever I did to keep it within the rules of the silencers. I developed the skill to work faster in collecting data for my own research. I had decided when I got married to Mason to help him find his way out when the time came. Determined to take down every member, including myself, if I could free him like the week of our honeymoon.

Our wedding and honeymoon were the first time in his life that he put this world in silence. He thoroughly enjoyed it with me. I picked up on it as we had so many adventures that week. It was something I decided that I would do as the only way I knew how to ever give him a suitable gift like the watch he gave me as a ring. We were getting closer to our four-year mark and still no rings. It looked bad on me just as much as him, but I didn't care, it wasn't about a diamond. We were working together, being together, and going through life together. We had learned to become one.

Chapter Fifteen

LYING IN BED, looking at each other after a shared moment. Mason propped up on one arm with the other stroking my face, and then my hair. "You know you're the most beautiful wife ever," he said as he leaned forward.

I moved closer to him and kissed him and then shifted myself to be in his arms as we lay there. "Mason," I said as I felt his embrace cover me like a warm fuzzy blanket. "If you could," I paused. "Think of something to dream about other than the life we have right now. What would you dream you could have?"

He exhaled a deep breath as he nuzzled his chin on the top of my head. "Back to the dream thing, again," he said, and then kissed the top of my head. "I supposed if we lived differently, I would still have you as my wife." He stopped as he shifted himself to be more comfortable. "I would have some fancy CEO job that bought us anything and everything."

"What kind of house would we have?" I asked as I moved my head back to look into his eyes.

He smiled as he looked down at me. "A glass house with five bedrooms, two offices, study room, men's den, and a living area." He stopped as we stared into each other's eyes. "A kitchen that is huge enough and equipped for you to make those recipes you stated your mom had stashed away."

I chuckled as I couldn't believe he remembered me telling him about them the week of our honeymoon. "Would you want any kids?" I asked as settled our laughs.

He took another deep breath. "Stacy, why get yourself worked up on dreams that isn't an option for us," he said as his eyes shifted to sorrow.

I looked away from him as I pulled him closer to me. "I just want to know if it was a dream that would you want kids?" I asked.

He kissed the top of my head. "If it's only for this dream purpose, then yes," he said. He shifted to lift both of us to a seating position, pulling the cover over my breasts. He brushed my hair behind my ear as we looked into each other's eyes. "You know that if there was a way I could make a better life for you without us ending up in body bags, then I would take you off and us live out this dream." I smiled as he kissed my shoulder. "I love you, Stacy Henderson," he said.

"I love you, Mason Henderson," I said as he shifted his head up to look me in the eyes. "And you're just enough for me." He smiled as he brushed his hand to the back of my head, gripping lightly as he kissed me passionately. It was the moment that I started to pray for a different lifestyle. I prayed for us to have a child as it was something I desperately wanted at that moment. He pushed me down as he got on top of me as I shifted my legs and started touching him. We had a shared moment that left me in tears after he fell asleep. I let him start snoring before I got up and pulled my robe around me. I walked over to the window, looked out at the busy chaotic street and cried.

My sobs woke him up as he came over to me and put his arms around me without saying a word. He lay his head on my shoulder, rocking with me as I held his arms, turning my head towards his chest, and cried. Stroking my hair, he kissed the back of my head. "You're getting yourself caught up in these dreams," he said. "It's dangerous when you start getting emotional."

His warning always raised fear in my veins as I knew he wasn't lying. I feared our lives each moment as one mistake could result in our last. I knew since being with him that my chances were running thin. I turned around to embrace him as he held me tightly. After several moments, we finally went to bed as he held me till I fell asleep.

It had been two weeks since that night he finally confessed a dream to me. We had done several jobs, not being able to rest much in between gathering information to closing an assignment. It had become solid work with lack of sleep. I woke up to smell Mason cooking, feeling slightly nauseas from it. *It's probably from working so much and eating snacks.* I got up from the bed, slipping my robe on as I walked into the kitchen. I walked over, putting my arms around Mason's back and kissing his back.

"Good morning, husband," I smiled.

"Good morning, my beautiful wife," he said. "Do you want some eggs?"

The nauseated feeling increased the longer I stayed near him. "No," I said letting go of his embrace as I walked over to the island countertop and picked up bread. "I will eat some toast."

"Suit yourself," he said as he slid the eggs from the frying pan to a plate. I placed two slices of bread in the toaster, smelling freshly brewed coffee. I got me a cup and poured it, allowing the scent to inhale in my nostrils. The smell of coffee was refreshing as I took a sip, enjoying its contents.

"Did you save any for me?" Mason asked as I turned around to pour more into my cup.

"Yes, some," I said as I walked over to the toaster. Pulling out the two slices out and placed them on a plate. We stood at the island countertop, eating our breakfast and drinking our cups of coffee.

The sound of his phone went off on the countertop. We both paused and glanced at it for a moment. He picked it up and answered it. "It's Henderson," he mouthed. "Okay. Yes, we will make our way over there now." He got off the phone and shoved a few more bites in his mouth. "We have to get to the warehouse now."

"New assignments," I said as I finished my cup of coffee. Mason finished his eggs and then walked away from his half drink cup of coffee. I picked it up and quickly drank the rest of it. We left the dishes on the counter as we went to the bedroom and got dressed.

He walked out of the bedroom. "Did you finish my cup?" He asked bringing the cup back into the bedroom.

I shrugged my shoulders. "You walked away from it," I said pulling my black flat bottom boots on.

"It didn't mean I was done with it," he grumbled as he walked off.

I chuckled as I fixed my hair and made my way out. We left the apartment. Mason kept on about him not having a full cup of coffee. I rolled my eyes as it was just one cup. We got to the warehouse and entered; all were gathered around the table that we sit at. Henderson at the head of the table. "About time the married ones arrive," he snorted. "Scott, Kyle, and Preston, you all will be traveling across the country. Ryan and James, you will take on Mason and Stacy's assignments for the next several weeks. Mason, Stacy, Jackson, and Thomas, you will be on this assignment." He tossed a folder over to Mason. "Our biggest payout yet with six million each."

We all looked around at each other as Mason opened the folder. "They want an entire department demolished?" Mason asked as he flipped through the pictures.

"We don't ask questions," Henderson said as he leaned forward on the table, pressing his knuckles into its surface. "You all will have a week to do the legwork, and then you must complete the assignment by end of the following week."

A strange feeling overwhelmed me as I held onto Mason's arm. Jackson and Thomas glanced but weren't looking in depth as Mason and I were at each person on the hit list. "Should we all focus on this one?" Mason asked.

"The client is hosting a party one evening that week for all of these guests," Henderson said. "You will take the building out after lacing each guest."

"You want us to gas them, and then burn the entire building?" Mason asked as his eyes shot up. I looked up at Mason, and then over at Henderson.

"It's a high paying job, Mason," Henderson said. "Something you ought to be thankful that even came across our desk."

Mason put the folder down. "It's very risky," he said as he shifted his weight. I pulled away from him as I saw the tension rising. "These people may have families with them. We've never taken out an entire building of the max. Are you sure your intel is right?"

"You've been working too many small jobs lately. Are you getting soft on me?" Henderson asked.

Mason put his hands on the table as we all watched with their expressions. He had anger flooding his face with redness. I slipped my hand over his hand. "I can start working on getting us the best angle to proceed," I said attempting to ease the built tension. "I can also hack into their security network to maybe where we can get it to be less overwhelming than it seems."

Mason looked down his arm at me. Henderson cleared his throat. "Then it's settled. Everyone needs to get heading out besides you four. Stacy get to work immediately on that hack," Henderson said, and then pulled away from the table. He turned around and walked off.

The others scattered. Mason shook his head as he looked back at the huge folder. I stroked his arm to try and calm him. Glancing over at Jackson and Thomas, they had been looking across the table. I glanced to see them staring at Ryan. Ryan tipped his head and then got up from the table. The reaction between them sent chills down my spine. Jackson and Thomas had walked in the opposite direction away from us.

Mason turned to me and put his hands on my shoulders. "Let me know what you find out," he said as he lightly squeezed my shoulders. He still looked angry as he walked away, heading towards Henderson's office. I glanced around in Ryan's direction, who was getting things from the supply room. I turned to look over at Jackson and Thomas who were in the corner discussing something. The feeling felt strange as I shook it off.

I grabbed the folder and went to the room with the lockers. I sat up my computer, pulling up the company's site and location. Working my fingers to find a tower closest to the company's building and start pulling data. I got through their firewalls and started working on the layout of the building. Downloading the company's emails mainframe, pulling data from it that seemed prominent to the case.

Preston walked into the room, closing the door behind him. "I'm about to head out," he said.

I got up from the chair, letting my laptop download files. I shook Preston's hand as he pulled me in for a hug. "Stacy, be careful. I don't feel like something's right about all of this," he whispered. "It's too big of a payout."

"You don't get caught across seas," I said pulling away from him. "While you're out there, get some pointers from Scott on ladies."

Preston smiled. "See you when we get back."

I waved him bye as I sat back down at my laptop. Taking a deep breath as I now had confirmation that my feeling wasn't just me. Preston felt anxious over this entire ordeal like me. I shook off the conversation and continued working.

I worked from my laptop for seven days, finally getting an angle. Mason, Jackson, Thomas, and I gathered by the big table. I had floor plans printed out, and different items to show where the party would be, and where we can set the gas to be released. I also stated how we can blend into the crowd, pack gas masks, and then complete the mission of burning it to the ground, causing an electrical fire with repeat failed maintenance papers to the county.

"This will work," Jackson said pressing his hand down on the table. "Great work, princess," he said. *Princess* sent cold chills as I moved over to Mason. Mason had his arms crossed, hand on chin and processing the plan.

"I agree it works," he said looking down at me. I looked at Jackson who had a grin on his face. "Let's head out tomorrow," Mason said. "The party is in five days. We don't need any distractions."

"Speak for the two of you," Jackson said as he leaned back. "We don't have any distractions."

"We shall see you both tomorrow," Mason said as he glanced at them.

Jackson took a step back, patting Thomas on the chest. They both turned and walked away. The way they acted sent chills as Mason walked around the table, looking over the plan. "How do you plan to reach their security cameras?" He asked.

I cleared my throat, shaking off the unsteadiness feeling I had from Jackson and Thomas. "I plan to hack their server and shut down their cameras before the gas is released," I said looking down at the floorplan. "Mason," I paused as he walked around to me. He put his hand on my shoulder, adjusting to pull my hair off the opposite shoulder. "I have an uneasy feeling about this assignment."

He kissed my shoulder. "You're tired. You've nonstop worked on these floor plans and processes for seven days. Any other details you found from their emails?"

I turned around to face him. "Mason, I have an uneasy feeling about our two partners," I said.

"You're tired, Stacy," he said as he wrapped his arms around me.

I looked away and embraced him as he put his head on top of mine. "Let's get home, spend a night together," he said, and then kissed the top of my hair. "You and I need a night. We haven't been able to dive under the covers in a few weeks."

I sighed, he wasn't wrong. We'd been busy between jobs and lack of sleep that had been three weeks since our last intimate night. I nodded. "You're probably right," I said. "Let's go enjoy our evening."

He pulled me to his side as we walked out. We got home and immediately started kissing each other, running into every piece of furniture on our way to the bedroom as we left a trail of clothing that was stripped from our bodies. His kisses felt more intense, and I was in the moment. Gripped sheets, moaned, and we had kissed for several hours. We finally finished having our shared intense moments and lay there, unable to sleep as he rubbed my back.

"Anxious?" He asked as he kissed below my neck on my back.

I turned over to face him. "Mason," I said still feeling uneasy. "I just don't feel like something's right with this one."

"Well," he said as he moved closer to me. "We were supposed to get some sleep, and we didn't get any." We both broke out laughing as I moved over on top of him. He held onto my hips as I moved on top of him. He and I shared another moment, leaving us both out of breath as the alarm went off. I fell on him, kissing his neck. "We have to go," he said brushing his hands through my hair.

Tears prickling as I didn't want to leave. My body had so many emotions rolling through them, I couldn't hold back the tears. Mason kissed me as I grabbed his wrists. "You have to stop crying," he said nervously. "We have to go."

I nodded. I pulled myself off of him and went to the bathroom, closing the door. I sat down on the toilet and cried. It felt so strange for me to get emotional over us not able to stay here. The apartment felt secure, cozy, and peaceful. When we left the apartment, it felt like we were on edge with every step away from it. I got in shower and pulled myself together.

Mason joined me in the shower, kissing me again. "Stop acting like it's our last time," he said as we were under the water together. He picked me up and cornered me. "I told you that we are careful, we will be fine."

"I trust us," I said with my arms around his neck. "I don't trust them."

Mason shook his head. "As long as I'm there, nothing will happen between any of us. They know who's lead here."

I nodded and pulled myself to him, kissing him. He pressed me tightly in the corner as we had a shared moment. A moan slipped out, and then we finished. He put me down as he put his hand on the back of my neck. "I love you, Mrs. Henderson," he said as we stared into each other's eyes.

"I love you, Mr. Henderson," I said. We kissed, finished showering, and then got dressed. I wore my white blouse, blue jeans, and sneakers. I put his watch on my left wrist, fastened my gold cross necklace around my neck, and parted my hair leaving it flowing down my shoulders. Mason wore a regular shirt, jeans, sneakers, and his favorite black leather jacket.

We locked up the apartment, putting the key in my laptop bag, and headed to meet up with Jackson and Thomas. We all met before heading in the direction of the subway. Mason wanted to split up, but Jackson suggested we take a longer route that went behind alleys. I wasn't for the plan, but Mason agreed. Mason and I led as they walked behind us. I didn't hold Mason's hand as we made our way the long route to the subway. We weren't far from our apartment, the route actually was less than two minutes as we rounded another corner.

A noise shuffled from behind us. We both went to look behind us. Jackson was behind Mason who wrapped his arm around Mason's neck. Before I could react, Thomas had an arm around my neck, a pinching pain pierced my neck. Darkness flooded my sight as I felt my body go limp.

I heard a slapping sound, and then a groan from Mason. My head pounding as I was coming too. I opened my eyes to see Jackson standing in front of Mason. He hit him again, and then Mason's face fell to the side with a groan. Mason's hands in metal handcuffs behind him, with both ankles cuffed to a chair. I rolled over to my side as I tried to get up.

I had my hands tied behind my back. "Jackson, she's awake," Thomas said as he appeared in my sight behind Mason.

Jackson stopped hitting Mason as he came over to me. He pulled me by my hair to my knees in front of Mason. A scream slipped through my mouth. He moved his hand back and slapped me. I fell slightly over to my right side as the burn stroked my left facial cheek. "It's about time you woke up," Jackson snorted.

I got back up as I looked at Mason. His eyes wide at the sight of me. Jackson got in front of Mason, punching him in his gut. Mason jerked forward in pain as his breath was knocked out of him. "No," I screamed as I tried to get to my feet. Jackson turned around and slapped me again. I fell over as I started crying.

A pain struck through me as our lives being taken by surprise. Jackson had full control of this environment as he had us both restrained. Thomas looked only to be following Jackson's commands, fear of us getting free. The anxious sensation that haunted me since being paired with them as partners rushed through my veins. I felt nauseas as I didn't know how to fight when we were drugged, restrained, and unable to find a factor out of this situation. Tears flooded my face as I sobbed in agony.

Jackson pulled me back to my knees, grabbing my hair and pulling my head up. "Look, Mason," he yelled as Mason had his head down. "Look at her!"

Mason looked up as his face full of sweat and blood, bruises on his eyes. His shirt covered in blood from the blows of Jackson. "Why?" I asked as tears rolled down my cheeks. "Why are you doing this to us?"

Jackson gripped my hair tighter as he looked at Mason. I glanced around and noticed we were inside our apartment. *They led us straight to a path beside our apartment.* I tried to look away as Jackson gripped my hair tighter. "Mason, boss, tell us where to find the clients contact?" Jackson yelled. "Because if you don't, then I will beat every inch of her until she's dead."

Mason spit to the side. Thomas had his hands by his side, gripping and closing them as he was nervous. I looked at him as if he had a face of fear written over it. "Mason," Jackson yelled. "Give us the information!"

"I don't have it," Mason said.

Jackson let go of my hair and got in his face. "I hope you enjoy this," Jackson said. He turned around and faced me, taking his right foot up, and plunging it into my chest. I fell backwards, hitting my head on the chair by our window. He came over to me and picked me up by my blouse. He tossed me over towards Mason. Mason started screaming as I was thrown around the room. A scream slipped through my teeth.

Jackson grabbed my hair, pulled me to my feet and walked me over to where Mason sat. Mason was trying to jerk his hands or legs free.

Jackson shoved me back to my knees in front of Mason. He gripped my hair tightly as Mason and I exchanged looks. Sweat pouring off his face as he tried to free his hands from behind him.

"Give us all the clients' information now," Jackson demanded.

"Just calm down," Mason yelled. "I don't have their contacts."

Jackson tilted his head as he took an opposite hand and punched me in the stomach below my rib. I gasped as the breath was knocked out of me, falling back on my hands, hitting my head on the floor. Jackson turned me over, cutting the rope off my hands.

"Jackson, leave her alone," Mason yelled as he tried to free his hands.

I looked up as Jackson flipped me back on my back. He straddled me as he pulled both hands above my head. "Hand me the liquor bottle," he demanded towards Thomas.

I tried to wiggle and fight him off. He pressed my hands down with one hand. "Pour it in her mouth," Jackson demanded as he moved his other hand to open my mouth. I tried to bite him. He slapped me and gripped my chin. Thomas hesitantly opened the bottle.

"Leave her alone!" Mason yelled as I heard the chair he was in shaking as he was trying to get free. Thomas started pouring the bottle onto my face. Gagging as Jackson gripped tighter, forcing my head back onto the floor. Thomas poured the entire bottle of alcohol with me gagging, choking, and then Jackson let my chin go.

He got up as I rolled to my side, coughing. "Give us the information," Jackson demanded to Mason.

Mason looked at him, and then down at the floor at me. "Jackson, I swear, when I get free I will kill you with my bare hands," Mason yelled as he jerked his body, trying to get free.

I looked up at Jackson as he shrugged his shoulder. "I've waited a long time to do this," he said. Jackson lifted his leg back and kicked me hard above my belly button. Every ounce of oxygen left my body as I couldn't breathe. A few seconds passed as I gasped for air. He rolled me over to my back and ripped my shirt off.

"Jackson, don't you fucking dare," Mason yelled.

Jackson got up and walked over to slap Mason. Catching my breath as he walked back over to me. He grabbed my ankles and pulled me across the hardwood floor. I tried to kick away. He swung my legs down as he quickly straddled me. My bra was exposed as I felt him grab my neck. I looked at him as I reached to grab his neck. "Mason, give us the information," Jackson yelled.

"Jackson, this wasn't part of the plan," Thomas sounded nervously.

"Shut up," Jackson yelled as he pressed firmly on my throat. "I told you, Mason. You don't give us answers and I will bruise every inch of her." Jackson said rubbing his other hand down my chest. A hard lump form in my throat. My body broke out in sweat as I started to shiver at his touch.

Mason fought to get out of the chair as Jackson glanced over at him. I glanced with my eyes as I feared for my life. Mason looked me in the eyes, fear striking both of us. We had been so careful till now. Jackson pulled me up to a seating position and got his lips to my ear. "I hope you enjoy every inch of me inside you," he whispered. "Whore!" He threw my head back into the floor.

My vision pulsated as pain radiated through me as Jackson did what he wanted since day one of meeting me. He had jerked every piece of clothing off of me, exposing my body. Mason yelled to a point Thomas gave him another shot in the neck. After Jackson had finished, I partially blacked out. He picked me up and threw me over his body, carrying me through the apartment, and then swung me on the bed.

I blacked out for a few minutes and felt something flung over top of me, weighing on me. I opened my eyes, seeing they had Mason half undressed over me. I tried to find energy but felt so weak and helpless. I blacked out again.

I heard some whispering as I opened my eyes again, my vision blurred. I came to see Jackson and a man exchanging an envelope. I tilted my head to focus on my vision. It cleared enough to see Detective Jones take the envelope and shake hands. "How badly beaten is she?" He asked.

"She'll be lucky if she makes it to the hospital," Jackson said. "We're going to give her another dose."

"Good," Detective Jones said. "You don't want her waking up after an incident such as this one."

"We'll call it in an hour or so," Jackson said. "By then, she should be gone. Mason won't be coming to for several hours."

"You do understand what this means?" Detective Jones asked. "You can't go back to Henderson."

Jackson nodded. "I have no intentions of working under them again. I plan to be the next leader."

"I hope you've been trained well," Detective Jones said, and then his phone rang. I felt my head fall back as I blacked out.

I woke up as I felt Mason moving off my body. "Get him in handcuffs," a man yelled.

"Stacy," Mason slurred. "Stacy!"

I opened my eyes as so many people were in the room. I was exposed as a woman paramedic draped a white sheet over me. "Honey, we're here to help you," she said as another person came to put something underneath me. "Get the stretcher," the lady yelled.

My vision blurred out, and then back in as they loaded me on the stretcher, putting an oxygen mask on me, attaching straps down my body. "Stacy!" Mason yelled.

"Get out of our way," the female paramedic yelled.

The sound of rustling rushed around me, so many people in every direction. Detective Jones came into my sight, looking down at me. "Let the hospital know when she's alert, I need a statement," he shouted. I looked around to see Mason, but never saw him. They got me out of the apartment building and turned me to load up on the ambulance. I looked as I saw four policeman bringing Mason out of the building. Mason wasn't wearing a shirt, only his jeans and sneakers. I went to move my arm but couldn't get it up.

"Mason," I said through the oxygen mask.

He looked over in my direction. Our eyes met but it wasn't like the other times. We were staring as he was being arrested. Pain in my stomach as it felt like a piercing pain. A police officer shoved him forward towards a car. Mason looked back over at me as we stared. The ambulance doors closed, and I couldn't see him anymore. Pain rushing through me as I blacked out again.

Chapter Sixteen

*Beep...Beep...Beep... PSSST...PSSST...*An unusual scent as something blew in my nose, laying on my face. I moved my hand to my face, touching a tube. A slight pain as I heard noises all around. A beeping noise from a monitor to my left. The sound of air was hissing as slight pressure was going into my nose. I blinked open my eyes as I looked around seeing myself in a bed slightly elevated to see a television that was cut off in my room attached to the wall in front of my bed. Looking to my left seeing huge windows with curtains. Looking to my right seeing a couple of windows with blinds closed. A noise of someone coming over an intercom echoed outside of my closed-door room. I pulled the oxygen cord out of my nose and shoved it off to the side. Next, I tugged at the blood pressure cuff, the sound of Velcro separating roared through the room with the beeping and hissing noise. I pulled the heart rate monitor off my finger. I moved myself to the side of the bed, feeling unsteady as I tried to get up.

I sat there for a few seconds. The door creaked open, and I shot my head up. A nurse in blue scrubs rushed over to me. "Mrs. Henderson, you need to stay in bed," she said as she grabbed my arm.

I shoved her off of me, releasing a scream. "Where is he," I yelled. "Where's my husband?" She kept her hands out but away from me a few inches.

"He was arrested," she said calmly.

I shook my head as my mind felt foggy. I saw the IV line in my left arm and started to tug at it. "No," she said grabbing it. "Please let me call the doctor."

"I have to leave now," I yelled.

"You need to stay put," she said. "We have to let the police know your awake."

I shoved her off of me. "What's going on here?" Another female walked into the room, I looked over at her as she was blonde with her hair pinned back wearing green scrubs and a white coat. "She's awake," the female doctor said as she put her hand with a tablet in it down. She closed the door behind her as she walked over to us. "Do you know where you're at?" She asked calmly.

"A hospital," I said through gritted teeth as I swiped my hair back off my face.

"Do you know your name?" She asked, keeping her hand out. The nurse stayed a few inches away as they both stared at me.

"Yes," I said. "How long have I been here?"

They glanced at each other and looked back at me. "You've been in a coma for four weeks," she said.

"Where's my husband?" I asked as I looked at the doctor with blonde hair.

"He's been arrested. He does have a trial today at eleven," she said putting her hand down.

"What time is it now?" I asked looking at both of them.

She looked down at her watch, "nine o'clock."

"I need to get out of here," I said putting my feet that were covered in socks on the ground. I stood up as I felt sluggish and wobbly.

"Woah, steady," the nurse said as she grabbed my arm. I jerked it away from her.

"Stop touching me," I said as feeling better each second.

"You've been asleep, your body may need to adjust," the doctor said.

I rolled my eyes as I waved my hand at her to shew her away. "Get this IV out of my arm," I snapped.

"We were told by Detective Jones to contact him as soon-."

"You don't call him," I interrupted. "I need to get out of here." The nurse reached for my arm again. I shoved her back.

The doctor took a deep breath. "I'm so sorry to do this," she said as I looked over at her. She glanced at her nurse. I looked back as the nurse had a needle in her hand and started to come after me. Reacting immediately, I reached out and grabbed her wrist, twisting it as I turned her around in front of me. Grabbing her throat as I took the needle with my other arm, jabbing it into her neck. She fell to the floor. I looked at the doctor who had sat the tablet down on the bed, with her other hand in her coat pocket.

"You don't know me," I said as she came after me. Grabbing her wrist up with one hand, grabbing her throat with the other as I walked forward, her stumbling backwards into the wall. The IV ripping out of my arm. I slid my forearm against her neck as I twisted her wrist into dropping the needle. "But you won't forget me after this," I snapped as I pressed tighter against her throat.

"You're pregnant," she hissed.

I loosened my arm as she slid down the wall. "I can't be pregnant," I said reaching down to grab the syringe she dropped.

"I had them run labs again today as I do so every few days for coma patients," she gasped.

I shook my head as I stood over her. She held her throat, coughing as she tried catching her breath. "You really screwed up trying to sedate me," I said as I plunged the syringe in her arm. She looked up at me as she inhaled a deep breath. I pushed the contents into her body. She fell over immediately. I looked around at both of them now lying on the ground.

I got the nurse first, dragging her across the room to the bathroom, leaving her on the ground. Every muscle ached with every ounce of energy draining, pushing through it all. I got back out and looked at the doctor, her hair color similar to mine. I knew that I wouldn't be able to walk out of this place without some type of disguise. I quickly stripped the doctor and then threw the gown they had me in over her as I dressed quickly in her scrubs. I pulled her over to bed, struggling with her weight and the height, pulling her up into it. I used the bed straps and restrained her as I tucked her in. Placing the oxygen mask over her nose, hooked up the blood pressure cuff and heartrate monitor. I pulled the IV machine over and slid the IV under the blanket next to her arm. I saw the blood droplets on the floor, quickly cleaning it and tossing it away.

I got the tablet off the bed, feeling in the doctor's pocket, finding her cellphone. I reset the phone, downloaded an app, and started to do a transfer of data from the tablet to my new phone. I downloaded all my information they had on me from the day of arrival to today.

Knock. Knock. I glanced over my shoulder as I pinned my hair up like hers was. "Hey, Doctor Maddy, room 2014 is needing you," a male nurse said.

"Just a minute," I said as the mainframe hospital network cleared my personal data. He closed the door behind him. I took a moment and looked around, spotting a bag over by the window. Going over to it, I found my gold cross necklace and black leather watch. I put them on and threw the bag away. Slowly exiting the room, I slid the phone in my white jacket and closed the door behind me as a Code Blue paged over the intercom. All the staff available rushed to that room. Sliding the tablet on the counter and rushed for the stairs. Making my way down a few flights, looking in each floor, I saw a few people in scrubs coming out of one room, seeing lockers. I quickly opened the door and rushed to grab the door that led to the locker room right before it latched.

I went inside, not seeing or hearing anyone as I started checking lockers. Locating a locker open, it had jeans, purple shirt, and boots with heels. I took off my doctor's coat, scrubs, and then changed quickly. I grabbed the phone I've confiscated, and left the locker room, tossing the doctor's scrubs in a waste bin on my way out. I went down the flight of stairs and left the hospital. Searching the phone maps, local courthouse, and then got in a cab. I got out a block before the courthouse, taking off running. I pulled my hair down as I came up to a small strip with different stores. I snatched a brown hat and black shades off one of the stands and kept going to the courthouse.

Entering the courthouse, asked for the room Mr. Henderson's trial was in. I was directed to the courtroom, and then went in, taking my seat at the back. I kept my hat and shades on as I slipped behind a crowd of people. I watched as they called Henderson versus New York State. I felt my heart race as the anxiety swept through me. I rubbed my hands on my legs as they began to sweat, like the walls were coming in on me, breathing hard.

The door to the courtrooms left opened up, a guard, and then him. I saw him in a blueish gray jumpsuit in metal handcuffs come out. He looked as if he hadn't shaved in weeks, and then his hair was longer. I inched forward in my seat as he had red eyes as he stood beside a man facing the judge. I felt nauseas as I watched. Detective Jones sat with the state, bringing up that I haven't woken yet. A sense of relief rolled through me as I realized the hospital hadn't figured out that I had escaped. After a few moments, the judge proceeded to put him in prison until his next trial hearing. My air being sucked out of me as I looked down at the ground.

Exiting with the crowd synching myself in between to be blended. I went down to the area of the guards and asked where he would be sent to. They advised me of his transportation date and should be able to have visitors in a few days. I left the courthouse and made my way to the prison that he should be transferred too.

I camped out near the prison, waiting for him off in the streets, snatching food from food marts. I kept a low profile, changing clothes, redoing my hair, and then going to the prison. A few days had passed since his hearing. I walked in and signed in under my name. They led me to a room with other visitors. We were assigned numbers and sat down at those stations. I watched as they brought him in. He glared at the prison guards, and then turned, seeing me at the station. He ran over immediately as a glass was between us. I picked up the phone on the wall as he did the same.

"Stacy," he said covering the phone with his hand. "It's not safe for you to be here."

"Mason," I cried. "I had to see you were okay."

Mason put his head down, swiping his other hand through his hair. "Hey," I said putting my hand on the glass. "Don't look away. I'm here," I said with tears streaming. He looked up at me as his eyes were filled with water. "Mason, I'm going to get you out of here."

"You go straight to Henderson," he demanded. "Go tell them what happened. I haven't been able to reach anyone as protocol." I looked away as I knew what he meant by protocol. I knew he referred to the silencer's rules. "Stacy, I'm so sorry!"

"No," I said looking back up into his eyes. "We're not going to do that." I stopped as I pressed my hand on the window. He put his against the glass on his side where mine was at. "You see, I'm here. I'm alive."

"They told me you more than likely wouldn't make it," he cried.

"I made it," I said. "I'm here now. I'm going to get you out of this mess."

He shook his head. "You know what happens when we get in here."

I shook my head. "No, Mason," I cried. "You can't give up now. You have to promise me you're going to stay alive. I will get you out of here if it's the last thing I do."

"I can't protect you," he said looking at the watch on my left hand.

I nodded. "I need you to protect yourself for the time being," I said. "I will get a handle of things out here."

"Stacy, I love you," he said as our eyes stared. I wanted to embrace him as he stood up. "I love you forever." He pressed his head against the window.

"I love you, Mason," I said. "Stay alive for me."

He nodded. I hung the phone up and then left the room. I got out of the prison and vomited in their trash can outside of the door. Holding back tears as I wiped my mouth. I pulled out the phone I had confiscated, pulling up my apartment address. I made my way back in a cab that I ditched a few blocks away. My apartment room door was cordoned off with tape, I wiggled the knob, it was locked.

"Stacy." I turned around seeing the landlord come up the hallway. "You're alive," Pete said. He was an older man that walked with back hunched over.

"I need inside," I said.

"The police don't want anyone in there," he said looking at me, and then at the door. "I guess it won't hurt since you were found there." He reached into his pocket, pulling out a ring of keys, and then putting one in my door. He unlocked it and walked away.

I took a moment as the memories flooded through me. Opening the door, going inside and closing the door behind me. I looked around at the apartment that left scars rather than security. My safe place from the work we done corrupted in the hands of Jackson.

I looked around, seeing that night flood through my sight. I saw the alcohol dried on the floor where they drowned me in liquor. Holding my stomach as I walked to the bedroom, seeing the bed bloody and messed up from that evening. Running to the bathroom, throwing up in the toilet, I sat down on the floor. Looking over everything as I remembered just hours before us in this bathroom making marked moments of marriage. I flushed the toilet, and then got up, going to the bedroom.

I went to the closet, finding my laptop bag, looking inside, seeing the computer busted. Throwing it to the ground, screaming in anger and frustration. I looked around, found my floorboard cut out, and then opened it. My security box keys and money. I pulled those out, shoving them in my olive-green laptop bag with the busted laptop. I put the floorboard back together.

I didn't make my way back to the warehouse immediately until I purchased a decent meal, ten pregnancy tests, and then a new laptop. Resting at a cheaper hotel on the far side away from the apartment, and warehouse. I ate feeling better, and I took pregnancy tests after tests. Crying with each positive test as I knew they weren't lying. Angry that this child that was inside of me wasn't Mason's. I curled up on the floor as I had one more test to confirm like the other nine.

Two weeks since Mason's trial. I transferred the data from my old laptop of the last job to my new laptop, sweeping its mainframe. Grabbing up everything, heading out, paying for a cab to head towards the warehouse. Dropped off a few blocks inside the city to not cause attention to myself if dropped off at an abandoned warehouse. I walked up to the door as the memory of my first time standing in front of this door with Mason appeared. The attack dogs were more than likely there, my mouth suddenly dry. I put my hand on the doorknob. The door opened, as I jerked back.

Scott came outside with his back of his head towards me, and then he turned. He jerked back as he looked at me. "Stacy," he said in shock.

"I need to talk with Henderson," I said looking down.

Scott shifted himself, and then finally motioned with his hand. He walked me in as I glanced to my left, seeing Preston, Kyle, James, and Ryan who locked eyes with mine. Scott led me to Henderson's office. I looked back at Scott who opened the office door for me. Inside, seeing Henderson smoking a cigar, sitting at his desk. His eyes shot up to mine and he stood up. Scott closed the door behind us.

"It's about time you showed your face," Henderson snapped.

I sat down immediately as the nerves were rushing through me. "Mason was arrested," I said lowly.

Henderson coughed, shoving his cigar in the ashtray. "Mason was arrested. You were in the hospital. Jackson and Thomas are no where to be found. What the hell happened?"

"Have you heard from Jackson or Thomas since we departed for the assignment?" I asked as I locked eyes with Henderson.

He shook his head. "Not a word from anyone," he said. "Why the hell is Mason in prison?"

I cleared my throat, holding back tears. "Jackson and Thomas attacked us."

"You better not cry," he demanded. "What do you mean?"

"They asked us to go a different route to the subway to not draw attention," I said. I took a deep breath. "The next thing I knew, we had arms around our necks with syringes being plunged into us. I woke up on the floor of our apartment. Jackson kept hitting Mason, asking him for your clients' information. He wanted all of them."

Henderson leaned forward as he listened. "They beat us both," I said. "Detective Jones was given some money, so he's in on it to."

"You think I'm just going to believe you," Henderson snorted. "You're a woman. You're too emotional. I knew when Mason brought you here it was a mistake. Now you have him locked up and you're here with a story that doesn't add up."

"I'm speaking the truth," I said as I threw my hands down on my lap. Looking down at the black leather strap watch Mason gave me, taking a deep breath. "Look, if you haven't heard from Jackson or Thomas in six weeks it's because they turned on you."

"Where have you been?" Scott asked. "We got intel that you escaped after waking up two weeks ago."

I put my head down, as I held back tears. "I visited Mason and went back to the apartment. I collected money I had stashed there and my laptop. They had it crushed, so I had bought a new one to transfer the data."

"What is the importance of that data?" Henderson asked. "You all acted poorly in ensuring this was under any radar."

I looked up, switching between both Henderson and Scott. "It was the night that changed everything for me. I transferred that data because I'm going to find the reason behind them turning on us."

"You plan on assisting us here?" Scott asked.

I nodded. "However," I paused. "I have to handle something first."

Henderson snorted as he chuckled. "You have to handle something first. What's more important than us finding them?"

"Nothing is more important than finding them and getting Mason out of prison," I said. "However, I found out that I'm pregnant." I looked down as I fumbled my fingers in my lap, embarrassment swept over me as the blood rushed to my cheeks.

"Mason can't have kids," Henderson said. I looked up at him as he sat back in his chair with a look disgust running across his face.

"What else happened that night Jackson and Thomas attacked you both?" Scott asked as he took a step forward.

I glanced over at him and looked down at the ground. "Stacy," Henderson said. "If there was something else that happened, we need to know right now."

I wiped my eyes as I moved my hands through my hair and then looked up at both of them. "Jackson told Mason he was going to beat every inch of my body," I said as the hair rose up all over my body. Wiping my face as cold chills shivered down my spine, goosebumps surfaced.

"What happened?" Henderson demanded.

My lip quivered as I fought tears back, putting my hand over my mouth. I looked away from the both of them. "Jackson raped me in front of Mason," I sobbed throwing my head down between my legs into my hands as the memories rushed through me.

Henderson slammed his hands down on the desk in anger. Several moments passed as I couldn't stop the tears, neither of them touched me. They allowed me to have my minutes crying. After I cried all that I could, I sat back up as Henderson handed me a handkerchief. I took a deep breath, wiping my face that was now wet and swollen. "Scott put everyone on this right now. Locate them," Henderson said. "If they move an inch, locate them and bring them back here."

"Yes sir," Scott said as he walked over to the door. He stopped before opening it and turned around. "Stacy, I truly am sorry for the both of you." He turned around, grabbing the doorknob, and then left the room.

"I have contacts that can assist you in-."

I put my hand up. "Henderson," I said. "My sister is a doctor. With your permission, I would like to visit her and get this taken care of by someone I personally know."

He nodded. "Do you want someone to take you?" He asked.

"I just want to be dropped off at the bus station," I said looking down at my laptop bag. "I will find my way from there. In the meantime, I need you to trust that I will be back and will assist in getting Mason free."

"His only battle now is ensuring he stays alert," Henderson said. "If any of our contacts get word that he's in there, they know what to do to ensure he never leaves"

I shook my head as I put my hand over my mouth. "Please," I begged. "Help me keep him alive."

Henderson nodded. "I'll do my best, but Mason knows what to expect," he said as cold chills rolled down my spine.

I got up from the chair. "Can Preston drive me to the bus stop?"

He nodded. "I will expect you back in a couple of weeks," he said coldly. We locked eyes for a moment, and then I turned around and exited his office. I took a breath as I looked over seeing Scott informing the others of the situation.

I walked over to them as they all looked down and away from me. "Scott, can Preston drive me?" I asked.

Scott looked at me, and then at Preston. "Get back as soon as possible," he said patting Preston on the shoulder. Preston walked over to me as we walked to the garage. We got in the car, and then he backed out, driving me to the bus stop.

"What happened?" Preston asked. "We're only being told to do a cold hunt for Jackson and Thomas."

"I don't want to talk about it," I said looking out the passenger window. "I just need you to help me with something."

"You know I will do anything to help you," he said as we both glanced at each other.

"Even if it breaks silencers' rules?" I asked.

He nodded. "I feel if Mason were here, he wouldn't object and probably would take a leap in front of bullets for both of us."

"I need you to tail Ryan," I said. "I think he's part of their plan. I think he's going to be a mole inside of this operation."

"You want me to tail the one who tried to kill both of us," he said as his voice dropped.

"Preston," I said looking over at him. "Just do it with no questions."

He sighed as he looked back on the road. "I think I would have rather took my chances with the attack dogs."

I rolled my eyes as I looked out the passenger window, placing my hand on my bag that covered my stomach. I wasn't sure what I was going to say to Liz in asking her for the biggest favor of my life after years of not seeing her. I put my hand to my mouth, propping my elbow on the windowsill as I bit my nails. I started to cry, wiping my eyes as quickly as they fell. Preston handed me a box of tissues from the backseat.

"I have lots of allergies," he commented.

I laughed and cried as I blew my nose. "Thank you," I said as I looked over at him. Our eyes met and a look of sorrow rushed over his face. He nodded and looked back at the road. We got to the bus station where he got out, opening the door for me, and then walking me inside. He purchased my ticket and then walked me over to where they loaded the buses.

"Stacy," he said as he fumbled with his hands.

I looked at him as I glanced to see others loading. "Preston, I have to go," I said starting to turn away from him. He grabbed my arm and pulled me to him, giving me a hug.

"If you were my little sister," he said as he embraced me. I accepted the embrace as I felt more tears prickling at my eyes. His action of comfort took away some pain that ached inside of me. "I would hug you knowing whatever you went through was bad."

"Thank you," I said, and then pulled away from him. I turned not looking back as I rushed over to my bus, loading it and took a seat near the back. He stood and waited for my bus to leave. I looked back down at the laptop bag that now holds so much weight. I kept my eyes on it as we pulled away from the station.

I did a quick search to find my sister had married to Eric Warren. I smiled as I remembered when I met him at Thanksgiving years ago. I looked up where she was practicing medicine. She was an OBGYN, a female gynecologist that handled female reproduction systems. I closed my laptop, putting it back in its bag as I rested my head back. The thoughts of the events and how I left going here last time rushed over me. Mason had given the option to choose here. Now, years later I was returning to do what we had been raised not to do. We had been taught that abortions are not part of God's plan for our lives. I looked up at the ceiling, wondering was Jackson and Thomas were part of his plan. Why cause me this pain?

We had one bus transfer, and then we finally arrived in North Carolina. I reached my destination with slight confusion as to who to contact. Last time I was fortunate enough to find mom and dad's neighbor to hitch a ride with to the ranch. This time I needed a ride to the medical care unit my sister Liz worked in. I felt a little unsure as I wasn't seeing anyone trustworthy.

After looking around for a few, I went inside and spoke with a customer care receptionist. She called a cab to pick me up. I got in, feeling slightly better in trusting a service used all the time in New York. We arrived at the Medical Unit. I paid the driver who then left shortly after. I stared at the red brick building with glass windows and a double glass door. I took a few deep breaths as this wasn't going to be easy.

I walked in and went to the receptionist. "Hey," I said lowly.

"Do you have an appointment?" She asked. She was a young lady with red curly hair, glasses, and very pale skin.

"No," I said lowly.

"Then we can't see you," she said not looking up from her computer.

Frustrated as the lady kept typing on her computer. "I'm here to see Liz-."

"Stacy," I heard a voice from behind this girl. We locked eyes as her face was shocked to see me. "Let her through now," she demanded to the receptionist. The receptionist looked at me and then pointed with her eyes to the door to my left.

I heard a buzzard noise as I opened the door. Liz came up to me and threw her arms around me. She embraced me as I felt like I couldn't breathe anymore. "Stacy," she squealed. "I can't believe you're here, where I work," she squealed. "Ginger," she said looking over at the receptionist. "Have Tucker take over my patients for the rest of the evening." I glanced over as the girl got up from her chair. Liz grabbed my arms and then smiled even bigger. "Follow me," she squealed.

I wasn't expecting this type of reaction and was shocked. I followed her over to a hallway that led to doors of offices. She stopped in front of one that had **Liz Warren** printed on a plaque outside the door. She took a key and opened it up. "Come on in," she said as she stepped to the side. "Let's catch up in here."

I walked inside seeing a room with a few bookshelves, two black leather chairs to the left, a desk filled with papers, a computer, pictures, and then a rolling office chair to the right. I glanced around the room as I took a seat in one of the black leather chairs, closest to the door. Flustered, my cheeks flushed red, my hands sweating, breathing heavy as she took a seat across from me. She started talking, flooding the room with chatter as I looked down at my fingers that were sweating. I tried to rub them on my pants, feeling anxious every speaking moment. She smiled, laughed, and continued to talk as I couldn't register a word she expressed.

"Liz," I snapped as the anticipation of my presence in her office rose. "I'm not here for a social visit." Liz, twenty-six years old now, dirty blonde hair pulled back in a ponytail, became silent, forming her lips into a line. "I need your help with something," I said as I nervously fumbled my fingers in my lap, not able to look at her.

"Stacy," she said with anger in her tone. "It's been four and a half years since any of us have heard from you."

I felt tears form in my eyes. "I know that you're upset with me, but I need your help."

"What possibly could I do to help you?" She sounded frustrated as she interlocked her fingers and sat them on her desk.

"You're an OBGYN," I said glancing up at her. "I need a pregnancy terminated."

Her mouth fell slightly, and then she sat back in her chair. She looked away from me as if she were in pain to hear the words from my mouth. She folded her arms across her chest. "How far along are you?"

My mouth felt dry as I looked back down at my hands. The pain inside of me rose as this was something I wanted for the longest time. I licked my lip, and then looked back at her. "I should be seven weeks," I cried. I dabbed my eyes as I sniffled.

She got up from her chair and walked around to me, placing her hand on my shoulder. "You don't look like you want to terminate this pregnancy," she said kneeling down beside me. "Are you sure this is the route you want to go?"

I nodded. I glanced over at her as another stream of tears rolled down my cheeks. "If it wasn't for how this baby was conceived then I would keep it," I cried looking away from her. "But it's not my husband's child."

"Oh Stacy," she said as she wrapped her arms around my neck. I grabbed her arm as the tears flowed out of me. We sat there for a few minutes, and then she grabbed a few tissues and handed them to me. "Let me get a room set up to ensure the timeline is accurate," she said. "And then, we will set a date for when you want this done."

"Thank you," I whispered as I dabbed my face with the tissues.

"Of course," she said patting my shoulder. "It's what family does, look out for each other." She gave me a light squeeze, and then left her office.

I sat there crutched over, my elbows on my knees, and my face buried in my hands. It had been seven weeks since the incident. Seven weeks that turned our lives around for the worse. I moved my right arm around my stomach, as if this tiny thing could feel my hand. *I'm sorry that I have to do this to you. It's not fair for you to be brought into this world from a tragedy that occurred to me.*

Chapter Seventeen

KNOCK. KNOCK. I looked up to see Liz had returned. "I've got a room for you," she said holding onto the doorknob. Her face looked in as much pain as I felt for what I was about to do. We both were raised better than this, but if it wasn't for that wrongful act I would be making a different choice. I nodded as I slowly got up from the chair, looking in front of me at her desk. A picture of her and her husband Eric on their wedding day sat there. I slightly smiled as the moment was precious, it reminded me of my own wedding. I followed Liz out.

We walked down the hallway to a different hallway. "This hallway is closed off," she said. "We keep it for some patients who want to be discreet."

I nodded as I clutched my laptop bag. We arrived inside a room that had a table and all sorts of equipment. "I need to do an ultrasound to confirm the conception time," she said as she walked around the table. "If you will put your bag in that chair, strip from waist down as I have to use a pelvic ultrasound exam."

I turned away from her, pulling my bag off my shoulder, and then stripping my waist down. I got on the table as she helped place a sheet over me, putting my feet in foot pedals. I felt my entire body shake as I lay there, feeling every single emotion roll through me. "Just try to relax," she said as reassuring as she could. She had gloves on, put a protector on the doppler, and then applied gel to it. She went under the sheet, pulling it up a little more. "You may feel slight pressure," she said as she adjusted the probe.

She inserted the probe, and I winced in pain. I put my head back as she turned her head to look at me, patting my arm. I glanced over at her as she started typing on a computer. "So," she said unable to keep quiet. "Did you go back for the man you left us for?"

I nodded taking a deep breath in as it felt painful. "What's his name?" She asked.

"Not now," I breathed out. "This is more than slight pressure," I said as she glanced over at me.

She looked behind the sheet that separated my sight from her and the ultrasound probe. "Do you think you can bare through it a few more minutes?" She asked.

I nodded as I put the back of my hands over my forehead, and then the memory of Jackson securing my hands flashed through me. Placing my hands down, over my stomach as she continued to do the ultrasound.

"Found the little booger," she said with a smile. We exchanged uncomfortable glances, and then she looked back at the screen. "Sorry, that wasn't right for me to say that."

I shook it off as she focused on the screen. "How far did you say you estimated to be?"

I looked away from her. "Seven weeks," I said lowly.

She pressed some keys on her computer, adjusted the probe. I winced again in pain and started to breathe through her moving the probe around. She hit a few more keys and pulled the probe out. We looked at each other. "You're measuring to be ten weeks," she said with no distinction in her voice of lying. "Are you sure you want-."

I threw my hand up. "I can't be ten weeks," I snapped. "The incident occurred seven weeks ago."

"Do you use birth control? Track ovulation?" She asked.

"My husband had a vasectomy," I said waving my hand in the air. "He's had one at eighteen and is way older now."

She cleaned up the probe and handed me a towel. "Stacy," she said sitting down on the stool. "In very rare cases, a vasectomy can reverse."

A breath exhaled abruptly from my lips as I put my feet out of the foot pedals. "Can I have a minute?" I asked as I sat up, putting my hand over my mouth.

"Take as long as you need," she said getting up from the stool. "Just make sure to say bye to me before trying to leave town." She walked over to the door and then left the room. I cleaned myself up as I processed the information unsure how to take it. This wasn't Jackson's child. I got up and walked over to my clothes, pulling on my clothes and shoes. I sat down in the chair, crying as I knew I couldn't abort this child now.

I was carrying Mason's child. Getting up from the chair, swung my bag over my shoulder, and then walked over to the door, opening it. Liz stood across from the door, propped up against it with her left foot on the wall behind her and arms crossed. "Do you still need my help?" She asked as she wasn't as chattery as earlier.

"I need to go see mom about something," I said as I started to walk away.

"Stace," she said taking a step from the wall and grabbing my arm. I stopped and looked at her. She dropped her head as she shook it.

"Is mom okay?" I asked, turning back to face her.

She shook her head as tears ran down her face. "You know it's been five years," she cried. "My birthday was a few weeks ago, and that's when you left."

I grabbed her arm as she looked up at me. "Mom and dad died two years ago," she sobbed, gasping for air. A shattering heart wrenching pain rushed through me as my mouth dropped. I stepped away from her, letting her go as I placed my hand on my head. Tears rushed down my cheeks as I wiped them away quickly. "We couldn't contact you after you left here. You disconnected your phone."

"How did she?" I couldn't manage to ask a full question.

"It was a car accident that took both of their lives," she said as she bent forward, trying to hold back tears. "I'm so sorry."

I turned away from her as I placed my hand on the wall, shattered, broken into a million pieces. I put my head against the wall as it felt like my world was crumbling around me. No ground to stand on, my husband was locked away, my team was a mess, and now my family was gone. I pulled myself together as I didn't have time to fall apart here. "Liz, I sent packages," I said catching my breath.

She nodded. "I put them in the safe like mom told me too," she said.

"I need to get some of it," I said.

She nodded and wiped her face as she stood up straight. "I will take you to it," she said as she walked past me. I followed behind her as we left the medical care unit and got in her car. We rode in silence to the ranch. The memories of our home with mom and dad flooded through me as I saw the porch swing. My favorite memory was mom telling me the story of dad, confirming the feeling I needed to decide.

We hurried inside and rushed upstairs to what used to be mom and dad's room. "I took over the ranch when they passed," Liz said opening the safe.

"You deserve it," I said.

She stepped to the side to let me in it. I grabbed one of the larger envelopes and closed it back. I shoved it in my laptop bag. "Thanks," I said as she locked the safe back. "Can you give me a ride to the bus station?"

She turned around and looked at me with a look of disappointment. "You just got here," she said. "You're expecting a child."

I licked my lips. "I know none of this makes sense," I said. "But I promise I will be back because I'm going to need the best medical doctor I know."

She slightly smiled and then nodded. We rushed downstairs as we went back to her car. I got in the passenger seat. "Stace, you know that was the only way I knew you were still alive," she said as she drove to the bus station.

I looked out the window from her. "I know nothing I do made a bit of sense to any of you. But I am a much stronger person because of him. I promise to be back so that you can help me with this," I said keeping my eyes outside at the road that passed.

"Are you in trouble?" She asked.

I shook my head. "You can't do that," I snapped as I pulled my hand to my mouth and started biting my nails. "You can't ask me questions."

She sighed. "Can you at least tell me when you will be back this time?"

"I have to handle some things," I said. "You have my word that I will make it back here. I just have to get some eggs back in my basket."

She laughed at the expression. She got to the bus station, and then we got out together. I embraced her tightly. "Don't give up on me," I said holding her face. "I will be back soon."

She pulled something out of her pocket, forcing it into my hand. I looked down to see five gathered photos. "It's your ultrasound photos," she said wiping her face. "You better both come back to me."

I smiled and then pulled away from her, watched as she smiled back as I walked away. Purchasing my bus ticket, and then boarded it. We departed the station when I turned on my laptop. I located the tower closest to the police station Detective Jones, sneaking into their server. I pulled his email account, letting my computer search key phrases to detect any communication through email. His other files from his laptop downloaded the data onto my computer. Siffling through the database seeing another interesting employee that was recruited a week ago.

I looked over the profile, downloaded her information to my computer. Searched the remaining files, finding Ryan and James profiles. I downloaded their emails and data to my computer. After I got everyone's downloaded, I did some research on safest secured areas of prison. I did find out that having a person locked in solitary confinement, or a chamber was the best of the options. *Hang in there, Mason!*

I got back to the city, avoiding the warehouse as I checked a room in an apartment, a mile from the warehouse. After finding something to eat, I went back to my apartment. Getting my laptop out and began digging up anything that I could to assist me in helping bring Detective Jones blackmail out. I searched up Detective Brown, locating her new home and finding her interests.

A few weeks had passed by as I tailed Detective Brown. She enjoyed morning walks in central park, sitting on a bench and enjoying a latte. While sipping on a latte, she reads a book, mostly mysteries as they tend to spark her interest.

I started to grow, not being able to fit properly in my pants. I bought new pants and then decided to head to the prison. I signed in and then was escorted with others to the visitation room. I sat down, waiting on Mason to arrive. Mason came into the room, sitting down. We looked at each other and then picked up the phones.

"Hey beautiful," he whispered.

I smiled as I placed a hand on the window. "Mason, I talked with Henderson weeks ago," I said. "We're all going to work on getting you out."

"I know some heat is picking up on my end," he said glancing around.

I nodded. "You have to trust me," I said as tears pricked my eyes. I dabbed my eyes and then sniffled. Nauseated even being in this room, speaking with Mason through a glass.

"Hey," he said putting his hand on the glass. "None of that, remember."

I nodded as I put my hand on my side of the glass in front of his hand. "Mason," I whispered. "I have to tell you something."

"Have they come after you again?" He asked.

I shook my head. "Mason," I said looking through the glass as our eyes locked. "You remember the night months ago when you and I discussed dreams."

He looked at me as his lips formed a line. A heartstring tucked as I had a feeling I should wait to discuss this, but I needed to tell him in case he didn't get out of prison before it was born. "You know when I asked if you could, would you want kids?"

His facial expression changed as he gritted teeth, forming wrinkles on his forehead as redness flooded his face. "Why haven't you got an abortion?" He asked in fury.

My mouth went dry as I didn't know how to explain. "I," I stuttered as my heart raced.

"How far along are you?" He asked.

"I'm fifteen weeks," I said lowly, keeping my eyes on his eyes.

He broke our stare as he looked down at the desk in front of him. He moved his hand from the window and slammed his fist down on the countertop. "You should have got rid of it," he raised his voice. I jerked back in my seat, keeping my eyes on him, as I took a deep breath. "Why would you even allow yourself to carry something from that night? Why do this to me?"

"Mason," I said trying to deescalate as he stood up. An officer came up behind him. "I need you to calm down so I can explain."

"You're choosing a child over me," he yelled slamming his fist down. "You're choosing his child over me!"

The officer behind him started to grab Mason. He shoved him off. I felt myself shattering in front of him as I watched him become physical with the officer, dropping the phone. I stood up, trying to scream for them to stop. Mason was restrained, angrily staring at me as they dragged him out. "No," I sobbed. "Mason, no!" I hit the glass as I dropped the phone and sat down in the chair. Wrapping my arms around my stomach as tears flowed.

After a moment, I pulled myself together and then got out of the chair. Leaving the prison, I made my way back to the apartment. Feeling the urge to scream, wanting to throw things, but refrained from it as none of it was going to save Mason from being killed in prison. I got on my computer, pulling Detective's Brown information and decided to make a new plan.

The next day, I went to Central Park. She purchased her latte from a coffee stand, carefully locating which hip her holster was on. She walked towards the benches. I had tailed her, finding a person step between us, shoving them forward as she turned to sit down. The person stumbled into her as I unhooked her holster and snatched her gun as she was helping the woman back to her feet. I placed the gun in my long coat pocket, as I sat down on the other end of the bench. I pressed my shades up on my eyes, swiped the hair from my lips, and then waited.

She took a deep breath as she finally got a chance to sit down. "Never a dull moment," she sighed. She was an African American with beautiful black curly hair and big brown eyes. Her complexion was beautifully glowing in the sunlight. She had worn a brown leather jacket, crème colored shirt and brown leather like pants.

"Detective Brown," I sternly said glancing behind my shades at her direction.

She immediately looked alarm as she sat up straight, head in my direction. "Do I know you?" She asked kindly.

I chuckled. "You know of me," I said shifting my head to face hers. She reached down to put her hand on her holster, realizing it wasn't there. I opened my jacket, exposing her handpiece in my coat, and then closing it back. "I know you pretty well," I said. "You've been here five weeks and don't know how to keep a hand on your holster. This isn't Georgia."

She shifted uncomfortably in her seat as she sat her latte down beside her. "So, what else do you know about me?"

"Top of your class. Several recommendations," I said. "Boring stuff. The part that interests me is how you moved from a Southern state, low populated area to here, a highly populated area."

"Interests you," she giggled. "You threatening a cop isn't going to make your day go well."

I smiled. "Who said I was threatening you?" I asked.

"You took my gun," she said as we stared at each other.

I nodded. "You know much about the Henderson case?" I asked.

She looked as if she were searching for her thoughts. "I feel as if I've heard of it," she admitted shifting herself to face towards me better.

"You have a mole in your department," I said.

"There's only a handful of us," she said. "I don't think either of them would be a mole."

I pulled my shades down to expose my eyes. "My husband isn't guilty of beating me to near death. My husband loved me as he once stated that we had become one," I said, and then pressed my glasses back up, moving my hand over to snatch her coffee. The smell of a caramel latte delighted my senses. I took a sip as she gasped.

"Now you're stealing from me, again," she said shaking her head.

I laughed. "I like your sense of style," I said taking another sip. "I need your help."

"Fine way of asking," she said. "I'm still a rookie in these parks. Not much help."

I shifted myself to look forward. "It's why you're perfect," I said. "You're new to the area, less of a threat to me for now. You're still training, but I rather capture you before they brainwash you."

She snorted. "You sure your husband didn't hit your head too hard," she said as she shook her head.

I stood up and faced her, putting my hand inside of my jacket. "I know you think I'm on bad terms already, but I'm going to teach you a lesson right now."

She stiffened up as she looked at me. "As of right now, I have you cornered. My hand is on your gun covered by a glove, no DNA to be detected, no fingerprints. You have one or two options of escaping," I said. "You can attempt to attack me, or you can scream in hopes a distraction will kill my focus. What you're not accepting in the factor is I am a professional of what I do best. You don't want to find out the hard way of what I do best," I said. I finished her latte, keeping it tightly in my hand.

She gulped as I had her full attention. "You have a mole in your department. I can provide you with the information I have for you do some research of your own," I said. "But know I am a woman with a time crunch. I need to get my husband out of prison before it's too late."

She looked away for a moment. "I saw the media coverage and file," she said. "You were beaten really bad. Are you sure he didn't do it like his file said?"

I pulled my glasses down slightly to look her in the eye. "You can start with that file," I said. "I'm only giving you a few days, and then I will be in touch."

"Do you have a phone?" She asked. "How am I supposed to be in touch when I locate something?"

I pushed my shades back up. "You don't get in touch with me," I said and turned to walk past her.

"Wait," she said getting up from the bench. "I need my gun back."

I looked her in the eyes and saw the look of a true law enforcement agent but also saw the look of someone who needed to earn my trust. "You have only a few days," I said reaching inside my coat pocket. Taking my other hand and pulled the clip out and bullet in the chamber. Handing her the gun, and then the bullet with clip. "Please don't disappoint me, you won't like the ending result," I said, and then left her there. I walked into a crowd, blending myself in as I do best.

I went to a local shop and picked up a burner phone. I got to a crowded area, and then I called the next person I wanted to speak too. "Preston," I said as he answered.

"Where have you been?" He asked. "Things are getting hot here."

"Which is why I can't go in yet," I said. "How is your research going?"

"Can you meet at your apartment tonight?" He asked.

I took a deep breath. "Meet me around the block at the bar," I said.

We disconnected our lines. I made my way to the bar, blending when needed, exchanging hats and shades, scarfs, and purses as needed. I got to the bar and sat down near the bartender. He suspiciously looked at me as I pulled down my shades. His face lit up as he leaned in towards me. "Heard you got hitched young lady," he said. "Also heard he beat you in."

I looked into his eyes. "You believe he beat me?" I asked.

He shook his head. "Not that boy," he said. "You want your usual?"

"Water," I said. "I don't drink anymore."

He nodded as he filled a glass with ice and then put some water from the tap in it. He slid it over to me and then winked. He walked away as I sipped on the water. A few moments later, Preston walked in with a brief case in hand. He came over to me and sat down. "I want you to have this," he said. "It's the information you requested."

I smiled as I took another sip. "How hot?" I asked discreetly.

"We're past boiling," he said glancing over his shoulder. "Henderson believes your story on Detective Jones, but he states it's hard to just cut him off."

"He needs to expose him, cutting him off will lead us to where his other sources are," I said. "Jackson and him definitely had a partnership that night."

Preston nodded. "You need to come by, it may help ease Henderson's tension."

I shook my head as I moved my coat, exposing my belly. He glanced down at me and then looked back forward. "You didn't get rid of it," Preston stated with eyes widened. "You must have a death wish."

"It's Masons," I said. Preston looked over at me in complete shock. "My sister believes his vasectomy has reversed itself."

"I've heard of that," Preston said. "Did you tell Mason?"

I looked away from him as I gripped my hands around my cup. "I attempted to do so," I said, and then took a sip of water. "He flipped out, believing it's Jacksons."

Preston nodded. "Well, if you need me to do something else, let me know," he said as he patted my arm.

"Preston," I said looking over at him. "Keep up the good work."

"Your research wasn't too terrible," he said. "Just keep a contact to a minimum."

I nodded. "Be safe," I said.

He smiled as he saluted from his temple and then turned and walked away. I placed some money on the bar, picked up the briefcase, and then headed out. I took a subway over to where my new apartment was located.

Emptying the contents of Preston's research, finding pictures. I took pictures with my phone, uploading them to my personal database. Images of Ryan, James, and Detective Jones at the station. Preston managed to snap several different images of Ryan and clients. I looked through the paperwork on case files Ryan had assignments, snipping photos and uploading them. Skimmed through the work, my eyes felt like numbers and information blurred. I fell asleep with papers in my hand.

I decided while I had to give the new detective some time to process our encounter and the case I gave her to review, I would do more leg work of my own. I had a team that I once joined to be part of Mason's world. Now, I couldn't trust them as our lives, Mason, mine, and our newest growing inside of me depended on it.

The next day, I started with Henderson, tailing his every move. I blended, snapping photos with my phone of him meeting regular clients. Uploaded them to my personal drive. Snapped photos of his encounter with Detective Jones. Him entering the warehouse, including the address on the photo.

After tailing Henderson back to the warehouse, I followed Scott. He was second in command, and I knew he was the second person I could trust when I needed too. To be sure, I had to do my work in following him. Like with Henderson, I took photos of him going home, typing the address on his photo. I watched as he mainly commuted from home to the warehouse. I did watch as it appeared he had been assigned a solo assignment. After he left, snapping a few photos, I rushed in finding the scene of a suicide. I took pictures of the crime scene and then uploaded it.

Preston, I knew his loyalty and trust with me, but I needed to have evidence on him. He worked with James where I was able to capture pictures of both in the act. Waiting till they left, sneaking in and snapping photos of the crime scene.

Finally, Kyle, he was much more discreet than the rest of them. I had the worst time gathering evidence as he lay low. Entering an apartment multiple times a day, I watched as he went to the warehouse, but didn't find anything to pin on him other than entering the warehouse.

Collecting the data, I uploaded everything on my personal drive. I lay back on the bed, papers scattered around me as I placed my hands on my lower stomach. Less sick as I entered my second trimester which made days better for me.

A sudden thud inside of me, twitching from the movement, I sat up, looking down at my stomach as I felt it again. Stroking my stomach, I smiled at the precious sensation. A few moments later, another wave of thuds as I continued to rub circles around my lower abdomen. "You're loved more than you ever will know," I said so grateful that I didn't have the abortion.

Thoughts of Mason I knew that he wouldn't be able to adjust to me being pregnant as I recalled his way of asking me to marry him. I lay back on the bed, thinking back at that night that I followed him once more to let him claim me as his and him as mine. Impatient I was when we married and the moment we entered the hotel room. Now, I laughed at how he revealed to me that it would be just the two of us. Oh, how that has all changed now that I lay there with tears forming, holding my stomach that continued to thud within me. *You're going to be as strong as your daddy.* I closed my eyes and rested.

Chapter Eighteen

The next day, I brought myself to Detective Clara Brown's house. She had a top-of-the-line security system installed. I got on my laptop, a few blocks away, disabling the alarm system. Made my way to her home, and scoped out the two-bedroom, one-bathroom small town home. A kitchen with a small dining area, living area that was a little small for my taste.

Scoping out her house, seeing her photos with family, past troop pictures. I dug through her unpacked boxes of paperwork; some were case files. Searching her main bedroom, checking out every nick and crack. I hung around for her arrival, reinstating her alarm system.

It was a little after six when I heard her door unlock. I hid in her pantry as she entered the kitchen, unhooking her holster and placing it with gun on the countertop. Shaking my head at the thought of her selfless act. She rubbed the back of her neck as she sat a bag down on the kitchen table. Looking looked at the bag, she dug out some files. I slowly made my way out of the pantry, not making a sound, grabbing her gun from the countertop.

I got squared behind her and held the gun at the back of her head. "Boom," I said. She jumped out of her skin as she turned and faced me, nearly falling on the ground. "You literally are so ignorant. I could have killed you in two seconds."

"How did you get past my security system?" She asked as she regained her composure.

I shrugged my shoulders. "I hacked your system, disarming it, and then blocked its signal to send you any the information that your alarm had been disconnected. After that, I've been here, waiting," I said as I looked around. "You have anything to eat around here?"

She glared at me as she made her way past me to the kitchen. "Left over casserole," she said as she pulled a pan from the fridge.

"Sounds delicious," I said as I sat down at the bar of her kitchen counter. "So, I've given you a few days."

She scooped some portions on plates and put them in the microwave. "Only one person on the case, odd," she commented as she put the pan up. "He was closer to the scene than any other cop."

I nodded. Knowing who the person on the file was, folding my hand with a gun in it over my other, watching as she propped herself against the countertop, waiting for the microwave to finish. "What else did you find?"

"It was a clear concise case," she said. "No evidence other than a husband drunk and beat his wife."

The sound of the microwave beeped. She brought the plates over to me, grabbing a couple of forks, and walked over to grab two wine glasses. "I don't drink," I said as she glanced at me sideways. She shook her head in disbelief and then poured me a glass of water. She poured herself a glass of wine.

"How far along are you?" She asked as she sat the cup down in front of me.

I looked down as my belly had looked more curved out. "I'm sixteen weeks," I said lowly as the smell of her casserole filled my nostrils. The smell was delicious, watering my mouth. She propped herself over and took a bite of food.

"I don't know whether to believe your story," she said as she took a bite. "However, I don't feel any other person I know would go this extreme to save their husband that beat them to death either."

"I need your help in busting this," I said, and then took another bite, absorbing the flavors. I moaned as the taste was undeniable amazing. "And I need this recipe."

She laughed. "My mama's good ole recipe," she said with an accent.

A hard lump formed as the thought of mom's recipes crossed my mind. "Do you have any other of Detective Jones cases?" I asked.

She shook her head. "I think we need to set up some kind of deal," she said as she took her wine glass in hand. "I can't just help you bust people in my department for the fun of it. I need some leverage to play around here."

"Your life isn't enough," I said sipping on the glass of water.

Her eyes shot up at me as she had another frightening look. "I didn't know my life was at stake," she said. "I mean I know my job is dangerous."

I took a deep breath as I sat my glass on the counter. "I can give you some information," I admitted as she needed some information to establish a bond. "I just need you to understand something," I paused. "Once you have this information, your life can end anywhere from seconds to years."

She adjusted her stance, putting her glass down. "You're very intimidating," she said. "I'm not sure if I want to know your secret."

"You want some sort of leverage," I said looking down as I contemplated how to proceed.

She sighed. "I did bring some other of his case files home," she said interrupting my contradicting thoughts. "You look like you're going to have a meltdown, so keep your information a little while longer."

I took a deep breath. She rolled her eyes as she walked over to her dining room table. Pulling out the folders, placing them across her table. I got up from the chair, holding the gun in hand as I made my way over to her, hesitating to watch her motives. "I have his files pulled from the last few months." Relieved as I knew something among these files would help us. She took a seat and then extended an offer to me. I walked around, sitting opposite her, laying the gun down beside me as I picked up a folder.

"You know it's going to take time to go through these," she said looking over at me. I glanced from the folder, meeting her gaze. "Just don't get your hopes up that we will find an answer over one night."

I nodded. She looked back down at the folder in her hand as I began with the one in my hand. We spent the greater part of the night looking for similarities between the files. Noticing a few of them that he was the first to the scene. She had a notebook and pen, taking notes. After a few hours, she needed rest. I decided to stay and work on what information I could find.

She got up the next morning, stumbling through to her coffee machine. "Do you ever sleep?" She asked.

"My husband is in prison under false accusations," I said. "The ones who attacked us, are getting away with it and have disappeared off the planet."

She rotated her head, rubbing the back of her neck. Letting a cup brew, adding sugar and creamer. The aroma of freshly brewed coffee entering my heightened senses, watering my mouth, craving its taste. She came over to my side. I slid my hand towards the gun as she took a few steps back. "I don't mind that," I said pointing my eyes to the cup of coffee.

"Isn't it bad to drink coffee while pregnant?" She asked as she sat the cup down beside me. I shrugged my shoulders as I moved my hand to her cup, inhaling the aroma. My mind flashed back to when Mason and I the day we were assigned with Jackson and Thomas had breakfast. We had spent a couple of weeks working endlessly, and then I took more than half my share of the coffee.

"What's that about?" She asked as she stood by the counter, looking over at me.

I snapped into reality, taking a sip of the coffee, shrugging my shoulders. She rolled her eyes as she sipped on her new cup. I looked back down as I shuffled through the case files. "Do you ever work with him?" I asked. "Detective Jones. Do you work with him on cases?"

Both hands cupped around her cup, blowing the top to cool it down. "Yes, we've been occasionally working together on some cases. He's a very kind man," she said. "I just don't think he's the one you think is behind the framing of your husband."

I got up, putting my cup down. "I need to handle a few things. Can you start working closer with him?" I asked. "I need you to force your way into his lifestyle, learning who's his multiple business partners?"

Her eyes shot up from her cup to me. "Business partners?" She questioned. "The man spills coffee on his shirt every day."

"Does he have to go home and change clothes every day?" I asked tilting my head to arouse curiosity.

She took the bait as she put her cup down on the counter. "He does take an early lunchbreak on certain days," she said. "He says that he has a gym membership."

"I need you to get closer to him," I said looking back at the folders across her table. "I need him caught in an act, and then I need my husband freed."

"You going to be around to help?" She asked.

"No," I said. "I promise to stop by another time, but eventually I do have to head out of town."

She nodded. "I will see what I can do to create a connection and follow this rabbit hole you're sending me in," she said as she picked up her coffee cup.

"You will be rewarded," I said as our eyes met. "My husband taught me that hard work does pay off. I just need you to trust me."

"You realize you've only held me at gun point both times we've talked," she said.

"Trust isn't easy for me to establish," I said glancing down at my phone. "I'll be in touch."

She waved me on as I grabbed my laptop bag and phone. Leaving through her front door, not setting off her alarms. I went up the street, going to a subway. At my new apartment, feeling insecure with myself, my confidence was slipping through my fingers as the thoughts of Jackson and Thomas scarred me. Sitting on the floor by the door, I thought of how Mason would handle this type of situation right now. I missed him dearly as my emotions ran high.

I located an electronic store, grabbing up some sensors, and other prominent material to enter my next phase. At the apartment and began developing my own security plan to ensure the safety of myself and the baby. I linked and synchronized items. Self-testing the sensors, linking it to my personal drive, and then working on the network drive. I unfastened Mason's watch, placing the detecting signal on the back of the watch, linking it with the two sensors placed with stickers on my left side of my chest, and the other on my lower stomach.

Over the next few weeks, I created an upload site that I linked to my watch. Running a trial run, sending the code to myself, ensuring its effectiveness through several potential circumstances. After all the tests passed, I developed my security plan to ensure my exit. It was one thing that I learned as a silencer, you must be great covering your tracks. It always helped to have a backup plan.

I was twenty weeks when I appeared at Detective Brown's house. It was early morning as she woke up around three o'clock. "You said unexpected," she said as she looked up from her bed at me.

"I never said a timeframe, or date," I said. "This is unexpected."

She grumbled as she worked on getting out of bed. I walked into her living area, sitting down in one of her white fluffy chairs. "No gun to my head this time," she grumbled as she pulled a robe around her and sat down across from me.

"How's the relationship building with Detective Jones going?" I asked jumping straight to business.

She wobbled her head. "It's a process," she said. "He's being accepting to me working more cases with him."

"Did you sign up at the same gym as him?" I asked as I crossed a leg over another and pulled my hands to interlock in front of them.

"I haven't got that far in investigating," she said. "Some things have me blocked at work."

"Get them unblocked," I said. "Time is of the essence."

She rolled her eyes as she huffed. "You better have other reasons than waking me for this lovely idea of a conversation."

"I do have some reasons," I said. "I have some information for you." I pulled out of the briefcase a few files and handed them over to her. She accepted them, immediately opening and reviewing. "Ryan Webb and James Matthews?"

"Yes," I said. "They're part of a team of hitmen."

She jumped at the word hitman as if it was surprising. "The term scare you, detective?" I asked.

Her eyes shot up from her lap to mine. "You have no problem turning in fellow team players," she commented.

I cleared my throat, and then sat up, leaning towards the arm of her chair. "I want to tell you my story," I said. "How it became of where I'm at your mercy of helping me."

"It's three in the morning; can this story wait till I'm more alert?" She whined.

I got up from my chair, walking over to her window, looking out at the street. Starting from the beginning of me leaving my home in North Carolina to being jobless. My time for rent due was nearing, and then I was offered an opportunity. My initial interview was someone snatching my purse and then being pinned against the wall near the subway by a man who stole my heart. I told my story through the night that my life had changed. She was good and awake after all the information. "I need to ask a favor of you," I said. "I like you and think you will be the one for the job." I stroked my stomach as thuds were radiating through more profoundly.

"You already have me doing favors," she commented.

I nodded. "Those are business favors," I said propping myself against her windowsill. "This other one is personal."

She nodded. Intrigued by her ambition, I smiled as I looked down at her hardwood floors. "My husband has been in this industry since he was four years old with no other option. I can tell you that he wasn't meant for this type of work but found himself in the grips of death. As right now, he's in a prison fighting every day to stay alive. It's the same for when he's outside of those walls."

She leaned in closer to have her full attention on me. "I need him to have a way out. So, when the time comes, I want you to provide him with that opportunity. I don't know how you will do it, but I know you're the one who can give him a new life."

"You're asking for an impossible favor considering your all beating death dates as it is," she said. "Are you sure he will want a new life?"

"When the time is right," I paused. "You will know when it's right. I hope to see him come home to me and our child."

She nodded as she now understood why my request was personal. "Mrs. Henderson," she said as she stood up. "How will I contact you when it comes time for your favors to be answered?"

I pulled a phone out of my pocket. "There's only one number programmed in it," I said handing her the phone. "You understand that I've now put you in the mouth of the arena of death."

She nodded as she took the phone from my hand. "Please only use this new knowledge as leverage when needed. I am trusting you, remember that's a hard thing to come by with me."

"Thank you for weighing so much on me," she said as she stared down at the phone.

I got up from the windowsill and walked to where our shoulders were side to side. "Just remember who you're dealing with. You may have power in your court with that phone," I said keeping my face forward, and then looking over at her. "But it only takes seconds for it all to be swept away from you."

Her face tightened, fear stricken, I turned forward and walked out of her house. Leaving her house, I headed to the apartment, collecting my other items, and disposing of unnecessary items. Catching a cab, I headed to the bar where this life began. "Wade," I said. "I need a favor."

Wade leaned in and ready to listen. "I have this key I need a specific person to collect with this letter. I will give him a passcode, *remember where you're grounded*. Can you ensure he gets these two items?"

Wade nodded as he collected the items and then placed them in the safe. "You be safe out there, Stacy," he said.

I tipped my head and then left the bar and headed to the last place of business before my departure. I walked up to the door, taking a deep breath, everything felt so different. The smell outside of this door was even different now. Inside, immediately having the team around me. Kyle grabbed my arm leading me to Henderson's office with Scott, not expecting anything less from the two. I went inside and sat down in front of Henderson who smoked another cigar.

"Well," Henderson snorted. "Funny seeing you again."

"I wish I could say the same," I said. "But I don't feel as comical as you." I looked over as Scott moved over towards Henderson's side, crossing his arms. Glancing over my shoulder at Kyle who stood guarding the door. "That's not necessary," I said looking at Kyle. He folded his arms as he looked over at Henderson.

"I came to put in my resignation," I said looking into Henderson's eyes.

Henderson laughed as Scott shifted himself intensely. He looked as if anger roared over him, and then the air shifted behind me. "You haven't been seen in months," Henderson said taking a puff on his cigar. "Then, you march in here like you have any right. I see you didn't take care of the problem." He looked down at my now rounded stomach.

"It's Mason's," I said looking down at my belly. "I had it confirmed with the timeline. This baby was conceived three weeks earlier." Scott's face loosened as he glanced at Henderson and me.

Henderson put his cigar up in the air and then looked at me. "You said you would help us get him out," he changed topics. "You never came back. Now, all of a sudden, the baby is his and you want to resign." He chuckled.

Hearing the sound of Kyle moving his arm, glancing to see his gun out, aiming it at the back of my head. Every hair standing on the back of my neck. *Stacy, trust yourself.* The words ringed my ears as I took a deep breath for all or nothing. I held up the arm with Mason's watch on it. "Before you pull that trigger, you need to know something," I said glancing at Henderson.

"You want to tell us that you have Mason's watch," Henderson laughed. "He isn't around right now, sweetheart. He can't save you."

Another breath abruptly inhaling, shaking slightly, hesitating. "This watch has a sensor on it. If you shoot me then it will automatically upload every data I've collected over the past several weeks on each of you in here to every law enforcement officer with an active email address. You will have only minutes before this building is filled with every tactical team available," I said as Henderson immediately stopped laughing.

"You're bluffing," he said putting his cigar out.

"The monitor has two signals that always go to it," I said glancing back as Kyle kept shifting his weight in anticipation that he was ready to kill me. "One senses my heartbeat, and the other senses our child's heartbeat." I stopped as I looked around the room. A silent room as they all weren't sure how to proceed when the rabbit took the gun from the gunman.

"Kyle," Henderson said with a stern voice. "Put the gun down." Glancing over my shoulder as Kyle's hand was shaking. I could tell by his expression he'd been waiting for his moment to take me out for years, an opportunity had rose and he was ready for it. He had sweat pouring down his face as I glanced back to Henderson. "Kyle!" Henderson shouted.

Frustrated, Kyle put the gun away and then turned and walked out of the office. A breath of relief filled my heart as the fear of being seconds away from death again dissipated. "I gave you an option before, you chose to stay with us," Henderson said interlocking his fingers. "That was a one-time opportunity."

"That you gave Mason," I corrected. "You and him talked after Ryan nearly killed Preston and myself after the assignment with the girl. Mason came to you asking for a favor."

Henderson sat back in his chair, speechless as he stared at me. "You truly were his favorite and best choice." Henderson rolled his eyes as he pulled out another cigar. "So, what terms do we need to negotiate your resignation and that you want have those senses trigger an alarming email."

I smiled as I looked over at Scott, who was just in amazement as Henderson. Glancing back at Henderson. "I want to resign immediately, leaving to head back to my home state. I will keep this connection on me until I appear there. After I feel that life is comfortable, and I am no longer fearing you will have placed a hit on me, then I will mail you the sensors. If by chance, you feel you can outsmart my sensors," I paused. "I've entrusted a specific person outside of this team with solid information. If my death appears, this person will make your yellow carded life then red carded. You may never see daylight outside of prison walls ever again if I die, or if this child dies."

Henderson puffed on his cigars. "Scott, bring Mrs. Henderson to her bus station," Henderson said as he waved his hand in the air in anger.

"One more thing," I said as I reached inside my laptop bag. "I need you to give this to Mason once out of prison." I handed him an envelope with a key.

Henderson accepted the items, glancing at them, and then up at me. "Any other requests?" He asked looking up at me.

"I think that covers it," I said glancing between the two of them.

Henderson looked over at me, then at Scott, and then back at me. "You truly are perfect for my hardheaded son," he said rolling his eyes. "If it wasn't for your expertise in the skills you have developed, I wouldn't be accepting your resignation except through the only place I've ever accepted them"

An unexpected humor rushed over me as I could tell he was aggravated with the circumstances. "I know you wouldn't have accepted me to leave any other way than a body bag," I said as I glanced down at my hands. "It's why I knew to ensure a security package for us."

"I'll accept your one-time resignation," he said as he stood up. He held out his hand towards me. I stood up and hesitated. Relieved, I built up the courage and shook his hand. "Take care of that grandchild the way it ought to be taught. By mercy, you best stay out of dangers way."

I finished shaking his hand and then watched as Scott held out his hand as well, shaking it. Scott went to the door and opened it. Taking a step towards the door, stopping, knowing the final piece to give Henderson. I pulled a paper out of my jacket pocket, and then walked back over to Henderson. I sat down the five ultrasound pictures in front of him that I've received at my first and only ultrasound. "Thank you," I said lowly and never looked back at him. I walked out the door. Scott walked by my side as we went towards the garage exit. Ryan, James, Kyle, and Preston staring at me. Scott got to the car, opening the rear passenger side. He walked around to the driver's side seat and opened the door.

He backed out of the garage and then started down the road. I pulled out my phone, putting in text message to the only person I knew I could trust with the next phase of my security plan. I typed in the bar's information and passcode, pressing send.

"You really would have made Mason proud of your work," Scott commented. "Again, I'm sorry that this went south for both of you."

I glanced up at him as he looked back at me, and then back at the road. "You ensure to help find Jackson and Thomas. We need them taken out, or else they're going to take us all out."

Scott sighed heavily. "It's not my place to extend this offer," he paused. "However, giving the circumstances, I believe Mason would appreciate it being an offer to you. Stacy, you end up in any trouble wherever you're going, you call me. I will get a team to you quickly. I'm not joking," he said. "You and Mason didn't deserve what you went through that night. If I could get my hands around Jackson, he wouldn't be breathing very long."

"I will ensure to take you up on that offer if the occurs," I said as I stroked my stomach.

We got to the bus station where he got out to open my door. He pulled out a card. "My number for your lifeline when needed," he said handing me the card. "Good luck out there, kid." He walked back around the car and drove off.

Going inside to purchase a final ticket out of this state, I boarded the bus, breathing a sigh of relief as we departed New York state. I stroked my stomach, looking down. "I hope you understand how lucky you are to be growing in there," I said. "I'm excited every day as it gets closer to time to meet you."

The one bus change and then headed to North Carolina. I pulled out my phone. "Liz," I said as she answered her phone.

"Stacy?" She asked.

"I'm going to need a lift from the bus stop to home," I said as a smile slid across my face.

She squealed in excitement. "When will you be here? I will pick you up myself," she squealed. "It's Stacy," she said attempting to partially cover the microphone. "She's coming home!"

I looked up our route, seeing our scheduled arrival time, providing it to Stacy, and then we got off the phone. Placing my phone back in my bag, I rested my head on the windowsill. A flood of memories of New York flashed over me as the bus traveled. Recalling Mason's first appearance to his last behind a glass window. Shattered at the sight of him being taken away, staring at me angrily. I looked down as I hoped when he got out of prison that he would read the letter and come home to us.

We arrived at the final stop. I unloaded the bus as I looked out to see Liz running towards me. Smiling, I paced over towards her. She wrapped her arms around me, jumping up and down as she was so excited for me to be there. Her husband slowly walked up, held his hand out to me, and then pulled me in for an embrace. We all hugged for several moments, allowing every anxious thought of returning to draw itself out as warm hugs, love filled my heart. We got in their car and then headed to the place where mom always stated that's where my roots are grounded.

Chapter Nineteen

OVER THE COURSE OF SEVERAL WEEKS, Liz and Eric accepted me into their home as my previous family home. I stayed in my room, buying baby items as I prepared for the arrival of my baby girl. Liz started doing prenatal visits immediately when I returned to her, doing scans and helping me pick out different things to prepare for little miss's arrival.

At twenty-eight weeks, it had been a long day, my body exhausted, and I sat on the porch swing. Liz pulled up in her car as she was coming home from work. She walked up the stairs and then sat beside me on the porch swing. "Whew, what a day," she said as she turned herself to face me.

I had been stroking my stomach, thinking of names for her. "Busy day?" I asked as I broke away from my train of thought.

"Yes," she said. "We've delivered five today. At one point, it felt like an assembly."

I smiled as I felt the little girl inside of me kicking. "You want to feel?" I asked reaching for Liz's hand. She smiled as she placed her hand on my stomach. She felt the little kicks and then squealed with excitement.

"Have you decided on a name?" She asked.

I shrugged my shoulders. "I have time," I said stroking my stomach. "Liz, when are you and Eric going to try for kids?"

She looked away, dropping her head immediately. I tilted my head, moving over and rubbing her arm. "Hey, what's that look for?" I asked trying to cheer her up. "We don't have to talk about it."

"No," she said wiping her eyes. "We do need too. I just wished I had better ways of telling you."

A look of concern crossed my face as I shifted to give her my full attention. "Dad and mom wanted us to go to Fourth of July in South Carolina where the huge fireworks are released." She stopped as she took a few breaths. "Mom wasn't feeling well and decided to let dad drive. I was in the back seat," she wiped her eyes again.

"Liz," I said shifting myself to be next to her, wrapping my arms around her shoulders, embracing her as she paused again to breathe.

"Dad had another stroke," she said. "He wrecked into oncoming traffic. The other family survived. Mom and dad didn't."

"You were in the car with them?" I asked in shock as she looked up at me with her wet swollen face.

"Stace, I should have driven us. I was texting with a medical student that I didn't want to drive. I didn't know that he would have another stroke," she cried. "I shouldn't have been so selfish." She placed her head on my chest as she brought her hands up to hold onto my arm.

"Nonsense," I whispered. "Liz, you didn't do anything wrong. Most kids our ages wouldn't even think twice if we didn't spend time with our family.

"I feel guilty every day about it," she cried.

I moved my hands to her face, forcing her to look at me. "They are in a much better place than we ever are," I said wiping her tears away. "It was their time. Nothing you could have done to prevented it."

She wept in my arms as I held her closely and tightly. "Did you get hurt from the accident?" I asked as she calmed down.

She nodded as she sniffled. "I had a piece of metal pierce my lower stomach. They had to do a full hysterectomy on me." I closed my eyes as I felt the weight of her pain fall on both our shoulders. I couldn't speak as I became breathless, trying to hold back tears. "So, Eric had to find out before we got married that I wasn't able to have kids."

I smiled, not meaning to at her circumstances, but as it reminded me of how Mason informed me of his secret. He waited until after we were married to expose that he had a vasectomy at eighteen. I held my sister allowing the moment of Mason to disappear as I shared my sister's pain. After she dried up her tears, she sat up and asked to feel the baby kick again.

She got next to my stomach. "This is your aunt Liz," she said happily. "I can't wait to meet you when it comes time to do so."

I smiled as I listened to her talk with my stomach. The moment was a time stamp I wished I could have kept forever as feelings of the baby kicking were exciting to my sister talking to my stomach. The sensation sent new warm vibes throughout my body.

At thirty-two weeks, I decided to place the sensors and signal detectors in an envelope. I wrote a letter to Henderson.

Dear Henderson,

I know that it's only been twelve weeks, but after some time to process my life with you and my life here. I decided to turn these into you as an acceptance to you ensuring that we were safe. Over the years of working with you, I can say I've never seen you react so kindly to a lady that learned to fight from day one of your training till her last day with you. I hope you can one day, enjoy retirement.

P.S. Your grandchild is a girl.

Sincerely,

Your beloved daughter-in-law, Stacy

Folding and sealing the envelope, I mailed it off, unsure how to feel as I was fully trusting him now to leave us alone. Breathless from the pain that Detective Brown hadn't called with any updates, no news of Mason's release. Slowly time passed by, every day feeling the familiar pain of his imprisonment, knowing that it feared me of the possibility that he won't make it out alive.

Liz and I had gathered at the table as I wasn't feeling well. "Tell us how you met," Liz paused. "Mason."

I smiled as the memory was so sweet to think about. "I met him at a bar," I said. "He had his hooks dug into me the moment we locked eyes on each other."

"Did you have a beautiful wedding?" She asked as Eric took a seat beside her.

"Liz," Eric said. "She may not want to give us all these details."

"Shhh…" Liz said. Eric gave her a look that acted as in why you just quieted me. I began laughing as the quarrel between them sent Eric tickling her. Entangled in laughter as they tickled each other leading to them kissing. I looked away, reminded of my last kiss with Mason was in the apartment moments before meeting with Jackson and Thomas.

I got up from the table. "Excuse me," I said as I walked past them to the stairs. Breathing hard while walking up the flight of steps as my belly has grew to an enormous size, stroking my belly from cramps, and then entered my room that had all the baby equipment inside of it with my bed. I grazed my fingers across the crib comforter, smiling at the items we picked out.

A knock at the door had me turn around as Liz came into the room. "I can't believe in a few short weeks, she will be here," Liz said as she walked over to my bed.

I sat down beside her, laying my head on her shoulder. "I can't believe it's here either."

"Do you think he will come back for you?" She asked as she lay her head on top of mine.

I pulled away, looking away from her. "You don't understand," I said feeling a pain in my heart.

"Then explain it to me," she begged.

"It's not that simple," I said shifting myself to look back at her. "I chose his life over my family. I chose what we did that went against everything we were ever taught as kids. I had to choose it to be with him. This would have been four years of us married."

"He's not dead, is he?" She asked.

I shook my head. "No," I said. "It's worse than being dead."

She arched an eyebrow as she looked at me with a look of sadness and concern. "There was only one way out of that place," I said. "However, I outsmarted the man in charge. I gave him no option to kill me off."

Liz's eyes widened as she looked horrified at the words. "You mean you should be dead right now?" She asked as she embraced me.

"Being there isn't as simple as being here," I said. "Life in those streets were a life of learning to survive every day."

"I don't know how you handled it," she said shaking her head in disbelief.

I felt a cramp and winced in pain. "Here," she said getting up from the bed. "You need to rest. We can talk more about this tomorrow." I lay down, holding my belly as a few more cramps invaded. I thought of Mason's awkwardness in asking personal questions. He took care of me from the moment I followed him, asking and demanding to trust him. *Yep, trust him. Mason, look at where it has got us.*

Officially thirty-eight weeks, feeling every bit pregnant. I sat down at the table, nauseas, but allowing Eric and Liz to cook. Liz brought me a plate over to where I sat. Filled with energy and smiles, she sat beside me. "Please tell me you have a name," she begged.

"I'm still debating," I said as I took a bite of my biscuit and gravy. Savoring the taste, interrupted by the sound of a ring roared through the air. I pulled out my phone from my pocket as this was the call I've longed for and my heart fluttered.

"Mrs. Henderson," Detective Clara Brown stated.

"Detective Brown," I said as I put my fork down.

"How are you?" She asked.

"I'm about ready to pop, but otherwise hanging in there," I said. "I assume this isn't a social call?"

"No ma'am," she said. I got up from my chair and made my way to the front porch. "I have some great news. We got him."

"Him?" I asked as I wanted to jump up and down.

Detective Brown shrieked, "yes, we have solid evidence that he has been unreported certain criteria to cases. He's been arrested and charged. I've already gone to the judge," she paused. "Mason should be out tomorrow morning."

I took a deep breath of relief. "Good work, Detective," I said cheerfully. "You made my day."

"Best of luck to you," Detective Brown said.

"I'm sure I will be in touch," I said. We disconnected our lines, and then a smile of joy rushed over my face. I found myself stroking my stomach. A sharp dull pain emerged through me as I dropped my phone on the porch. Liz and Eric were out the front door in a matter of seconds.

"Let's get you to the clinic," Liz said. "You may be going into labor."

Eric picked up my phone, handing it to me as he helped me down the stairs. I got in the passenger seat as Liz drove us over to the clinic. We went into their private hallway, and then she did an ultrasound and pelvic exam. "Stacy," she said after checking me. "You're dilated to a three."

I smiled as I knew it meant we were about to head to a hospital. "You get dressed. I will be right back," she said leaving the room.

A smile burst across my face as it was all happening together. Mason was about to be released, and I was about to deliver our baby girl. Getting myself dressed and then headed for the door. Unsettling sounds erupted outside of the door, slowly cracking it open. Liz was pinned up against the wall across from the room I was in. Seeing Jackson and Thomas, heart racing, hair standing, and holding my breath.

"We know you're her sister," Jackson said through gritted teeth. "Where is she?" I immediately pulled out my phone, connecting to their phone, syncing their information and navigational tracking system to my phone through the app I created.

"I haven't seen her in years," Liz panicked with her hands up as in please don't hurt me. She had tears streaming down her cheeks. "She hasn't called or anything, please, don't hurt me."

Holding my breath, heart racing, peeking through the cracked door, a notification sound came across Thomas's phone. "Looks like Mason's getting out tomorrow," Thomas said showing Jackson his phone.

Jackson shoved Liz again into the wall. A soft shriek fled her throat. "If you do happen to hear or see her, give me a call," he said shoving a card in her shaking hands.

"Let's go pick him up from the prison exit gate," Jackson said as he hit Thomas's chest. They walked away from Liz as she slumped down, breathing hard in panic. Listening for the rear exit door to close, I waited to crack the door open wider.

Glancing down the hallway. "They're gone," she said. I looked down at my phone and saw the tracking system had begun. "Stacy, let's get you to a hospital." Liz stood up straight as she patted my arm. I looked down the hall in the direction they left, and then down at my phone. "Stace," Liz said moving her head under my eyes, waving her hand. "We need to get you to the hospital."

"I," I stopped as tears pricked my eyes for what pain I was about to cause her. Contemplating her demand and their plan, knowing they had been off the grid for months, untraceable. Now, they were going back to finish the job. "Liz, I'm so sorry," I said looking up at her eyes.

Her lips trembled as she grabbed my arms. "No," she said. "You're in labor. You must go to the hospital right now."

I glanced down at the phone, and then up at her. "I need your keys, now," I said shaking my hand. She begged with her eyes for me not to leave. "Now, Liz!" I yelled as I knew time was running thinner by the second.

"No," she said with tears streaming. "You can't drive. You could have this baby going down the road."

"It's not your place," I said as I grabbed her shoulders. "I need your keys now!"

She looked down, and then back at me with her eyes big and blue, red and wet. Heartbroken, she fumbled in her pocket as she grabbed the keys out. "Why him over us?" She asked.

"Not now," I said leaning in for a brief hug. "Her name will be Sierra Elizabeth Henderson," I whispered in her ear, sobbing she drew her hands up. I kissed her cheek, and then hurriedly down the hallway. I gripped the phone in my hand and the keys in my other hand.

Another pain as I got to Liz's car. "Okay, baby girl," I begged. "I'm going to need you to stay baking for a few more days. Mama has to make sure," another pain emerged as I opened the door. I slid in as my pep talk wasn't going so well. Cranking the car, hooking the navigation system up, and then driving off. I attempted to dial the number on my phone, but another pain erupted. "You need to stop being stubborn," I said breaking every traffic law. Determined to beat the clock's time, I went to dial the number again, and then my phone slipped out of my hand into the passenger floorboard.

You're not making this easy for me! Frustrated, I kept in the direction of New York State. Driving through the day, getting to the prison by late evening. Pulling my car around to the exit gate. I scoped out for other cars as I maneuvered to pick up my phone. Another pain emerged, breathing in and out. Struggling, I reached for my phone as a few more pains flowed through me. Sweat dripping, pain intensifying, breathing hard, finally a break for a few moments, and then unaware of my eyes drifting close.

The morning hour hit; I watched as the gate opened. Struggling with contractions through the night, dropping my phone multiple times, sweat was pouring down my face. My phone dropped in the passenger seat as another sharp pain erupted. I looked over at the gate of prisoners leaving. Mason was one to appear, and I tried to move myself to a position to get out. Witnessing a black SUV pulled up to him without hesitation he got in without resistance.

Multiple pains from physical and emotional flowing through me as I knew he was in more danger than beforehand. I reached over in the glove department, finding a handgun. *That a girl Liz, keeping a gun like dad taught us at a young age.* I got it out, putting it in the seat beside me. Placing the car in drive and followed the SUV. I got my phone as a final attempt to call. Dialing the number on the card I had tucked in my pocket for the emergency line I desperately needed.

"Hello," Scott said.

"Iiiiii…" A pain emerged as I kept my eyes on the road.

"Stacy?" Scott asked.

"Scott," I said with fast breathing breaths in between. "Jackson and Thomas have him. I need you to track my phone and," I screamed as another pain erupted.

"Stacy, we're headed to you," Scott said. "Get yourself to a hospital."

"No, we have to get Mason," I said breathing hard.

"I have your coordinates," Scott said.

I dropped my phone as another pain erupted. Hunched over, I followed the SUV as it quickly turned down a street and then parked in front of a different abandoned building. Throwing the car in park, as I grabbed the handgun Liz had stored in her car. I opened the car door, easing myself out as I reached in to grab my phone.

I called Scott back. "Stacy, get to a hospital," Scott demanded.

"How far out are you?" I asked as I bent over the hood of the car as another pain emerged.

"Stacy, get yourself to a hospital. We have it from here," he said sounding worried.

I dropped the phone as I grabbed the gun out of the seat. Sweat pouring down my face as I wobbled towards the building that they went in moments beforehand. Another pain emerged as I gritted my teeth, not making a noise outside the door. After the pain went away, I slowly opened the door, putting my hand up with the gun, and the other to support it.

I walked inside, easing my way forward as sweat dripped. I heard noise around the corner, and then through some plastic drapes. "Mason, our main man," Jackson said. "Where's your wife?"

"I don't know," Mason said as he spat out blood.

"You really going to make us torture you again?" Jackson asked, and then another motion was heard. Then, Mason groaned in pain. I slipped through the plastic coverings, locating Jackson, Thomas, and Ryan on the other side. They all looked up at me except Mason who couldn't see me yet.

"Let him go," I yelled as I had my gun pointed at them.

Another contraction rose as I tried to push the pain away, shaking as my body quivered, and then a groan slipped through my lips.

"Well, well," Jackson said as they all stared at me. "Ryan, did you not tell me that Mason had a vasectomy beforehand?" I took a few steps forward, getting beside Mason. He looked up at me as I glanced at him, face bloodied.

"Yes," Ryan said as he dropped his head.

"I guess I have a child expected any moment now," Jackson said with a grin crossing his face.

"Stacy, get out of here," Mason slurred.

My hand started to quiver as another pain emerged more intense than the last one. Jackson walked over to me as I tried to breathe through it, hands shaking. "Jackson," Mason slurred. "Leave her alone!" Jackson smiled as he reached towards me. The pain finally faded. I bent over, breathing heavily as I couldn't focus on my aim.

Jackson laughed as he walked over to Mason. "Looks like I stole your girl, reproduced, and now finally going to get that information I needed," Jackson laughed. "Life is grand!"

"Jackson," I yelled as I moved my hands back in aiming position as I stood straight up. He looked over at me as I started to pull the trigger.

A sound echoed through the building from a gunshot. "NOOOO! Mason screamed. A pain emerged as warm liquid dripped down my belly. I stumbled back as I looked at Thomas who had pulled his gun out on me. Falling on my knees as my gun flailed out. I moved it back into position, shooting in their direction. Ryan, Thomas, and Jackson all went running in different directions. I fell over on Mason's chair as he fell over, and then I fell on my back, looking up at the ceiling.

The pulsation thudding in my ears as everything else was tuned out. I dropped the gun, feeling it being taken from my hand. I glanced to see Mason had got his way up as the wooden chair they had him in broke. He threw the gun down, coming over to me.

Every painful sensation roared through my body, unable to breathe as I began panting, hearing the thud from each pulse echo my ear. Mason got his hand on my back, and then the other under my knees as he swooped me up in one motion. He hurried out the door as I heard tires squall.

I glanced around, my vision blurring as everything was happening so slow but quick at the same time. Preston opened the back door as Mason put me in the car. He ran around to the other side, getting behind me as he yelled. I glanced around as everything was silent but the pulsating thudding. I looked up at Mason as he looked at me.

"Keep breathing," his mouth formed. I wanted to kiss him as I had wanted to since the night of our tragedy. "Breathe, Stacy, breathe!"

We arrived at the hospital as multiple people opened the door and pulled me out, putting me on a gurney. Mason held my hand as I looked at him. They put an oxygen mask on me. "Mrs. Henderson, we have to rush you to surgery."

I pulled the mask off, looking at Mason who had blood all over his face. "Her name is Sierra Elizabeth Henderson," I said squeezing Mason's hand. He moved forward, kissing me, our touch sending the familiar warm sensation I missed.

"Keep breathing for her," he whispered. They shoved him back as they put the mask back on me. I looked up at the fast-paced rolling lights as my eyes went backwards.

My life started from infancy being held in mom's arms. I grew up seeing Liz in mom's arms as we all gathered together for a family photo. A few years passed by as Liz and I was outside playing at the ranch. It then showed us growing up, church, family gatherings, special holidays. I felt myself in a timelapse as I rushed into the night of Liz's twenty-first birthday. I hugged her as she put the gold chain necklace around my neck.

I watched as I picked up the glass at Wade's, Mason sat down beside me. My body reacted watching how I nervously backed away from the bar, running out to behind the man who stole my purse. I snatched it as I felt my body shoved into back wall platform, Mason invading my personal space as he flipped out my ID. The scene flipped to him holding my hand with the second shot as he moved in closer to me. "Why don't you put that shot down and follow me?" He asked staring into my eyes. The scene moved forward into his eyes to outside of the warehouse for the first time. "Trust me."

The words echoed as I watched myself escape the attack dogs, ending up in bunkroom with Preston, Jackson, and Thomas. Preston and I were in the dressing room as I fussed at him for not taking this seriously. It then switched to me in the short red cocktail dress and sneakers sitting beside Mason, staring into his eyes.

Like a rollercoaster speeding downhill as the motion went inside Mason's eyes to where I saw him standing in front of me with a gun to my throat. My body quivered in fear, and then it switched to Mason sharing his story of his mother at my apartment. He leaned into me as it switched to me making the choice to choose him. The tension between us as we were breathing hard. He put his forehead against mine and then created the barrier that held in place for over a year.

Mason leaned forward as he put his hand around my gold cross necklace. The scene switched to the shooting range as Preston was mad about his aim. Jackson came up and I pressed the gun to his manhood.

I dropped down as my breath was taken away as Mason placed his hand on my bare skin back at the celebration gathering. I had worn the long red dress with the back that was out from my neck to my spine. He moved his hand to my hand as the scenery switched to us standing in front of the altar holding each other's hands. He placed the watch on my wrist, and then we moved into kissing.

The kiss that moved me to the hotel where he kissed me passionately. I watched as our honeymoon replayed, showing Mason's face of enjoyment as we did multiple activities. "I will never get enough of you," Mason said, and then kissed my shoulder.

I saw myself going into the shoulder kiss, and then coming back away when Mason said he dreamt in a different world that he could have a family, job, and a house. His hands wrapped around my stomach as he comforted me when I started crying by the window, flipping to the shower where he said, "we're careful, nothing is going to happen to us."

Then, suddenly, a white light emerged through my life as I saw myself standing, staring at the white light. "Stacy!" Mom and dad shouted.

I put my hand up to look through the light. "Stacy!" They yelled again.

"Mom! Dad!" I yelled.

"We're over here," they yelled in synchrony. I finally caught a glimpse of them and ran to them. They embraced me with their hug. "Come on, let's go home."

"Wait," I said as I felt an urge to look back.

"You don't want to look back," mom said. "It's very painful when you can't go back."

Tears emerged as the feeling felt intense to look back. "Mom, dad, I was pregnant. If I look back will I see her?" I asked as I felt a tug to turn around.

Dad looked at me and then embraced me. "We don't know what we see when we turn around," dad said. "Just know you can't go back." He pulled away from me as I stood there for a moment with each of them holding my hands. I glanced over my right shoulder, looking slightly. The white light filled my vision as I took my last breath.

Chapter Twenty

~ Mason ~

THE NURSE WHO SHOVED ME AWAY as they rolled Stacy away, kept her hands up as she directed me to the waiting room. I sat there with my hands over my face as I recalled the last interaction I had with Stacy. Looking back at the memory of her crying as I got angry with the idea of her keeping the pregnancy. I didn't understand why she kept the pregnancy! I kept my head down as I waited for hours.

After several hours, two doctors came out. Finally! I stood up as they both walked over to me. They both were female doctors and then proceeded to point to the chair. My life was in cruise control as they both had looks of deep regrets on their faces. They broke the news to me that Stacy's gunshot wound was too much as she had been in active labor and bleeding for hours. They had a small clear plastic bag that they handed me. I looked at the contents of the gold chained necklace, and the black leather watch. Shaking my head, heart pounding, sighing heavily that I just lost my wife, the one who changed me.

Frustrated, I wept in my own arms. After several moments, they advised me that I had a baby girl that is very healthy. She was located in the nursery. No interest in looking at this child that wasn't even mine. I didn't even want to see it as I knew who the father was, disgusted, as I wanted to kill him with my bare hands for what he did to us. Stacy was gone.

I thought back to the many times we discussed children as she wanted them. Wishing she hadn't kept this one, then she would be here with me. My mind was a mess as I thought of us. It took me quite some time to build up enough courage to go to the nursery. I wasn't sure how I could handle this piece that she left behind. Anger and resentment towards the child that when I got to the hallway of the nursery, I looked in seeing a small baby wrapped in a pink blanket with a white hat on her head. The name on the card above her head stated, "Unknown for baby's name, Henderson for Parent's last names" that was written in black permanent marker.

I pressed my forehead against the glass, looking down at the ground as I allowed tears to slip. My once beloved beautiful wife left me behind this child that's not even ours. Banging my head on the glass slightly in frustration. A hand slipped on my shoulder, looking to my right, Henderson positioned himself to put his back against the glass.

"You really messed a lot of things up," Henderson said as he pulled out a cigar and lit it.

I shook my head slightly as I had my hands balled up beside me. "I don't understand why she kept his child. He hurt the both of us, and now they killed her," I said angrily.

"Pull yourself together," Henderson scolded. "We have bigger problems than what they did to you. We have lost contact with ten of our clients. We've lost our cleaner due to some other detective getting involved. And now, we have this," he said slightly turning to look at the baby. "Babies are nothing but death grabbing our chests in this life."

"You think I didn't ask her to abort the kid? It's not even mine," I snapped as I raised up to look at him. "This child doesn't even share my blood."

Henderson turned, looking at me red in the face. "You're such an idiot," he said throwing his hands up.

Shocked by the comment, I threw my hands back as I became offended by his phrase.

"Stacy, may she rest in peace, was an extraordinary being," Henderson said as he puffed on the cigar. "Let me tell you about your wife these past several months while you've been in the slammer."

I shifted myself to lean my back against the nursery windowsill and crossed my arms and ankles to listen to him. Henderson shifted to where he could see the nursery behind me. "It took her two weeks after she woke up to visit me. She informed me of her side of the story. Not believing her but knowing I hadn't heard from anyone from the team I had assigned to you in weeks. She eventually broke down advising what Jackson did to her in front of you. She then informed me that she was pregnant."

I slightly nodded as I had my eyes down, processing every word from him. "I told her that I would give her a couple of weeks, then I needed her back. She went missing over the course of ten weeks. When she finally returns to visit us," he paused. "I've never had anyone so clever that she had so many tactics in place for her departure. I just wish she was smart enough to have stayed away."

He cleared his throat. "Your wife turned in her resignation," he said, and then puffed on his cigar again. A nurse with a cup of coffee walked up to the two of us.

"Sir, there's no smoking allowed," she said looking between the two of us. Henderson took his cigar and threw it in her cup. She became angry and then walked off mumbling under her breath.

Henderson rolled his eyes as he shifted himself to look me in the eyes. "She had managed to create a device that hooked to the watch you gave her that sensed her and the baby's heartrate. She then informs me that she also had someone outside of the team as a second backup to her plan of resignation." Henderson shook his hand as if he were angry. "It's a shame to see such a waste in today's event," he admitted. "She did advise me that the baby was in fact yours after she went home to have it aborted by her sister. This isn't Jackson's child," he said pointing at the baby.

I turned around, facing the nursery, looking down at the small baby. "I think I know what I have to do," I said as I felt the sensation of Stacy standing next to me. I looked to my left as if she had lay her head on my shoulder, staring at the beautiful life she and I created.

"There's another thing," Henderson said. I glanced over at him as he reached in his pocket, pulling an envelope and a golden key out of his pocket. "She asked me to give this to you when you were out of prison." He handed me the items as I accepted them, fumbling the key in right hand, and then staring at the wrinkled envelope. Henderson put his hand on my shoulder. "I expect you back immediately once you get things settled here."

I nodded as our eyes met. He patted my shoulder, and then walked away, putting his hands in his business pants. I propped myself against the wall as I opened the envelope to read the letter Stacy had written.

Dearest Husband,

I want you to know that I never meant to leave you in horror of my decision to keep the baby. I did attempt to visit my sister and having it aborted. However, after she done the initial exam, we found out that the time line of conception was three weeks earlier than we all assumed. This is when I knew I couldn't take it from us. I also knew that I had to make a new choice in my life whether to continue to be part of your world, or to take matters into my own hands.

If you're reading this, then you must be out of prison. I hope you understand I have resigned from the silencers. I now needed to focus on a new life for our daughter. I know this may come shocking to you as five years ago when you gave me a timeline, I had made the cut off by three minutes which was the same as our wedding time. Ironically, you married me exactly one year from the time I chose to be part of your world. It was the best decision of my life to come back to you.

Now, time has changed as we have new factors in play. I hope that after you get yourself back into life that you will take the time to visit us on my parent's ranch. I know that Liz and her husband Eric will be as warm to you as they were of my return at ten weeks pregnant.

In addition to some changes, I've decided to hire for us a secret contact. I've done my research and met with her on multiple occasions. I do feel she will be the perfect cleaner to keep you out of trouble. Her name is Detective Clara Brown. I have provided you details to contact her once on your feet. Please don't give her up to the rest of the silencers. She needs to be private for your discretion. You can trust me with her as I've already done the research to seek her commitment to us.

In a final note, I want you to know that making the decision to leave you is the last thing I wanted. I worked so hard and long to be yours as you're mine. We've made something of our relationship to become one. I truly want you to know that when the time is *right for you to make a decision to choose a different lifestyle. You deserve a life that doesn't have you on edge of your last breath. I want you to choose me. Choose a different life for yourself.*

I love you more than life itself as you have made me a stronger woman.

Your beloved wife, Stacy

I saw another paper inside of the envelope and looked at it. It was an ultrasound of the baby. Shoving everything back in the envelope and placed it in my pocket. I took the clear bag with her gold cross necklace, sliding it onto my neck, attaching the key to it. I slipped on the watch and then looked back at the nursery. *Stacy, I love you too.*

It took me a few days to finish getting the baby's birth certificate with the name **Sierra Elizabeth Henderson,** she had other testing they had to complete, and then the hospital provided so many items as I had no idea what to do with them. We left the hospital together, awkwardly. Scott assisted in ensuring the baby was secured in Stacy's sister's car. "You sure you don't want me to go with you?" He asked as he saw the nervousness that I had with putting the items in the car.

"No," I said. "I need to do this one alone."

Scott patted my shoulder, and then I got into the car. We left and headed South. I attempted to listen to what the nurses had told me about feeding and changing, but it was a mess. The baby cried, spit up, and had so much poop. I was disgusted as this wasn't the idea I had in mind when leaving prison.

We arrived at the ranch driveway, taking a deep breath, and then feeling my palms sweaty as I made my way slowly to the house. Placing the car in park, and then got out, looking around at the scenery. I closed the car door as I absorbed everything about this home Stacy once lived in. My heart was torn into a million pieces.

The sound of the front door swung open, I jerked my head to look over as a man had a shotgun in hand and came down a couple of steps. "Who are you?" He yelled. I put my hands up as this wasn't the warm welcome I expected that Stacy had mentioned.

Silent, processing this unpredicted moment, I watched as their door opened again. A woman with darker hair than Stacy's but looked similar to her stepped out. She went beside I assume her husband as she kept behind him as if he was going to protect her. "Are you Liz and Eric?" I asked, keeping my hands up.

The man shifted, holding his gun tighter. The woman took a step down as she looked over at the car, and then at me. "You're Mason," she said as she ran down the steps. I glanced as the man lowered his gun, reacting by putting my hands down. The lady ran up to me, tears welling in her eyes. "Mason, where's Stacy?" The man came up to her side, wrapping his arm around her, kissing the top of her head as she had tears roll down her cheeks.

"I need a place for us to stay," I said walking backwards to the car. I opened the rear seat and pulled out the car seat. The lady ran over to me, crying as she looked over the baby.

"Come in," she said. "Eric grab his bags." Eric nodded to both of us and went to grab the bags out of the car as we walked in. "She's beautiful. She looks just like Stacy." We walked up the porch, and then into their home. I was led to the right in a living area where I sat the car seat down. "Do you mind?" She asked looking up at me. I stepped back and nodded as I looked around the small room. She unbuckled the baby, swooping her in her arms while she cried.

"Auntie Liz has you," she said as I shot my eyes back to her. The man entered the house, putting our bags by the stairs, and then walking over to his wife. "Look Eric, she has our eyes," she said looking up at him. "She has Stacy and my eyes."

"Mason," Eric said. "I'm sorry for pulling the gun out. We've been more cautious since Stacy's departure." He held out his hand as I accepted and shook it. They pointed out for us to sit down. I sat down across from them two as Liz held the baby.

"Liz, Eric," I said as I watched them staring at the baby. "I know we don't know each other at all, but I need to ask a favor of the two of you."

They both looked up at me. "I have no idea how to raise a baby," I admitted. "I know Stacy had plans for her and this child, but I must return to-."

Liz cleared her throat, interrupting me. "Your family, Mason," she said as Eric wiped her face. "Your problems, our problems. It becomes our family problems."

I lingered on her words as they stung my tongue. No one ever spoke words as such to me, willing to accept me and adjusting as they were being. I watched as she cradled the baby with her husband holding them both, staring at the small baby in front of them. "I know Stacy trusts you," I said. "I have to go back to work. I assume she didn't talk about it."

Liz looked over at me. "Can you stay one day?" She asked. "I can show you around, but first I want to hold this precious gift you brought to us."

I nodded. "I can," I said.

They held the baby for a few minutes, and then Liz got up and went upstairs. She cleaned the baby up and then came back downstairs to the kitchen where she made a bottle. Eric and I stayed in the living area as we watched her move in grace, grabbing up what she needed, and then feeding the baby from a bottle. Eric talked about being a General Surgeon as Liz was a female doctor that delivered babies all day. They both had met at a hospital they worked at while in school.

Liz talked about her parents, and then the ranch. Liz motioned for me to follow her upstairs, and I did. She went into a room that had an assortment of baby furniture and a full-size bed inside of it. Liz lay the baby down in the crib. "Stacy was going to stay here," she said as she kept her hand on the baby, watching her sleep. "Did you name her Sierra?" She asked.

I nodded as I was looking around the room. "Sierra Elizabeth Henderson," I said as I walked over to the bed. I saw pictures of Stacy while pregnant, when she was a teenager, and then when I met her years ago. I breathed a heavy sigh as the moment swept over me.

"Can you tell me what happened to her?" Liz asked through held back tears.

I looked over at her as she stood up, crossing her arms, looking at me. I shook my head. "It was something we both got caught up in," I said looking down at the floor.

"I begged her to stay," she cried. "She demanded my keys. I knew she was in labor and tried to get her to stay with us."

"She was a very stubborn woman," I chuckled. "Very determined."

"That's the truth," she laughed as she wiped her face. "Mason, she loved you so much. I don't know any woman that is in actual labor would put them on hold to run and save their man. Stacy was a rare gem."

I felt tears prick my eyes as I looked away. "She did something I never in my life had thought anyone would do for me," I said, and then walked over to the crib. "She loved me till death parted us."

Liz grabbed my arm, squeezing it lightly. "Will you ensure her body gets brought here?" She asked. "I would rather have her buried beside our parents."

I nodded. "I will make arrangements," I said looking down at the peacefully sleeping baby. She looked so much like her mom. I moved my hand to stroke her cheek and then walked away from the crib. I walked out of the room.

"There's another thing," Liz said as she walked out of the room. "Stacy always sent us," she paused as she wasn't sure how to speak about whatever she needed to tell me. "Just come here." Motioning me to follow her to the master room, she walked over to the closet where a gun safe was locked up. Entering a code, hesitating as she slowly opened its door, and then stepped to the side.

I walked over to it, seeing it filled with envelopes. I glanced at Liz, surprised, and then sighed as I bent down to pick up a package. I opened it up, seeing money inside it. Looking back at the safe, and then back at Liz who had stepped back and kept her eyes lowered. I tossed it back in the safe, closing it for her. I couldn't look at her as I wasn't sure how I could process this information. "Did she say where these envelopes came from?" I asked glancing over at her.

"No," she said not looking up at me. "She sent them to mom first. It was a way of letting mom know that she still was alive without telling us directly."

I looked up at the ceiling as this was something I never expected of Stacy. "Did she ever speak of it?" I asked as frustration rose inside of me and then feared as now I was going to leave our daughter with them.

Liz looked up at me with eyes filled with water. "No, Mason," she said clenching her teeth. "Stace kept her job a secret. We just knew that when we couldn't get in touch with her that this was the only way our hearts rested. She sent them frequently. Mom was the one who started placing them here. Then, I found out by checking the mail one day. Mom told me it was Stacy's way of communicating with us. I wished I could say I handled it well, but I was angry with it. We stored it here. So, when Stacy came to me a few months ago, she did ask to get some. Well, we've used the money to purchase the baby items. Other than that, I've kept the money locked in here."

"You understand that you can't say a word about this to anyone," I said.

She nodded. "It's been our secret this long," she said.

I shook my head as I wiped my eyes. A migraine formed as this visit was turning out to be more painful than it was expected to be. "I need you to keep Sierra," I said as we walked downstairs.

"We don't mind," she said as she wrapped her arms around her husband at the bottom of the stairs. I walked over to the front door, looking out at the porch.

"Look," I said looking back at the both of them. "I have to work. It's been part of my life much longer than Stacy was in it. It's not a job that I can just walk away." Eric tightened his stance. "I need to settle some affairs, and then as soon as I can return. I will be back here."

"Will you take her from us?" Liz asked as her lip trembled.

I shook my head. "I have no idea how to raise a child, much less take her from two who can help me raise her. I can't promise to be here every few days, or even weekly, but I do promise that I will stop by as much as I possibly can."

"Mason, you should know before Stacy departed," Eric said. "Two men jumped Liz at her medical office."

I shook my head as I pulled a few photos from inside of my jacket pocket. I handed the photos to Liz. "Where these the men?" I asked as I glanced away from her.

She looked over them and then handed them back. "Yes," she said lowly as she clutched her husband tighter.

"They know Stacy was shot. They saw from the news media that she was killed," I said putting the photos back in my jacket pocket. "You should always keep a weapon nearby for any emergencies, but you shouldn't be bothered by them." I looked back at them.

Liz placed her head on Eric's chest as he kissed the top of her head. "If you need me," I said pulling out a card. "Call me."

Eric took the card as he held it out in front of them. "Just make sure you come back," Liz said as she wiped her face. "We want you to be part of her life just as much as we are a part of hers."

I nodded, glancing back at them. "Take some money and buy a new car. I need to borrow yours for a while," I said, and then turned around walking out the door. Hurrying down the steps, getting into the car, I felt so many emotions unravel as I was leaving a little part of me with them. I barely knew them and had to fully trust that they were the best thing for Sierra.

I drove back to New York state, making a phone call to Detective Clara Brown. She advised me that she would be at a public meeting place in Central Park. I followed her instructions, sitting on a bench, looking around for her arrival. After several minutes, a dark colored lady with her hair large with curls, wearing shades took a seat on the bench. She had blue jeans, a green shirt, and a brown leather jacket.

"Mr. Henderson," she said as she glanced over at me.

I shifted in my seat as I looked away from her. "I don't know you," I said uncomfortably. "But my wife left me a letter that stated she's done the legwork on you. I also know you were the one to bust Detective Jones."

I looked back over at her as she pulled her shades off, exposing her brown eyes. She folded her shades and then placed them inside her jacket. "Your wife was intimidating," she admitted. "She held me at gun point twice."

"You let her walk away," I said shrugging my shoulders. "She must have been convincing."

She smiled with a chuckle. "Your wife found me," she said as she crossed her legs, and then placed her hands on her knee. "She even came to my house twice. I won't forget her last visit," she said.

"I know my wife trusted you," I said. "But I don't trust just any cop. I trust the cop that becomes part of my team."

"You want me part of the silencers," she commented as she didn't flinch. I glanced over at her as I shifted myself to face her.

"You are saying a bold word there," I said. "You sure that you're ready to be part of this arena."

She looked down at the ground, shaking her head. "Your wife unfortunately recruited me to your death arena," she said as she looked over at me. She stood up from the bench, placing a hand on her hip. "I'm at your disposal."

I got up from the bench. "I'll be in touch," I said as I turned away.

"You as scary as your wife?" She asked as I took a few steps.

I turned around to look at her as our eyes locked. "Scarier," I said, and then turned and walked away. I glanced back as she watched me fall into the crowd. She had a look that wasn't fearing for life, but what in the world have I signed up for. A smile slipped across my face as I shifted through the crowd towards the subway. I headed back to work, as now I had to focus on regaining our clients and then taking out Jackson and Thomas.

I arranged for Stacy's body to be transported. Kyle assisted in allowing me to see her body before departure. I looked at her iced body. Placing my hand on her cold face. My body shook to the core as I never felt her so stone cold. "My beautiful wife, Stacy," I said as stood in the mortician's room. I was alone with my wife. "I'm sorry that I dragged you into my world, promised you a life with me, and then had it snatched away. You didn't deserve what you went through with me. Your sister, Liz, and her husband, Eric, are going to help raise Sierra." I stopped as I closed my eyes. "I wish I could have given you the dreams you talked about." I took a deep breath as I kept my eyes closed. "Now I will ensure to keep our daughter alive better than I did you. Rest easy, my love, until we meet again."

Acknowledgements:

I am thankful for my salvation in Jesus Christ, and my creativity to write this novel and its future sequels. I want to thank individuals who have supported me through my writing and book design. I want to thank my dad, J. G Beck and stepmom, R. Beck, for encouraging me through my creative writing years. I want to thank my beta reader for providing amazing feedback and tips for improvement. I want to thank my aunt, P. G. Flynn, for her continuous support. The following supporters were great encouragements to me, D. Pena, K. Beck, K. Collins, and E. Collins. Most importantly, thank you for taking the time to read my novel. Please feel free to leave a review.

About the Author:

Katelyn Beck is a resident of Surry County, NC. She is a mother of two children. Katelyn has enjoyed creative writing since she was thirteen years of age. She published her first YA Novel with Publish America Books in July 2013, Why Me? Her second YA Novel was published with America Star Books in August 2015, Why Me? II Changes for him, Changes for me. Her inspiration for the Why Me series came from her love for Young Adult Fantasy novels and action adventured movies. The Why Me series was about a girl with gifts of the mind (mind-reader, telepathy, and many more gifts) who went into battle with the leader of the gifted. She started writing the Choice series when she graduated from Surry Community College in 2015. This series has been an eight-year work in progress. A Choice with A Promise to Keep was published in April 2023. A Choice with Hidden Secrets was a continuous story of the fictional character, Amberoanie. Katelyn has been very passionate about God, her kids, writing, and the awareness of Human Trafficking. This series is completely fictional with the events and characters being made up.

<u>Follow Me on Social Media:</u>
Facebook: Katelyn Beck, Author
Instagram: @writtenbykatelynbeck
TikTok: @katelynbeckauthor

Other Published Works:

A Choice Series:

Amberoanie, seventeen years old, runs away from her drug addicted mother. She ends up on the streets where she becomes a victim of them over the next several years. A Choice offered by Senior Richards, a wealthy older man, for her to stop a Human Trafficking Orchestrator at a local university. A trilogy that will keep you on the tip of the page till the end.

Please feel free to provide a review either via Amazon or my website: www.writtenbykatelynbeck.com

www.ingramcontent.com/pod-product-compliance
Lightning Source LLC
LaVergne TN
LVHW010147070526
838199LV00062B/4285